CW01668726

DEDICATION

This work is dedicated to the memory of

Hugh Shortt
Curator 1937–1975

A tribute and bibliography of his works appears in Part 1 of this Catalogue

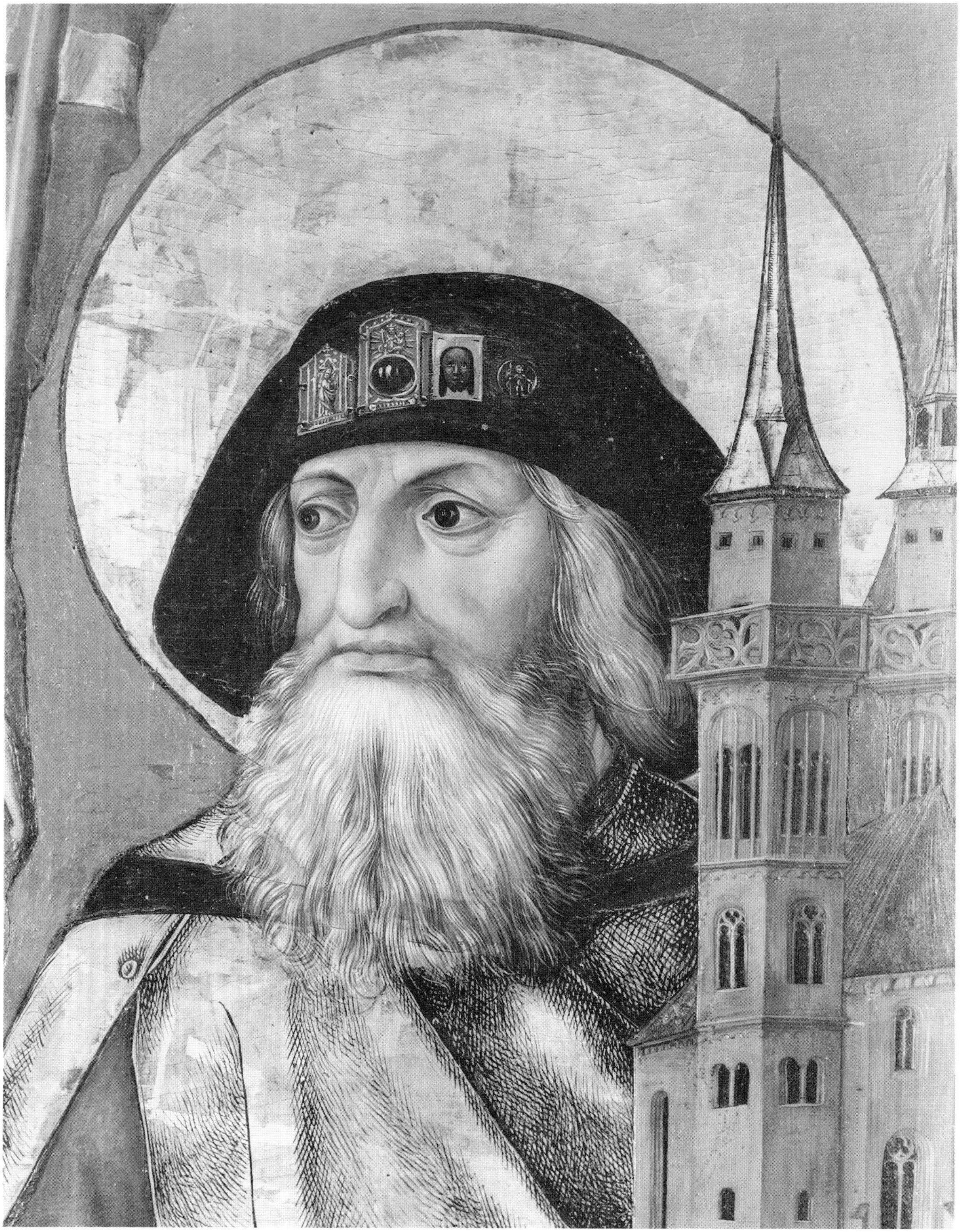

Detail from an altar-piece, dated 1487, depicting St Sebaldus as a pilgrim. His travel souvenirs include a mirror-badge (? from Aachen), a memento of painted cloth from Rome and, from Neuss (near Dusseldorf), a medallion similar to a pewter badge found at Salisbury. Nürnberg, Germanisches Nationalmuseum, no. Gm 143.

SALISBURY MUSEUM
MEDIEVAL CATALOGUE

Part 2

PILGRIM SOUVENIRS AND SECULAR BADGES

Brian Spencer
with illustrations by Nicholas Griffiths

Published by
Salisbury & South Wiltshire Museum

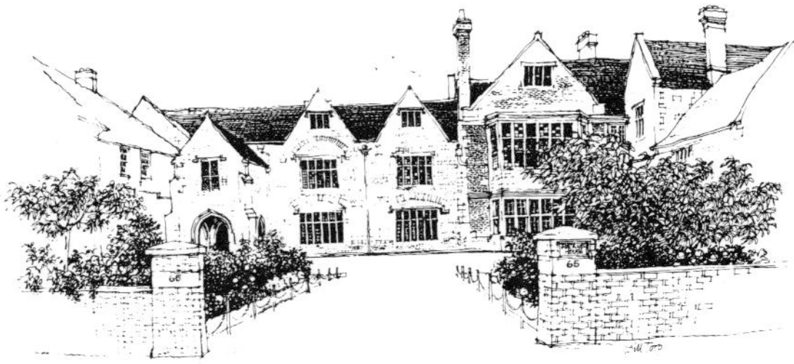

Published by Salisbury and South Wiltshire Museum
The King's House, 65 The Close, Salisbury, Wiltshire,
SP1 2EN, England

ISBN 0 947535 12 8

Editors: Peter Saunders
Eleanor Saunders

Cover photographs and design: David Cousins
David Pitt

Typeset and printed by BAS Printers Limited,
Over Wallop, Hampshire.

The Trustees of Salisbury Museum are grateful to the Council for British Archaeology for a grant toward this publication.

Front cover: badge, Our Lady of Tombelaine, Cat 36
Back cover: badges, Cat 2, 123, 86, 125, 16, 147, 178, 217

Contents

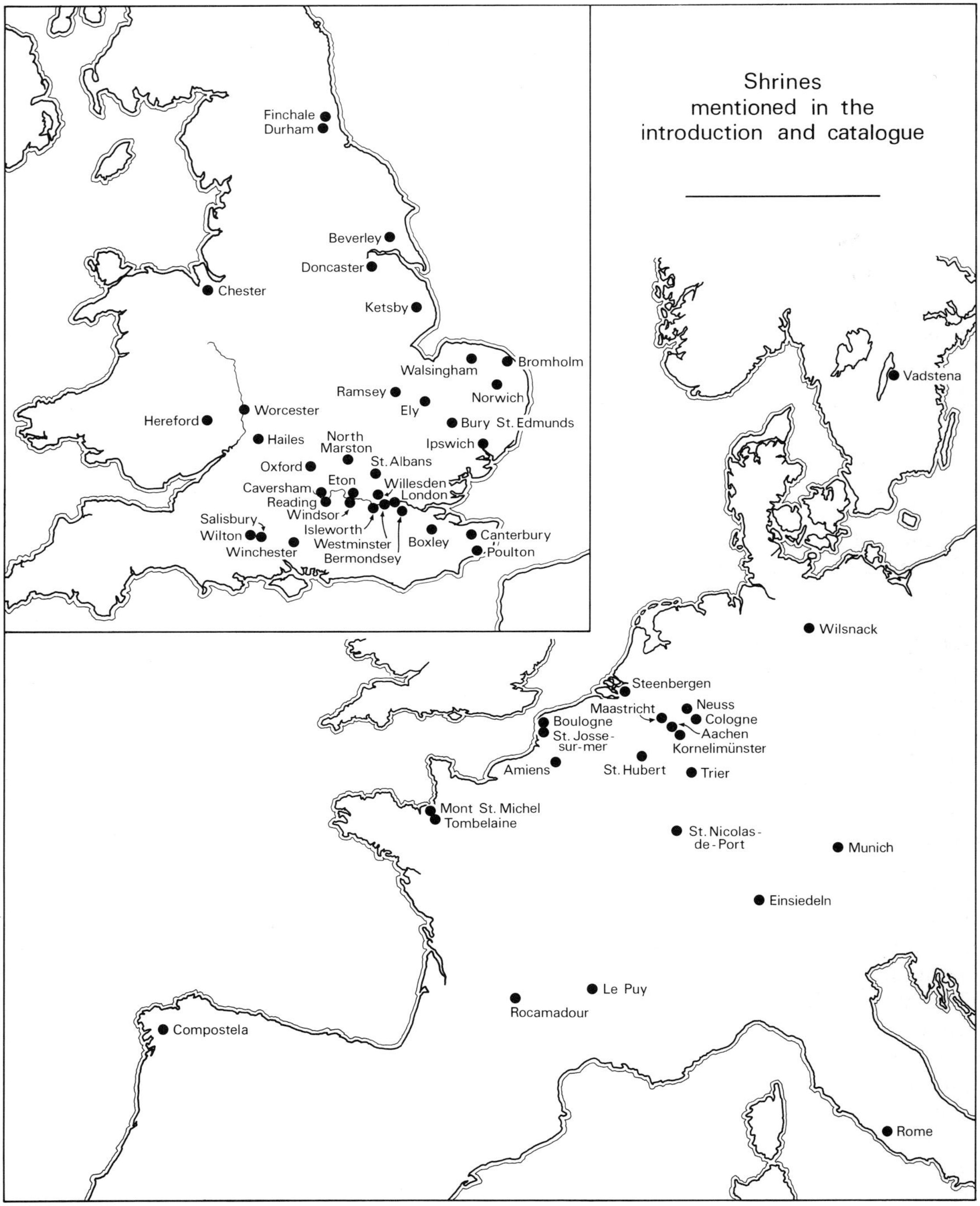
Shrines
mentioned in the
introduction and catalogue
Finchale
Durham
Beverley
Doncaster
Chester
Ketsby
Walsingham
Bromholm
Ramsey
Norwich
Ely
Hereford
Worcester
Bury St. Edmunds
Hailes
North Marston
Ipswich
Oxford
St. Albans
Caversham
Eton
Willesden
Reading
London
Windsor
Salisbury
Isleworth
Wilton
Westminster
Boxley
Canterbury
Winchester
Bermondsey
Poulton
Vadstena
Wilsnack
Steenbergen
Maastricht
Neuss
Cologne
Boulogne
Aachen
St. Josse-sur-mer
Kornelimünster
Amiens
St. Hubert
Trier
Mont St. Michel
Tombelaine
St. Nicolas-de-Port
Munich
Einsiedeln
Le Puy
Rocamadour
Compostela
Rome

Pilgrim souvenirs

INTRODUCTION

Going on pilgrimage was one of the most popular ways by which medieval men and women actively sought the path to salvation. Yet by the fourteenth century, instead of being a purely religious or penitential exercise, pilgrimage had for most people become something of a social occasion that combined an element of tourism with religion. Nowhere is this more obvious to us now than in the matter of collecting souvenirs. When William Wey, fellow of Eton College, returned from a pilgrimage to the Holy Land in 1458, he carried a bagful of the mementoes he had literally picked up there – 'a ston of the Mounte of Calvery, a stone of sepulkyr, a stone of the holy cave of Bethleem . . .' He carefully listed them all, even though he had been well aware of official notices in Jerusalem forbidding the removal of objects as souvenirs and condemning the equally deplorable habit of leaving behind graffiti (Williams 1857, p xxix). Aside perhaps from impecunity, William had little excuse for making off with these fragments of the holy places, for, as he himself tells us, it would have been perfectly possible to have purchased purpose-made souvenirs, such as miniature replicas of the holy sepulchre or reliquaries containing 'earth from which God fashioned Adam'.

All pilgrims wanted to carry home visible proof of their travels, and by the time of William Wey, and indeed long before, manufactured souvenirs, usually in the form of metal badges, were available to pilgrims almost everywhere. The badges were normally worn on the hat (see Frontispiece). Pewter and silver badges commemorating pilgrimages to Our Lady of Eton, for instance, were on sale at William Wey's own college at the very time that he was undertaking his own long-distance journeys. An unknown contemporary of his brought one of these Eton souvenirs home to Salisbury. This (Catalogue no 45) and a number of other fragile and disparate pilgrim signs, which have survived in Salisbury's soil, sometimes merely as fragments, are discussed in the catalogue below.

For Christian pilgrims in much earlier times, Jerusalem and Rome (Cat 88) had been the only objectives of real importance. Then in the late tenth and eleventh centuries the shrine of the apostle St James the Greater, at Santiago de Compostela in north-west Spain, rose to prominence and by the twelfth century had probably become the most popular pilgrim resort in Christendom (Cat 85-7). Simultaneously new places of pilgrimage were springing up along the various routes to Compostela and, thereafter, intricate networks of pilgrim centres, large and small, developed across the whole of Europe. With this multiplicity of shrines came also the phenomenon of the mass pilgrimage, with pilgrims flocking in vast numbers to shrines rendered important or specially inviting as the result of, say, a famine or an epidemic, or because of a jubilee or a particular feast-day or a newly-reported miracle or, as in the case of Salisbury, following the canonisation of a local saint (Cat 1-7).

At such times pilgrim resorts were often faced with an influx of visitors far exceeding the size of the permanent population. Thus an average-sized medieval town like Wilsnack in north Germany with around 1000 inhabitants could expect to receive 100,000 pilgrims every year, most of them during the summer months. At Munich (population *c.*10,000) pilgrims were counted at the gates by dropping peas into a bowl: 40,000 were counted during one exceptional day in 1392. Roughly the same number were arriving on average days at Rome in 1450. At about the same time observers in England were struck by the crowds of pilgrims who thronged the roads and left their home towns almost deserted. In 1496, 142,000 pilgrims were counted at the gates of Aachen in a single day (Spencer 1968, p 137). Accidents arising from the crush of pilgrims were not uncommon and numbers had sometimes to be restricted by the closure of a city's gates.

Every major pilgrim centre and its hinterland was faced with daunting logistical problems. Pilgrims had to be supplied with food and shelter and with adequate stocks of basic necessities like shoes and knapsacks. In the late twelfth century victuallers at Mont-Saint-Michel (Cat 84) were said to have 'set up tents and turned the paths into streets. There was plenty there of divers wines, bread and pasties, fruit and fish, birds, cakes and venison' (Evans 1969, p 77). A guide to Compostela, written earlier in the twelfth century, describes the shops that surrounded a paved courtyard behind the cathedral. Here were sold 'casks of wine, shoes, deer-skin bags, purses, straps, belts and all kinds of medicinal herbs' (Vieillard 1938, pp 96-7). Here, too, the guide-book tells us, it was possible to buy the distinctive form of souvenir which had been adopted by the organisers of the pilgrimage, namely, 'the shells which are the signs of St James'. These scallop-shells, gathered from the shores of Galicia and later reproduced in metal and jet (Cat 85-7), were perforated with two holes so that they could be worn suspended round the pilgrim's neck or attached to the clothing, knapsack or staff. During the second half of the twelfth century the provision of purpose-made souvenirs began to spread to other major shrines like Canterbury, Cologne and Rocamadour.

By the fifteenth century, and perhaps before, the souvenir content of the pilgrim trade at Compostela and all the main sanctuaries had become pre-eminent. At Le Puy in southern France the shops around the church were by then concerned exclusively with souvenirs. They stocked not only badges of the various local shrines but a wide range of trinkets and devotional bric-à-brac (Cohen 1976). At Rome the trade centred on St Peter's basilica. Souvenirs, which by the fifteenth century included the contemporary equivalent of picture postcards painted on pieces of paper or parchment, were sold in the forecourt, on the steps, in the portico and even in the cloisters. At Rocamadour the badge stalls alone filled a particular square, while at Canterbury (Cat 8-34) the badge-sellers were to be found just outside the cathedral gate in Mercery Lane. It was here that one of Chaucer's pilgrims, the Miller, was said to have gone shoplifting, picking for himself 'a bosomful of signs of Canterbury brooches' (Furnivall & Stone 1909, lines 171-83).

For those who could afford them, pilgrim badges of gold and enamel were also to be had. Thus in 1455, 25 *sous tournois* were paid for a gold badge bought for the duchess of Orleans at Sainte-Cathérine-de-Fierbois (Laborde 1852, p 354). By comparison, in 1504 ordinary leaden badges were costing one *sou* per dozen in Paris (Lamy-Lassalle 1971, p 273). Instances of pilgrim souvenirs of various materials, from silk to jet, are referred to in the catalogue below. But the great majority, and almost all those found at Salisbury, were made of a eutectic alloy, combining about six parts of tin with four of lead. This fitted the general requirement for a cheap, mass-produced article. With its low melting-point, the alloy was suitable for the swift production of souvenirs by multiple castings. Moulds, sometimes casting several items at once, were usually of fine-grained stone – often steatite, slate, chalk or Bavarian lithographic limestone. Occasionally they were also of bronze, baked clay, wood (Cat 86) and cuttlebone. Moulds of the best quality were probably the work of goldsmiths, who also intermittently undertook commissions for pilgrim badges of precious materials.

No pilgrim-badge moulds have yet been found at Salisbury, though the recent recovery from the river Avon of several stone moulds for making costume accessories and of discarded, faulty castings and scrap metal point to the local production of small pewter objects in the fifteenth century. One of these moulds (alongside an associated find, a cast pewter buckle from a similar mould) is illustrated here (Figs 324-5; private collection) since it broadly resembles the simplest kind of mould used for casting pilgrim signs. Characteristically, the matrix for one side of the object is cut (in reverse) on one face of a block of stone, which is fitted with sockets and dome-headed lead lugs to ensure an accurate, tight fit with a corresponding block on which the mould for the other side or back of the object was cut. Unlike many continental badges, English pilgrim signs were hardly ever cast in one-piece, open moulds. Reverse moulds took care of a badge's pin and clasp and often introduced enough modelling to hollow out the back and save metal in casting and add rigidity to the finished product; sometimes the counter-mould was also used to work in a little concealed thickening at vulnerable points (Figs 133, 135, 141) (*cf.* MacGregor & Spencer 1987). Aspects of some of the pilgrim souvenirs relating to Salisbury's own sanctuaries (e.g. Fig 7; Cat 6, 142) suggest that they, too, were being manufactured locally in the fifteenth century. Evidence from the better-documented centres of the pilgrim trade makes it plain that pilgrim signs were almost invariably made and were certainly always sold at the particular shrine concerned. Sometimes, as at Walsingham (Cat 48-57), the church itself seems to have run a manufacturing workshop within its own walls. On the production of secular badges and other non-religious wares at certain shrines, see below pp 96–7.

Though arrangements varied from place to place, the manufacture and sale of pilgrim souvenirs was everywhere fairly strictly controlled. Regulations sometimes sought to safeguard a monopoly for all the inhabitants of the resort involved or for certain sections of that community – particular families, perhaps, or, as at Compostela, special craft guilds. Most often they bolstered up the church's claim to exclusive rights or to at least a share in the business, since the sale of badges afforded both a useful income and a means of advertising. As early as 1199, the pope granted the authorities of St Peter's Rome, the sole right to make and market pewter badges bearing the images of St Peter and St Paul 'with which visitors adorn themselves for the increase of their own devotion and as proof of their accomplished journey' (Baluzius 1682, pp 305-6). Similar regulations at other shrines usually meant that local inhabitants could only manufacture badges under licence from the church or by hiring the church's moulds. Disputes between the shrine proper and the surrounding town were not infrequent. Over a period of two centuries, shopkeepers at Le Puy, claiming traditional and hereditary rights to sell souvenirs and other paraphernalia to pilgrims, fought a bitter legal and commercial battle against the monopoly imposed in favour of the hospital of St Mary there (Cohen 1976, pp 198-211).

At Steenbergen in North Brabant, where an image of St Wilgefort was the attraction, the church alone was allowed to sell badges made of silver (Heeringen, Koldeweij & Gaalman 1987, p 97). At Aachen, on the other hand, only the goldsmiths were permitted to make silver and silver-gilt badges, while the production of cheaper badges (Cat 37) fell to the city's mirror-makers. However, both of these guilds were unable to cope with the enormous demand at times of mass pilgrimage, namely, every seventh year, when the cathedral's great relics were exhibited to pilgrims over a period of several months. To ensure adequate stocks, the souvenir trade was then thrown open to all, including outsiders, provided badges were sold exclusively in Aachen. It was this provision that encouraged Johann Gutenberg, goldsmith and inventor of printing, to reveal his interest in the achievement of cheap reproduction by undertaking the mass-production of Aachen pilgrim badges at Strasbourg in 1438, ready for sale at Aachen during the summer festival of 1440 (Köster 1973). At the chief resorts like Aachen and Canterbury, then, pilgrim signs were being sold at the rate of tens and perhaps hundreds of thousands every year. In 1466, 130,000 badges were sold in a fortnight at the Swiss monastery of Einsiedeln.

Why were badges so popular with pilgrims? For one thing, they were often of practical value on the journey. They helped to mark the pilgrim's status as someone who was entitled to expect support, hospitality and safe-conduct along the way. As proof that a pilgrimage had been completed, they could serve a useful purpose after returning home. They might be the kind of evidence required by an employer or a sponsor, for example, and they would certainly need to be produced if the pilgrim wished to be admitted to a local confraternity dedicated to a chosen shrine. They were not, however, accepted as legal evidence of the performance of a penitential or penal pilgrimage imposed by a court of law. Pilgrim badges were also sought after as personal remembrances and aids to devotion.

A badge was, moreover, much more than an ordinary memento or a trifling present to give to a relative or friend, for it had been in contact with the shrine or image that it was intended to commemorate. The pilgrim, either in person or at the hands of the shrine-keeper, would have touched the shrine with the badge or he would have bought the badge in the belief that it had already touched and even been blessed at the shrine. Touching was in accordance with the medieval appetite for physical contact and tangible reassurances in matters of devotion and religious belief. More significantly, the practice enabled the pilgrim to return home with benefits that were thought to arise from such close encounters with holy relics. A little of the saint's virtue and the divine grace that were deemed to radiate from saintly relics and wonder-working holy objects and places were transmitted to the badge, which then became a secondary relic and a talisman exercising its own powerful magic. Even the string from which a Canterbury souvenir had once been suspended was found to be a contact relic sufficiently potent to work a miracle for its owner (Robertson 1875, p 254).

It is therefore easier to see why the church was able to defeat or repress illegal badge-makers, not only by the use of litigation and excommunication, but by refusing to allow unauthorised or suspect badges to touch the shrine. It is also easier to understand why pilgrims often wore their pilgrim signs long after the completion of their journey and sometimes took steps to ensure their long-term preservation and why pilgrims were not averse to acquiring several badges at one sanctuary so that they could afterwards apply them individually to a number of different purposes.

As secondary relics pilgrim signs were thought to be important enough for pilgrims to present them to their own parish church. Here badges found their way into reliquaries, altars and treasuries. Some pilgrims left the souvenirs they had acquired at one shrine as votive offerings at another. Others made their badges the subject of a bequest while others still took their pilgrim souvenirs to the grave. Wealthy pilgrims sometimes arranged to preserve their pilgrim signs by having them stitched to the illuminated leaves of devotional books.

Fulfilling their function as amulets and prophylactics, some pilgrim badges were kept about the house, nailed at entrances or suspended over the bed or on the wall in the belief that their protection might extend to the whole family and perhaps to friends and neighbours, too. Concern for livestock and crops led to the fixing of pilgrim signs on stable-doors, cowsheds, drinking-troughs and beehives and to the burial of others in gardens and arable land in the hope of fending off weeds, insect pests and vermin (Köster 1981, p 453). The occasional discovery of pilgrim signs in the footings of buildings suggests that they may also have been used in magical foundation deposits.

Virtually all the pilgrim badges found at Salisbury, like the vast majority of those (now amounting to a few thousand) found elsewhere, however, have come from medieval watercourses. Find-spots are specified in some of the catalogue entries below, and in all other cases objects can be assumed to have been found in the bed of either the Avon or of the Millstream between 1975 and 1987. That so many badges should have been found at or near river-crossings and other watery places must owe much to the soft, anaerobic properties of river-mud which undoubtedly have helped in the preservation of these flimsy objects. But such a vast proportion of surviving badges have everywhere been found at river crossings and riversides that the complete explanation of this phenomenon is again likely to lie in medieval superstition. The bulk of pilgrim badges may have found their way into rivers as propitiatory gifts, or thank-offerings, thrown there by returning or returned pilgrims. The practice was doubtless rooted deep in folk belief and had many parallels among the superstitious habits of travellers in earlier and later times (Spencer 1978, p 250).

Belief in the ability of pilgrim signs to overcome evil led metal-founders to incorporate them in the moulds of bells and smaller products like fonts, mortars and lidded tankards. The badges so used were sometimes the founder's choice, sometimes the client's. Since badges were usually made of a eutectic alloy, when a bell was cast any badges embedded in the mould, along with inscriptions and conventional ornaments modelled in wax, would melt away and their shapes be filled instead by molten bell-metal. For the bell-founder the decorative value of the replicated badges was a secondary consideration. They were placed on the bell, sometimes at four points of the compass, primarily to ward off demons and to avert thunderstorms, which folk-belief had long ascribed to the ringing of church bells. At the same time, it was thought that when a bell was rung the apotropaic properties of the badges incorporated in it would be transmitted to those who were within earshot. In Germany and Scandinavia especially, these replicas on the surfaces of bells are now the main source of knowledge about many types of pilgrim signs, the fragile originals of which have either perished or have yet to be discovered (Köster 1957, pp 54-5).

Another illustration of the magical aspects of pilgrim signs is to be found in their occasional conjunction with mirrors (see Frontispiece). With the development of the mass pilgrimage during the second half of the fourteenth century and later, and the measures that had to be introduced to ensure proper crowd-control, the possibility of personal contact with relics at some shrines grew more remote and it often became necessary to take relics out of churches and exhibit them from galleries to the enormous crowds assembled on the ground outside or on neighbouring rooftops or in specially constructed stands. It then became the practice for pilgrims to hold up little mirrors towards images or relics that could now only be seen from afar, in the belief that by catching their reflection the mirror would encapsulate some of the virtues issuing from the relic (Köster 1983B). As with a true touch-relic, these benefits could then be taken home and shared with relatives and friends. Pewter frames, often suitably inscribed, from such mirrors have been recovered at London. From a much wider range of places, including Salisbury (Cat 37, 79; Fig 126) has come evidence of pilgrim badges that appear to have incorporated a mirror in their design.

Pilgrim souvenirs of the twelfth and thirteenth centuries have yet to be found at Salisbury. The collection of badges and related items discussed below, however, provides a fund of information about the practice of pilgrimage in later medieval Salisbury and about many aspects of popular religious belief and iconography. Pilgrimages were such everyday events that, like visitors to a cricket match or concert today, pilgrims left few written traces of themselves or of their objectives. Even though only a minute fraction of the original output has survived, pilgrim souvenirs help substantially to fill the gap in our knowledge.

They suggest that most of Salisbury's citizens undertook pilgrimages that could be completed, there and back, in three weeks or less and that their main objectives lay within a triangle bounded by Dover on the south-east and Walsingham in the north-east. They also bring to light a number of more adventurous souls who journeyed to far-away places in Germany, the Low Countries, France, Spain and Italy and they include many reminders of the attractions to pilgrims that lay within Salisbury itself and in its neighbourhood. There also remain a number of souvenirs whose symbolism is difficult to understand and whose place of origin is impossible to identify.

Except when stated otherwise, all the objects described below can be assumed to be of tin-lead alloy. It can also be assumed, again with a few stated exceptions, that all the badges were provided with integral pins and clasps. The pins are mostly vertical (Fig 141) but occasionally horizontal (Fig 144). Many openwork badges were also fitted with clips (Figs 18, 110) for holding a backing of coloured cloth, parchment or paper or of shiny metal foil, while some badges may themselves have once been brightly painted (Cat 36). The two openwork metal badges worn by the pilgrim depicted in the Frontispiece were mounted on a lining of red cloth.

Several donors have contributed items to the Museum's collection and their names are, with gratitude, recorded in the catalogue entries. A number of other items have been deposited on loan with the Museum by the following individuals to whom the Salisbury Museum is also grateful:

Mr J. Auld, Mr A. J. Essery, Mr R. Hooper, Mr B. N. Lee, Dr M. B. Mitchiner, Mr S. Moore, Mr P. Shaffery, Messrs R. & I. Smith, Mr S. Wheeler and Mr M. A. Tizzard.

ABBREVIATIONS USED IN CATALOGUE

H	height
W	width
D	diameter
BM M & LA	British Museum, Department of Medieval and Later Antiquities
Drainage coll.	Salisbury Drainage collection, see Saunders 1986
MOL	Museum of London
OS Diary	*Old Sarum Diary*; W. Hawley's manuscript diary of 1909–15 excavations, in Salisbury Museum
pc	Private collection
Sal. Mus. Cat.	*Catalogue of the Salisbury and South Wilts Museum*
Sal. Mus.Rep.	*Salisbury and South Wilts Museum Annual Report*
Wilts. Arch.Mag.	*Wiltshire Archaeological and Natural History Magazine*

Salisbury Museum accession numbers are given in italics.

Provenance

Unless stated otherwise all the objects catalogued below were found in the bed of the river Avon or of the Millstream at Salisbury between 1975 and 1987, see above p 11.

CATALOGUE

St Osmund of Salisbury

Probably Norman by birth, Osmund was for a time William the Conqueror's chancellor and took part in the compilation of Domesday Book. From 1078 he was also bishop of Salisbury. He built the first cathedral at Old Sarum, formed a chapter of canons and drew up a constitution that was to set the pattern for the organisation of other cathedrals. Revered for his purity and love of learning, bishop Osmund died in 1099, was buried at Old Sarum and was soon venerated locally as a worker of miracles. In 1226 his body and tomb (most of which survives) were moved to the Lady Chapel of the new (the present) cathedral of Salisbury and for over two centuries were the focus of his cult (Shortt 1959; Stroud 1984A and 1987). In 1228 the pope authorised enquiries into his virtues and miracles with a view to canonisation, a process which in the event proved to be one of the longest in medieval England. The project was revived in 1387 but it was not until 1457, after the investigation of another selection of miracles that had occurred since the 1380s and after the expenditure of vast sums of money in Rome by the cathedral chapter (Malden 1901, pp xxxii and 172ff.), that Osmund was finally pronounced a saint. Within six months his bones had been translated to a magnificent new shrine at the centre of the Lady Chapel.

1 Pilgrim badge in the form of a lozenge-shaped plaque on which the mitred bust of a bishop is depicted in low relief on a diapered ground. Angels, with wings outstretched, support each side of the plaque; the head of only one of them has survived. On the right and at the base remain two fragments of an outer frame, rectangular, or possibly architectural, in form. It was to the top of this frame that the pin would have been attached to the badge, the pin's position being indicated by the vertical mark of the mould-joint at the back of the badge. The bishop's head is flanked by the letters O and S and the further letters M,O,N, and D appear at the points where the angels emerge from the sides of the plaque, beginning at the bottom right-hand side and moving clockwise. 1457 or soon after. H. 35 mm. Given by Mr B. N. Lee. *190a/1987* **Fig 1**

2 Pilgrim badge similar to Cat 1. St Osmund is again depicted with the same form of mitre, but there is no inscription and no trace of an outer frame. One of the four supporting angels is missing. Angelic supporters were again to figure on another sort of Salisbury badge, also representing the apotheosis of St Osmund (Cat 3). *c.*1460. H. 34 mm. *90/1987* **Fig 2**

Badges such as these were doubtless among the souvenirs provided for the crowds of pilgrims who were drawn to Salisbury by the news of St Osmund's canonisation (which was to be the last in England until 1935) and by the special indulgences promised to those who made offerings at the new shrine. As yet no other badges of this type are known to have been found outside Salisbury.

3 Pilgrim badge: a solid plaque of pointed oval shape on which is depicted the bust of St Osmund, borne up by the demi-figures of four angels. Late 15th century. H. 30 mm. *212/1987* **Fig 3**

Another badge of this type, belonging to the Museum of London (82.255/2) is depicted in Fig 4. This is one of several virtually identical examples found at London; for another see BM M & LA 71, 7-14, 48, originally published in Cuming 1868, pl 17e and pp 224-5, where, unaccountably, it is attributed to St Narcissus of Cordova. The survival of variants like that in Fig 5 (found near the north end of Cannon Street railway bridge, London, 1982) points to a very considerable output.

Osmund, again, was probably the saint commemorated on certain badges of circular medallic form. On these the mitred bust is depicted against a neatly diapered ground (Fig 6, found at Bull Wharf, London, 1979). As on the lozenge-shaped and vesica-shaped badges described above (Figs 1–5), the mitre is given a distinctive lanceted shape. Other examples of this particular type of badge have been found at London (e.g. London Museum 1940, pl LXII, 9), but as yet none has been recorded as having been found at Salisbury.

The iconography of all these badges may have been inspired by the silver-gilt head of St Osmund commissioned for the shrine in 1457 (Malden 1901, pp 217–8). On the other hand, the imagery may simply have been derived from, and intended to compete with, a popular type of souvenir worn by contemporary pilgrims to Canterbury (e.g. Spencer 1978, fig 5c; 1980, p 19, no 74). This, too, was of circular medallic form and depicted a reliquary-bust of St Thomas Becket between the letters S and T or T and O. In *c.*1480 one example was painted as a still-life subject by the Flemish illustrator of a Book of Hours (Oxford, Bodleian MS Douce 219/220, f 16v), confirming a late fifteenth-century date for these Canterbury products, a date that could otherwise have been presumed from archaeological evidence. The solid, medallic forms of the St Osmund badges (the plaque-like form again appears in Cat 7 below) were also part of a much wider fashion in hat ornaments belonging to the second half of the fifteenth century. This fashion was further reflected in some of the souvenirs issued at other centres of pilgrimage both in England and abroad (*cf.* Cat 9, 38-9, 117-8).

The bust of St Osmund was also depicted on flimsy, bracteate badges. These were manufactured by using a die to strike the subject or device onto a flan of thin sheet metal, rather than by casting from molten metal, the method of multiple production used for nearly all the other badges described in this catalogue. In the case of a bracteate badge found (1987) in late fifteenth-century spoil removed from Butler's Wharf, Bermondsey, London, the nimbed and mitred bust of St Osmund, flanked by the letters S and O (for Sanctus Osmundus or Signum Osmundi) and surrounded by a barbed quatrefoil border, has been stamped onto a diamond-shaped flan of brass (Fig 7, *225cc/1987*). The badge is perforated with two stitching-holes. In another instance a similar, but larger bust has been embossed on a rectangular flan of tin foil (from the Thames, Queenhithe; MOL 85.78). A strip of lead recently found at Salisbury provides further evidence of the use of irons for striking badges of St Osmund. The lead had been used to test the die of a circular, bracteate pilgrim sign measuring some 32mm across (illustrated in Mitchiner 1986, p 192). Unfortunately the trial-piece was too narrow to accommodate more than a portion of the inscribed border. But the central motif is intact, namely, the nimbed and mitred bust of St Osmund flanked by the letters S and O and accompanied, on the left, by the top of a crosier.

The use of dies on metal foil as a means of mass producing pilgrim signs, a practice first referred to in the middle of the fourteenth century, was widely adopted at continental shrines during the second half of the fifteenth, and in England was taken up at long-established, major shrines like Canterbury and Walsingham, Norfolk. Thus Canterbury offered its clients circular and diamond-shaped bracteate badges of wafer-thin silver or brass, among them badges depicting the reliquary bust of St Thomas between the letters S and T (e.g. MOL 85.231/1 and Heeringen, Koldeweij & Gaalman 1987, p 72). The same mode of production was also adopted at shrines like Eton (see below p 30) or Salisbury, where the popular phase of the pilgrimage coincided with the development of the technique.

In addition to badges of St Thomas, another striking analogy for the bracteate badges of St Osmund referred to above is a circular silver badge stamped with the bust of St Antony, wearing mitre-like, patriarchal headgear and a Tau-cross on his left shoulder, and flanked by the letters S and A (MOL 87.220) This badge, found at London, is likely to have been a souvenir from St Antony's Hospital in London, pilgrimages to which were being conscientiously promoted during the second half of the fifteenth century (*cf.* Cat 91).

4 **Pilgrim badge:** the bust of a bishop set within a hexagonal frame, with trefoils at the angles and swags lining the sides; perhaps a stylised development of the conjoined angels on the earliest badges described above (Cat 1 and 2). Late 15th or early 16th century. H. 25 mm. *91/1987* **Fig 8**

The late date and Salisbury provenance suggest that this badge, too, may have been made to commemorate the silver-gilt head, or at any rate the cult, of St Osmund. The badge has no stylistic links whatever with any of the various and better-known souvenirs of the reliquary-bust of St Thomas of Canterbury (*cf.* Cat 16-26).

5 **Pilgrim badge:** standing figure of St Osmund, holding in his left hand a model of a church with a central spire. In doing so, he also raises up an outer garment to form (now damaged) folds. The robe is thus drawn aside somewhat to reveal the horizontal, dipping folds of his chasuble. In his right hand he holds up a document with the semblance of a written text on it. At his feet kneels a pilgrim, his hands joined in prayer. This suppliant is linked to the figure of the bishop by two undisguised runners, similar to the one bridging the bishop's mitre and the cross on the top of the spire. At the foot of the badge is an incomplete label faintly inscribed *s o . . . nd* in black letter. Second half of 15th century. H. 56 mm. *191a/1987* **Fig 9**

St Osmund is here celebrated as the founder of Salisbury Cathedral. Following the convention normally adopted for founder saints, he is shown with a model of the cathedral church. In addition, however, he is given a document to hold and this, along with the pilgrim figure, may be a reference to a story well-known in fifteenth-century Salisbury that during Osmund's lifetime a pilgrim had been miraculously whisked from the Holy Land to Salisbury in a day, bearing a letter for Osmund given to him by the Virgin Mary (Malden 1901, p 69). Alternatively the document might be an allusion to the Institution of St Osmund, the unique, written constitution which he gave to the cathedral at its foundation, or even a reference to the liturgical Use of Salisbury, the distinctive character of which also dated from the time of this Norman prelate. When the cathedral chapter decided in 1387 to press for the canonisation of their founder, one of their main objects is thought to have been to promote the Use of Salisbury which at the time was steadily being adopted as the normal liturgy in most English churches (Edwards 1967, p 80).

6 **Pilgrim badge:** a mitred bishop holding a crosier in his right hand and a model of a church in his left. A faulty casting has produced a blob instead of a cross on top of the church spire. The figure stands in a canopied frame with borders of pierced quatrefoils down the sides, supporting a low, flattened arch topped with crocketed pinnacles. On the back is not only the usual pin and clasp but a bar of extraneous metal left from the inlet of the mould. Possibly a waster. Second half of 15th century. H. 41 mm. *195a/1987* **Fig 10**

7 **Pilgrim badge** of circular medallic form on which the standing figure of St Osmund is depicted against a diapered ground. He is holding a crosier in his left hand and in his right a model of Salisbury cathedral, represented with a central tower and spire, topped by a cross. His chasuble has Y-shaped orphreys and the infulae or latchets hanging from the back of the mitre are visible on either side of the head. A central stitching-loop is cast in one with the back of the badge. End of the 15th century or early 16th. D. 30 mm. *190b/1987* **Fig 11**

The mode of attachment, replacing the normal pin and clasp, is unusual and was probably copied from the stitching-rings that were a feature of many contemporary bracteate badges, especially those sold at Walsingham and abroad (*cf.* Cat 38-9). To the backs of these thin, die-struck badges a central ring was often fixed at right-angles by a spot of solder. The figure of a bishop in an attitude similar to that of St Osmund in Cat 6-7, except that the crosier is held obliquely across the body, is engraved on the bezel of a copper alloy finger-ring, found at Salisbury in 1986 (pc). Serving both as signet and iconographic ring, this may afford further tangible evidence of the popular cult surrounding St Osmund at Salisbury in the late fifteenth century. The ring and many of St Osmund's pilgrim badges would doubtless have been worn as charms against toothache, paralysis, insanity and other misfortunes which had been the subject of authenticated miraculous cures through the intercession of St Osmund.

St Thomas of Canterbury

Thomas Becket was born in Cheapside, London, nineteen years after the death of St Osmund of Salisbury. Thomas's obvious ability led to rapid advancement and by the age of thirty-seven he was chancellor of England and close friend of the king, Henry II, whom he was to serve well as statesman, ambassador and soldier. In 1162, Henry, expecting their amiable relationship to continue, secured Becket's election as archbishop of Canterbury. But Becket became an exemplary churchman, throwing himself into the duties of his new office and soon finding himself in bitter conflict with the king over the respective jurisdiction of church and crown. In 1164 he was obliged to flee the country. When he returned from exile on 1 December 1170, the quarrel between king and archbishop broke out again. In a moment of fury, Henry asked his courtiers who would rid him of this turbulent priest and four knights, taking the king at his word, set out for Canterbury and there killed Becket in a side chapel of the cathedral on 29 December 1170.

That event staggered the whole of Christendom, and from then until at least the middle of the fifteenth century Canterbury was by far the most important centre of pilgrimage in England and one of the three or four foremost pilgrim resorts of Europe. Evidence of the mass appeal of St Thomas of Canterbury is provided by the extraordinary number of Canterbury souvenirs that have survived, especially at London, but also as far afield as Scotland, Ireland, France, Germany, the Netherlands, Norway and Sweden. At least forty Canterbury badges or fragments of badges are believed to have been found at Salisbury, constituting among local finds the largest group from any single shrine. One of Salisbury's churches, too, belonged to the eighty or so parishes that chose to dedicate their own church to England's new saint, thereby electing St Thomas to serve as their patron and protector. Indeed, every church in the land probably had an image or picture of St Thomas of Canterbury until the campaign against his cult by Henry VIII destroyed most of them. The prolific finds of Canterbury badges, lost or discarded before Henry VIII's time, afford modest compensation for these immense losses.

Canterbury was the first English shrine to manufacture souvenirs for pilgrims and its mould-cutters were to set the trend of English fashions in this field by a massive output of stylish pilgrim signs commemorating Becket's martyrdom and the events that led up to it or depicting his sumptuous shrine as well as lesser shrines and relics, which all formed part of the official medieval tour of Christ Church, Canterbury.

8 Pilgrim badge: incomplete standing figure of St Thomas Becket depicted as archbishop. He is shown in full archiepiscopal vestments, beginning at the neck with the amice, a piece of linen with an apparel (embroidered panel) attached, tied in front to form a kind of stiff collar. Next, hanging from the shoulders is the vestment specially pertaining to archbishops, the pallium, forming the outline of a Y, fringed at the end, over the chasuble, the outermost mass vestment of pointed oval shape. Beneath the chasuble can be seen in descending order the lower edges of the dalmatic and tunicle and of the alb. Beneath the tunicle emerge the two fringed ends of the stole. The alb has an apparel at the hem, enriched with diaper-work, and below this are glimpsed the episcopal sandals (closed shoes). The cuff of an episcopal glove can be seen on the left hand and, while most of the maniple, hanging from the left wrist, has been lost, its decorated ends have survived. Third quarter of the 14th century. H. 67 mm. Mitchiner 1986, p 61. *193a/1987* **Fig 12**

The archbishop's right hand (the fingers are missing) is raised in the act of blessing, while the left holds the shaft of the cross-staff, the top of which would have been level with his mitre. This simple hieratic pose had by this time become one of the conventional ways of representing St Thomas in all branches of English art. Many other badges of this subject are made to assume the same sway, or S-shaped curve, of the body, by which fourteenth-century artists sought to suggest grace and to inspire reverence. A few also succeed in conveying the popular medieval idea of Becket as an exceptionally tall man. A later version of this badge was impressed in the mould of a bell *c.*1450 and is thus reproduced on the bell itself at Lyneham, Wilts (Walters 1920, p 126, fig 91; for other types of badges preserved as casts on church bells, see Cat 37 and 122).

9 Pilgrim badge: a lozenge-shaped plaque on which is depicted the standing figure of an archbishop on a hatched ground. He wears a mitre and other vestments and holds an archbishop's cross-staff in his left hand. A nimbus surrounds his head and his right hand is raised in blessing. Though the badge has the usual pin and clasp, it has also been punctured with a secondary fixing-hole, near the apex. Late 15th century. H. 29 mm. *215/1987* **Fig 13**

Presenting the same subject as the previous badge after the lapse of more than a century, this pilgrim sign well illustrates the tendency for souvenirs at Canterbury and other long-established English resorts to start large in the fourteenth century and to diminish through the fifteenth. Several Canterbury badges of medallic form are known, some cast in pewter (Spencer 1978, fig 5 c,d), others stamped out of thin sheet brass or silver. But this is the first recorded find of a lozenge-shaped Canterbury badge, even though the form was widely popular in the second half of the fifteenth century, finding favour, for instance at Salisbury (Fig 7) and at Windsor (Cat 113).

10 Pilgrim badge: St Thomas riding a dappled horse. He wears a mitre, an apparelled amice, dalmatic, cope, a glove with monial (*cf.* Cat 31) and fashionable, pointed shoes. He holds the shaft of his archiepiscopal cross in his left hand, while his right hand would originally have been raised in the act of blessing or intercession. The horse is led by a groom. He wears a cape and a close-fitting, belted tunic, buttoned down the front and sleeves, and he holds a knobbed staff, perhaps a mace, in his free hand. End of 14th or early 15th century. H. 75 mm. Mitchiner 1986, p 55. *193b/1987* **Fig 14**

Both archaeological and stylistic evidence suggest that this type of souvenir was introduced at Canterbury shortly before 1380 (Spencer 1982, pp 309-11). Its introduction and manifest success almost certainly coincided with the period covering the fourth jubilee of Becket's martyrdom (1370) and the Black Prince's funeral (1376; *cf.* Cat 151). It was evidently at this time that the Canterbury pilgrimage was at its most fashionable and that Canterbury badges reached the highest technical and artistic competence. This badge from Salisbury lacks the crispness and meticulous detailing shown by badges of the best period (*cf.* Spencer 1987, p 221, no 60).

Of the many surviving examples of the badge, however, this is the one that corresponds most closely with a remarkable stone mould in the British Museum (Spencer 1968, pl vi, 1; Alexander & Binski 1987, p 396). The mould shows that the complete badge would have a dog running alongside the horse, and in the background, as it were, two or three winding shrubs providing openwork links between the figures and a baseplate. The trefoil from one twig still adheres to St Thomas's foot in the Salisbury badge. Emphasising the sense of occasion, the attendant is sometimes the picture of elegance, with a sword and a dagger at his waist and a three-line whip in his hand; for the badges appear to have been made to commemorate Becket's triumphal return to Canterbury on 2 December 1170, after an absence of six years in exile. Other souvenirs of this event show Becket sailing across the Channel (Spencer 1987, p 221, no 59) and the occasion was celebrated liturgically at

Canterbury by an annual festival called the Return of St Thomas. Four weeks after his return Becket was murdered and there soon arose a tendency to liken his last days to the Passion of Christ. Later, somewhat simpler, versions of the above badge (Cat 10) show Becket more suitably attired for riding, though still wearing his mitre and episcopal gloves. A portion of one of these is correctly attributed to Canterbury in Mitchiner 1986, p 52 (no 79), but an almost complete badge from the same mould is incorrectly identified with the Holy Blood of Hailes (*ibid.*, p 112), as are a badge of St Matthew and St Maternus from Trier and two souvenirs from Windsor depicting King Henry VI on horseback (*ibid.*, p 190; *cf.* p 54 below).

11 Pilgrim badge: fragment depicting the figure of Edward Grim, tonsured and holding an archiepiscopal staff, from a large badge commemorating Becket's martyrdom. Grim, a Cambridge clerk who happened to be at Canterbury, was the only person to remain with the archbishop when he was attacked in the cathedral. A portion of the border also survives. Second quarter of the 14th century. H. of complete version, 65 mm approx. *190h/1987* **Fig 15**

The complete badge would show an altar in front of Edward Grim, half-concealing him, and on it a chalice and retable (or, in other versions, a missal and crucifix). Becket would be shown facing Grim and kneeling in front of the altar as the four knights, wielding swords, attack him from behind (Spencer 1968, fig 3 b,c; Spencer 1987, p 222, fig 61). The scene would be framed by a border of pierced quatrefoils with four large trefoils adding corners, as it were, to the circular composition. The idea of Becket praying or even saying mass, instead of facing and resisting his assailants, is at variance with the facts, and had presumably been introduced to add to the sense of sacrilege.

The scene of Becket's murder inspired some of the most exquisite mould-cutting of the fourteenth century. The resulting badges were of such delicate openwork, however, that few have survived intact. A century later the same subject was being less elegantly commemorated on small pewter or brass badges of medallic form.

12 Pilgrim badge: a fragment depicting a knight advancing and brandishing his sword; probably from a scene of Becket's martyrdom similar to that described above (Cat 11), but larger. A surcoat covers most of his body-armour. Mid 14th century. H. 39 mm. *190i/1987* **Fig 16**

Becket was set upon by four knights, Fitzurse, le Bret, de Moreville and de Tracy. On pilgrim signs of the circular, openwork type described above, the most prominent knight, usually second from the right in the group of four, is shown cleaving Becket's skull with a downward stroke of his sword; he generally carries a shield, sometimes emblazoned with bears' heads (perhaps a punning device for Fitzurse, deriving from the Latin *ursus*, bear). Further in the background, another knight thrusts his sword vertically point-downward, into the archbishop's skull. Sometimes the third knight lunges with his sword at Edward Grim, striking him on the arm. The fourth knight (as in this fragment, Cat 12) is invariably shown preparing for action, unsheathing or flourishing his sword. This figure, judging from its size, belonged to a particularly large version of the badge, examples of which can be estimated to have measured as much as 140 mm across.

Concurrently other badges set the martyrdom scene in a rectangular frame, beneath a two-arched canopy. A naive version of one of these is represented by the following fragment:

13 Pilgrim badge: the figure of a knight and the left-hand corner of the frame from a representation of Becket's martyrdom. 14th century, probably first half. H. 26 mm. Given by Mr I. Smith. *200c/1987* **Fig 17**

Portions of identical badges found at London make it possible to say that this fragment like Cat 12, depicts the last of the four knights who enter from the left, shoulder to shoulder, like a latterday chorus line. With their arms concealed, all four figures are alike except for differing shields. They provide an interesting, and for Canterbury uncommon, example of banality in the field of pilgrim souvenirs.

14 Pilgrim badge representing a sheathed sword overlain by a buckler, probably a memento of the weapon with which Becket was martyred. Like actual 14th-century hand-shields recently found at London, the buckler is represented as having a central boss, sexfoil in this instance, a reinforced outer edge and an intervening field of applied decorative reinforcement, here depicted as a conventional branching vine-scroll in openwork. Like many medieval badges, especially the larger sort, this pilgrim sign is fitted with a series of malleable clips for the attachment of a coloured backing to show off the openwork. The 'bow-tie' quillons suggest a late 14th or early 15th-century date. H. 75 mm. Mitchiner 1986, p 192, where it is attributed to Glastonbury. *193d/1987* **Fig 18**

Variants, one of them also recently found at Salisbury, have a lion-mask in place of the foliate central boss (e.g. BM M & LA 98,7-20,2). Elsewhere, badges of similar configuration have been found, but with totally dissimilar forms of openwork ornament, among them one where the mitred head of St Thomas is at the centre of the buckler (MOL 86.18/2).

There is more consistency in the designs of a comparable and much more common series of badges which take the form of miniature swords slotting into scabbards. The scabbard is cast in one with a solid buckler or fist-shield (Spencer 1982, pp 313-4; 1987, p 222, no 62). These have been found in late fourteenth-century contexts at London and, like Cat 14 above, were also carried to points beyond the capital. The scabbard and buckler from one example has been recovered from a bank of the Windrush in Oxfordshire, while part of another has turned up at Salisbury:

15 Pilgrim badge: part of a miniature scabbard overlain by a buckler, which is covered with a diaper pattern. A pin and clasp are cast in one with the back of the scabbard, into which a separately cast sword, its quillons trimmed with hideous devils' heads, would originally have slotted. On most other badges of this sort, the diaper ornament is omitted from the scabbard and a boss, occasionally very emphatic, is depicted at the centre of the buckler. Late 14th or early 15th century. H. 41 mm (*c.* 145 mm when complete). Given by Mr I. Smith. *200a/1987* **Fig 19**

Sometimes souvenirs of the sword that delivered the final fatal blow to Becket incorporated a kite-shaped shield in place of the circular buckler described above, the shield being charged with bears' heads (*cf.* Cat 12; Spencer 1968, pl iv, 8). An example of a sword-badge with such an escutcheon is known to have been found at Salisbury in 1986 but cannot be illustrated here since it was not submitted to the Museum for recording. The sword from a plainer fifteenth-century version of the badge was also recently discovered at Salisbury (Mitchiner 1986, foot of p 159).

This type of badge owed its existence to the fact that the final blow to St Thomas, severing the crown from his skull, was delivered with such force that the sword shattered on impact with the pavement and was abandoned there. This weapon was preserved and subsequently exhibited to pilgrims at an altar set up at the spot where Becket had been slain. The sword was popularly regarded as a relic of major importance. Even Erasmus, who was sceptical of popular religious beliefs, made a point of kissing 'the sacred rust' of the sword when he visited Canterbury in the early sixteenth century.

16 Pilgrim badge: the bust of an archbishop wearing an apparelled amice at the neck and a richly ornamented mitre topped with a cross; at the base is the word *THOMAS*. Early 15th century. H. 86 mm. Found in Endless Street, Salisbury; Drainage coll. (E.T. Stevens). *Sal. Mus. Cat.* 1864, p 56 and 1870, p 10; Saunders 1986, p 10. *iiE504.* **Fig 20**

Throughout the fourteenth and fifteenth centuries the most popular of all Canterbury badges were those commemorating a reliquary known as the Head of Thomas (*Caput Thome*). This took the form of a richly jewelled, mitred bust and contained the portion of Becket's skull that had been hacked off by his assailants. The reliquary seems to have come into prominence after being refashioned at substantial cost for the third jubilee (1320) of Becket's murder. Several hundred medieval badges celebrating this object of popular devotion have been found at London alone, exceeding by themselves the number of surviving pilgrim souvenirs from any other shrine in Christendom. They have also turned up in other medieval towns like King's Lynn (Spencer 1980, p 19, nos 70-75) or Bristol (Barker 1978, fig 1, no 2), as well as abroad. Over a hundred examples are known to have been found at Canterbury, where they far outnumber other types of Canterbury badges.

At least fifteen more are thought to have been found at Salisbury (one of them is illustrated in Seaby 1987, p 18, fig V351B), enough to give a slight indication of the wide variety of sizes and types that were made over a period of two centuries. Cat 16 above is a good example of one of the largest sorts, where the bust is shown in silhouette without any surrounding canopy or frame. Consistent with nearly all other mementoes of the head-reliquary, St Thomas's face is modelled in comparatively high relief (the modelling was to become more perfunctory during the fifteenth century), while the neck and shoulders are virtually flat, a design that made for weakness at the junction of the head and neck. A very large proportion of the badges of this type have broken in half at this point, or in some instances were perhaps deliberately folded and broken (Cat 18-20). While many badges similarly show the face with a cleft chin, the mouth on this badge lacks the exaggerated downward curve, sometimes emphasised by a drooping moustache that is a feature of nearly all other badges of this subject.

17 Pilgrim badge: bust of St Thomas with carefully wrought enrichment of the mitre, amice and lower border, which, in the case of another slightly smaller Salisbury find is inscribed *CAPVT THOME* (Mitchiner 1986,p 155). Late 14th or early 15th century. H. 80 mm. *Sal. Mus. Rep.* 1987-88, pl 3a. *225n/1987* **Fig 21**

18 Pilgrim badge: mitred head from a bust of St Thomas. Second half of 14th century. H. 52 mm. Drainage coll. (Brodie). *Sal. Mus. Cat.* 1864, p 55 and 1870, p 11. *iiE505* **Fig 22**

Two badges recently found at Bankside, London were also cast from the mould that produced this Salisbury find (MOL 86.202/6-7); they retain the neck and shoulders missing from the Salisbury badge and add 34 mm to its height and the word *THOMAS* at its bottom edge. A few almost identical badges are also known. But even those others that differ markedly in size, quality, detail and date are remarkably consistent in their stylised portrayal of St Thomas's expression around the mouth (*cf.* Cat 17-22 and Spencer 1968, pl vi, 2-4 and fig 1d). This continuity may reflect either the handing down of moulds and designs or, more likely, conscious attempts to capture the likeness of the reliquary they were intended to commemorate.

19 Pilgrim badge: mitred head from a bust of St Thomas. Late 14th or early 15th century. H. 37 mm. Given by Mr W. Wareham. *143/1978* **Fig 23**

Other badges from the same mould (MOL 8804 and another found at Canterbury, 1987), show that the sloping sides of the mitre were once trimmed with crockets and that the lower part of the bust was inscribed *CAPVT : THOME.* The original height was about 60 mm.

20 Pilgrim badge: head from a bust of St Thomas. Early 15th century. H. 44 mm. *192c/1987* **Fig 24**

21 Pilgrim badge: head from a bust or figure of St Thomas. Early to mid 15th century. H. 28 mm. Given by Mr I. Smith. *200b/1987* **Fig 25**

22 Pilgrim badge: head from a bust of St Thomas. Late 14th or early 15th century. H. 42 mm. Given by Mr B. N. Lee. *2250/1987* **Fig 26**

Several other badges commemorating the so-called 'head of Thomas' reliquary in this silhouette form, as distinct from those enclosed in frames of regular shape, are known to have been found at Salisbury recently. Not all of them have been submitted for recording, however. One is illustrated here (Fig 27; pc) as a typical version of the subject in the middle of the fifteenth century.

23 Pilgrim badge: A mitred bust of St Thomas flanked by upright swords and set in a circular frame with widely-spaced dot-and-circle ornament. First half of 15th century. D. 29 mm. *195b/1987* **Fig 28**

For another, almost identical badge found at Salisbury, see Seaby 1987, p 18, fig V352A). At London part of an identical badge came from a foreshore deposit of *c.*1430 at Swan Lane, while a rather grander specimen was found at Queenhithe with five, little-circulated groats of 1413–34. The frames of examples found at Canterbury lack surface ornament but have trefoils sprouting from the outer edge instead. The general design appears to be a development from one of Canterbury's stock souvenirs in the late fourteenth century, showing Becket's bust in a circular frame (*cf.* Cat 25-6), usually inscribed *CAPVT THOME.* Swords similarly appear on the fourteenth-century seal of the Commissary-General of Canterbury. On pilgrim badges the swords may simply stand for Becket's martyrdom but they also probably allude to the so-called Martyrdom, Sword or Sword-Point, mentioned above (Cat 15). This was the altar set up on the spot where Becket was murdered. Here was exhibited the sword that delivered the fatal blow to Becket's head.

The silhouette types of badges described above (Cat 16-22) remained in vogue from the middle of the fourteenth century onwards and into the second half of the fifteenth. Framed versions of the subject, on the other hand, are almost as numerous, many of them having been excavated from closely-datable archaeological contexts. From these dated specimens it is clear that the framed badges enjoyed an even longer period of production, from the early fourteenth to the late fifteenth century, when they began to give way to badges of solid, medallic forms (*cf.* Cat 9).

24 Pilgrim badge: a smaller version of Cat 23, again showing Becket's bust between two upright swords. First half of 15th century. D. 17 mm. *Sal. Mus. Rep.* 1970-71, p 21 and cover; Salisbury Museum 1973, fig 61; Saunders 1986, p 10. Given by Mr W. Hodgkinson. *16/1971* **Fig 29**

This is the smallest known example of what seems to have been a fairly popular type of Canterbury souvenir. One of the cruder products of Canterbury's mould-makers, on the other hand, is illustrated by the next item:

25 Pilgrim badge: a small representation of the reliquary-bust, set within a broad circular frame, inelegantly inscribed + *CAPVT THME.* Early 15th century. D. 34 mm. *11c/1988* **Fig 30**

26 Pilgrim badge: a mitred bust, presumably that of St Thomas, in a circular frame with pearled edges and a band of close-set raised dots within circles, perhaps intended to resemble cabochons. Late 14th century. D. 21 mm. Mitchiner 1986, p 111. *193c/1987* **Fig 31**

Virtually identical frames were used for late fourteenth-century badges commemorating a royal saint (Cat 103-5). Mitchiner identifies this Salisbury find with the same royal cult, but another copy from the same mould (Thomas Hugo collection, BM M & LA) confirms that the bust wears a mitre and amice, not a crown and shoulder-cape. A similar badge from Salisbury was sold in lot 149 of a sale held by City Forum Auctions on 28 January 1988. A comparable badge found at Canterbury has a loop projecting from the base of the frame (*cf.* Cat 209). It may also be noted that circular frames similarly enriched with pseudo-gems had been tried at Canterbury as early as *c.*1320 (Spencer 1968, fig 1d) and were to continue in regular use there until the late fifteenth century, alongside settings which depended less on 'jewelled' surfaces and more on shapes, such as barbed quatrefoils. In general it may be suggested that the frames of pilgrim signs afford many insights into the probable forms and fashions of contemporary jewelled brooches.

While most circular frames bear either a basic pearled or dot-and-circle ornament, as in Cat 23, 24 and 26 or a caption or an invocation to St Thomas (such as *ORA PRO ME*, Pray for me) a number were also worked up to look like contemporary jewelled brooches. Other common forms of frames were square, multilobed or star-shaped or were based on intersecting rectangles, canopied niches or the Lombardic letter T. Thus the letter T, generally crowned, was used to surround figures of the archbishop enthroned (Smith 1846, p 205) and to frame representations of Becket's head-reliquary. On the example illustrated in Fig 32 (found at London, 1982), the reliquary is flanked by censing figures. Fragments of similar badges have been found at Salisbury and include the following:

27 Pilgrim badge: fragment of a large Lombardic letter T (for Thomas) which originally would probably have framed a representation of Becket's head-reliquary. Late 14th century. H. 55 mm. *10a/1988* **Fig 33**

28 Pilgrim badge: fragment of a similar, but smaller, letter T. Late 14th or early 15th century. H. 23 mm. Given by Mr I. Smith. *200n/1987* **Fig 34**

Portions of these large Lombardic letters, which are often found, are capable of being misunderstood, e.g. Mitchiner 1986, p 179 and p 262, where the top-stroke of the T is described as a flowering hill and confusingly linked with St Albans and with the type of badge illustrated below in Fig 321, and vertical strokes of the T are identified as ships of Our Lady of Boulogne. While the letter forms the outer structure of many badges, others take the T as their central motif:

29 Pilgrim badge: consisting, when complete, of a quatrefoil of veined leaves (i.e. a four-leaf clover) with a Lombardic T (presumably for Thomas) at its centre. 14th or 15th century. W. 23 mm. *209a/1987* **Fig 35**

An intact specimen, found at Canterbury, is illustrated in Fig 36. Several others have turned up at London, e.g. BM M & LA 71,7-74,58 (Cuming 1868, pl 17, no 10). These badges are good examples of 'reinforcement', whereby a secular and traditional good luck symbol, the four-leaf clover, is augmented by the amuletic use of the saint's initial. Another group of badges depicts a similar four-leafed figure, occasionally with a stalk and tuft of grass at the base, but omits the letter T; comparable quadrilobate motifs also appear on ampullae (Cat 140-3 & Fig 186).

The Lombardic T is also the central device of two or three different sorts of circular badge. These have more explicit stylistic links with badges of well-attested Canterbury origin. Thus a badge, found at Salisbury in July 1985 (pc), has a Lombardic T as its motif, encircled alternately by six diamond-shaped settings, each with a cluster of imitation seed pearls, and six collets, each containing an imitation cabochon gem, an ornamental arrangement already familiar from its use on a well- known type of Canterbury badge depicting the head-reliquary (*cf.* London Museum 1940, pl lxvii, 11).

Although badges commemorating St Thomas's head-reliquary were manifestly the most popular of all Canterbury souvenirs, the climax of the pilgrim's tour of holy places in Canterbury cathedral was clearly the shrine of St Thomas itself. It was to this magnificent structure that Becket's body had been translated in 1220. At the Reformation the shrine was obliterated but pilgrim souvenirs have left us with a schematic record of its appearance. These are large badges of delicate openwork and most of them have survived only as fragments. The solid, relatively strong fragment catalogued below is the portion which has most often remained intact:

30 Pilgrim badge: gabled chest cast in slight relief and represented as if encrusted with jewels. On the lid is a suggestion of the gold trellis-work to which loose gems and other precious offerings were attached. A small figure (which on some other examples is given the wings of an angel) points with a stick at the largest gem of all, the enormous ruby given to the shrine by the King of France in 1179. This detail bears out an observation written down by one 15th-century pilgrim from abroad that a little statue of an angel stood at the shrine pointing a wand at this famous jewel. Above the chest are depicted two model ships, typifying one of the most distinctive, yet commonest, kinds of votive offering left at the shrine, in gratitude for a safe homecoming or passage at sea. Late 14th century. H. 30 mm. *109/1988*
Fig 37

It was in this chest or feretory that Becket's bones were kept and, when the badge was complete, the chest would have been represented as raised up high on pillars, well out of the pilgrim's reach. Immediately beneath the chest would have been shown a recumbent effigy of the archbishop, his hands joined in prayer and his cross-staff or crosier at his side. This figure, in turn, is invariably depicted resting on the shrine's box base, which is perforated with the sort of niches into which pilgrims could insert their heads or ailing limbs (Spencer 1987, p 222). At the sides the badge would be adorned with flying buttresses or by figures swinging censers.

31 Pilgrim badge in the form of a pair of episcopal gloves of gauntlet type linked at the cuffs by a tassel and by a shared episcopal ring attached to the little fingers. The gloves are represented with monials (jewelled mounts) on their backs and with embroidered orphreys round the cuffs. 15th or early 16th century. H. 28 mm. *191c/1987*
Fig 38

32 Pilgrim badge virtually identical to Cat 31. *224/1987*. Not illustrated.

33 Pilgrim badge: fragment of a badge very similar to Cat 31, showing one glove with tasseled orphrey and ring. *225p/1987*. Not illustrated.

At least two other, similar, badges have also been found at Salisbury. A specimen from the same mould as Cat 31 was discovered at Brooks Wharf, London (Cuming 1867, pl 16, figs 3,4; now in the Canterbury Museum). Though many variants of this badge have been found, the gloves depicted on them are invariably shown with orphreys and with the ring worn over the glove on the little finger. Embroidered flowers or heraldic shields are occasionally substituted for the monials, however. In some instances the thumb-pieces are further emphasised by delineating stitches along their seams. Often, as with Cat 33, only one glove out of the pair has survived. One such fragment was recovered from rubbish deposited in the middle of the sixteenth century in the resonance passage under the choirstalls at the Whitefriars, Coventry (Woodfield 1981, p 101, fig 8c). Episcopal gloves doubtless figured among the relics and vestments preserved in many cathedrals. The gloves commemorated by the badges, however, appear to have belonged to a shrine of importance, judging from the considerable number and wide distribution of the surviving souvenirs. Canterbury is therefore a likely source. There, St Thomas's gloves, adorned with great orphreys, were listed among the cathedral's minor relics, along with other personal memorabilia such as his buskins (half-boots) (Legg and Hope 1902, pp 34-9), the possible subject of other pewter souvenirs found at London. A badge, recently found at Canterbury, in the form of an archbishop's pallium, may fall into the same broad category of saintly personalia. Several badges comparable to, but different from, Cat 31-3 have also been discovered in the Netherlands (Beer 1932, pl 27; Heeringen, Koldeweij & Gaalman 1987, p 73); with the exception of one example found at Nieuwlande in 1987, it is improbable that any of them originated from Canterbury, however. One further category of badge should also be taken into account. This consists of a pair of unadorned gloves designed as a pendant, with a loop at the junction of the cuffs (e.g. MOL 88.20/2) and seems more likely to be a lover's favour or a token of betrothal (Kurath, Kuhn & Reidy 1952+, s.v. glove, 2 & 2c).

34 Pilgrim sign: a Canterbury bell of truncated cone shape with a quadrilobe suspension loop and the (reversed) inscription *CAMPANA + THOME* (Thomas's bell) in Lombardic capitals round the lower edge. When found, the bell was fitted with a makeshift clapper of brass wire. Late 14th century. H. 42 mm. *1966/1987* **Fig 39**

The bell would originally have been fitted with a lead-tin alloy clapper held in place by a flimsy split-pin inserted through the hole in the top of the bell. In this instance, having lost or broken the clapper, the Salisbury owner, a Canterbury pilgrim of Chaucer's time, appears to have substituted a large brass pin. The pin, in turn, lost its domed or spherical head. Unlike the original clapper and split-pin, the bell itself would have been cast in high grade pewter, at least 95% tin with added copper and bismuth, to judge from the analysis of similar Canterbury bells found elsewhere.

Similar Canterbury bells retaining their original clappers have also been found at Salisbury (one is illustrated in Seaby 1987, p 18, fig V353). For a somewhat later type of bell found at Canterbury see Spencer, in Blockley forthcoming. William Thorpe, an itinerant Lollard preacher, spoke disparagingly of Canterbury bells when he was being examined for heresy in 1407. Excited by musicians and cheer leaders, he implied, pilgrim-parties grew so rowdy that they became a general nuisance: 'what with the noise of their singing, and with the sound of their piping and with the jangling of their Canterbury bells, and with the barking out of dogs after them, they make more noise than if the king came there away, with all his clarions and other minstrels' (Pollard 1903, p 97).

The Virgin Mary

Though eighty English churches chose St Thomas of Canterbury as their patron, his name ranked only twenty-second in the list of favoured dedications. The Virgin Mary, on the other hand, came top of the list, far ahead of any others in popular esteem. Salisbury Cathedral was one of over two thousand English churches dedicated in her honour. The stories of her miracles, widely known from the twelfth century onwards, emphasised her power of intercession between God and man and the universality of her interest and appeal.

It was everywhere accepted that she had been assumed into heaven and that she therefore left behind no earthly remains. But many churches claimed to possess such relics as her girdle or pieces of her garments or even entire garments and these helped to create local centres for her cult. More important in this respect were images of the Virgin, particularly those which were thought to work miracles. During the thirteenth and fourteenth centuries miracle-working statues or paintings of the Blessed Virgin appeared in countless churches. Devotees could therefore recognise her not only as an omnipresent protector, like her son, in every place at once, but also as a familiar localised figure – Our Lady of Ipswich, Our Lady of Willesden, Our Lady of Doncaster, Our Lady of Caversham, Our Lady of Worcester. Some of these local shrine-figures, like Our Lady of Walsingham or Our Lady of Aachen, achieved much more than local or short-lived fame, but most served a particular neighbourhood and the needs of the mass of poorer folk, who perhaps could not afford to go on far-off pilgrimages. The pilgrim trade sometimes catered for devotees of the more localised cults of the Virgin by the provision of appropriate pilgrim signs. At the same time some pilgrim centres, as the next catalogue entry shows, were able to offer their clients, over and above pilgrim signs, more general aids to the veneration of the blessed Virgin.

35 Figurine: the Virgin Mary enthroned as Queen of Heaven. With walls 1-2mm thick, the figure was hollow-cast in a multiple mould and was left open at the base (on the technique of hollow-casting, see also Cat 142). Subsequently the back appears to have been cut away below the lower edge of the veil exposing the rather rough, grainy interior of the casting. Thus, only the section of the figure above the shoulder is now depicted completely in the round. The Virgin wears a crown with four large acanthus-like fleurons and, on the breast, a conspicuous hexagonal brooch, jewelled at the angles. Her kirtle is drawn in high at the waist and is adorned at the neck and cuffs. Her cloak, too, has an ornamental border. Her elegant throne has a turned wooden framework and traceried side panels and stands on a substantial plinth with carved enrichment. English. Late 13th or early 14th century. H. 85 mm, W. 28 mm, depth 25 mm. Spencer 1987, p 224. *191s/1987* **Fig 40**

Combining dignity and tenderness, this figure is one of the better-class products to emerge from techniques that had been employed during the thirteenth century by mould-makers and pewterers at Canterbury and other English sanctuaries for the multiple production of comparatively large, hollow-cast pilgrim souvenirs of tin or pewter, such as ampullae for holding doses of holy water, free-standing statuettes of saints and three-dimensional ornamental finials, perhaps intended for the tops of pilgrims' staves. Like contemporary folding triptychs of pewter, good instances of which have been found at Tamworth Castle, Staffs., and King's Lynn (Spencer 1987, *loc.cit.*), the Salisbury figurine is perhaps to be regarded as an example of the ordinary man's devotional equivalent of the rich man's ivory. Its sparing use of metal invites comparison with the gold figure of the Virgin belonging to Richard Beauchamp, earl of Warwick (d. 1439), which stood 20½ inches high and weighed 95¾ ounces troy. The market for cheap figurines for use in the home of the humbler pilgrim seems to have been given further stimulus in the fifteenth century with the introduction of statuettes of the Virgin and other fashionable saints cast as solid figures of lead or moulded and fired in pipeclay or terracotta. One such leaden figure, a bishop, perhaps St Osmund, has been found at Salisbury (pc).

As for pilgrim badges proper, without the presence of contemporary captions or other explicit evidence of locality it is now impossible to identify with certainty the places of origin of many badges commemorating images of the Blessed Virgin or celebrating other specific or local aspects of her cult. Nor is it always possible to draw a distinction between pilgrim signs and badges that may simply have been made as devotional trinkets and amulets. But among the badges found at Salisbury are some that can be positively linked with certain English pilgrimages and a few others that seem likely to relate to Salisbury itself. The list starts further afield, however, with badges that can be recognised as souvenirs from abroad.

Our Lady of Tombelaine

36 Pilgrim badge: The Virgin seated with the Holy Child. The badge depicts the Virgin with a disproportionately large head and an ample abdomen, accentuated by a close-fitting, richly patterned kirtle and a slightly sagging girdle with D-shaped buckle at hip-level. She wears a heavy crown and with her right hand grasps a lily on a long stalk, which is linked to her waist by a three-petalled flower and to her hair by a rose. With her left hand she clasps the infant Christ who stands beside her, dressed like a miniature adult in fashionable houppelande. He touches the embroidered borders of her cloak and gown and in his left hand holds a globe representing the universe. When the badge was found, traces of red paint still survived around the globe. Northern French. Early 15th century. H. 57 mm. *Sal. Mus. Rep.* 1986-7, pl 5. *102/1987* **Fig 41**

Features like the large head may have reflected idiosyncrasies present in the cult-figure commemorated by the badge. Another badge in a private Swiss collection (Lamy-Lassalle 1968, fig 1a) is so similar that it must be from the same workshop as the Salisbury find. It repeats peculiarities like the dot-and-circle motifs on the Virgin's knees but also differs in a few details; the bench is narrower, the trefoil end-stops being moved to the top of the plinth which is inscribed *ave Maria* in black letter, and beneath the infant Christ are shown a pair of manacles, presumably representing a pilgrim's votive offering. The inscribed badge was found in the Seine at Rouen, as was a more degenerate version of the same subject (Musée des Antiquités, Rouen; *ibid.*, fig 23). Another badge (Prague, Museum of Decorative Arts), which is very similar indeed to the Salisbury find, though less complete, was recovered from the Seine at Paris. In this instance, the houppelande worn by the Holy Child is drawn in at the waist by a girdle and its low collar, open at the throat (a fashion suggesting a date of *c.*1410-20), is here emphasised by the addition of ornament (Koenigsmarková 1980, p 67). Other closely related badges are to be found in the Kunstgewerbe Museum, Cologne (Moses 1930, pl 91; Haedeke 1976, p 66), the Musée de Cluny, Paris (no 17988) and the British Museum (M & L A 1913, 6-19, 22 and 33), while another, recently found at Canterbury, was offered for sale by Spink and Son, Ltd, of London in 1989. Other badges recovered from the Seine at Paris possess some features that are similar to those of the Salisbury find and were possibly manifestations of the same cult. A few of these are inscribed *Tombelaine* in black letter on the plinth at the foot of the bench (Forgeais 1863, pp 48-51; Lamy-Lasalle 1971, p 284). Tombelaine was the name given to a tiny island near the coast of Normandy, some three kilometres from Mont-Saint-Michel. Here a chapel, founded in the twelfth century by the monks of Mont-Saint-Michel, became the focus of a cult of the Virgin. The success of the pilgrimage to Notre-Dame de Tombelaine could be attributed directly to the immense popularity of Mont-Saint-Michel itself (*cf.* Cat 84).

Another Salisbury find that is likely to have been brought back as a souvenir from France is illustrated in Mitchiner 1986, p 265. This badge depicts a figure of the Virgin and Child standing in a gateway beneath a steeply-pitched, tiled roof and between twin, cylindrical towers. Other examples of the badge have been found at London. Unfortunately no badges of this type are, as stated by Mitchiner (*loc. cit.*), inscribed with the word Tombelaine. That they are nevertheless of French origin is suggested by the discovery of several examples in France, at Paris, Rouen and Lyons, for example (Musée de Cluny 17977; Lamy-Lassalle 1968, fig 22; Tricou 1957, fig 62), and by the use of the same conventional aedicule to frame figures of various French saints (Forgeais 1865, p 153; Musée de Cluny 18020, 18026).

Our Lady of Aachen

37 Pilgrim badge: fragment depicting the lower part of a seated figure of the Virgin and a small section of a circular border, which is fitted with clips behind for the attachment of a coloured backing. First half of the 15th century. H. 26 mm: height of badge when complete, 120 mm approx.
10f/1988 **Fig 42**

This Salisbury find is from the same mould as another fragment recently recovered at Canterbury (Fig 43, pc) which also retains the Virgin's torso as well as the figure of the Christ-Child, standing, naked and with face upraised, to her left. This larger fragment, in turn, is identical to a relatively complete example of this entire badge (Stockholm, Statens Historiska Museum 17033:3), found during excavations on the site of the Cistercian monastery at Alvastra, Sweden (Rydbeck 1957, figs 1,2; Andersson 1989, pp 72-3). From this it can be seen that within the large circular frame the enthroned figure of the Virgin is flanked by two female saints standing on pedestals and that the frame was furnished with four stitching-rings. Linked to the top of the frame is another, smaller, shield-shaped frame, rebated behind and fitted with clips for the retention of either a separately-cast mount, perhaps a shield of arms, or, more probably, a mirror cut to the same shape. Also rising from the top of the circular frame is a niche-like superstructure, in the upper part of which , above the shield-shaped 'mirror' frame, is depicted a robe hanging, with its sleeves stretched out, on a horizontal rod.

This garment was Aachen's famous relic of the Virgin's night-gown, which, along with three other relics (Christ's swaddling-clothes and loincloth and the cloth used at the beheading of John the Baptist) and the miracle-working statue of Our Lady of Aachen, helped to make Aachen cathedral the most important shrine in Germany and a shrine of international resort, especially during the summer months of every seventh year when the major relics were exhibited. As at Canterbury, the manufacture of pilgrim badges seems to have begun at Aachen during the second quarter of the fourteenth century. Of the hundreds of thousands of badges that were subsequently made there, perhaps no more than a score have survived, in whole or in part, and detailed knowledge of their variety of design and imagery depends largely on the selection of badges which happen to have been recast on the surfaces of some ninety fourteenth- and fifteenth-century bells (Köster 1972, p 149; Köster 1957, 1973 and 1983B, passim). Their evidence suggests that badges of the type found at Salisbury were comparatively unusual and that the most popular Aachen badges of the late fourteenth and fifteenth century possessed three circular frames, set one above the other, with a mirror invariably in the smallest, middle frame. A late fifteenth-century mirror-badge, probably orginating from Aachen is represented on the hat of the pilgrim in the Frontispiece.

38 Pilgrim badge of lozenge-shaped, medallic form on which is depicted the Virgin Mary standing on a crescent-moon and holding the Child on her left arm. The edge of the badge, originally scalloped, is lined with a border of alternate pellets and tear-drops. To the right of the figure is a letter A, very faintly drawn. A bar perforated with a stitching-hole and set centrally, at right angles to the badge, is cast in one with the back. Possibly Flemish, *c.*1500. H. 42 mm. Given by Mr W. Wareham. *143/1978* **Fig 44**

No precise parallel for this badge is known but similar badges were used as still-life subjects in the borders of Flemish Books of Hours, *c.*1480-1520 (Köster 1965, pl 6). The letter A may conceivably be the initial of the place of pilgrimage (*cf.* Cat 138, 144). The crescent moon emphasises 'the steadfastest stableness of Mary perpetual. The moon lasts never in one, in fulness nor wasting, tokening this world changeable and all other earthly things; whilk Mary under her feet treads down ilk one, alway' (from the *Speculum Humanae Salvationis* in Huth 1908, chap. 37).

39 Devotional badge of circular medallic form on which is represented the Virgin and Child. Mary is portrayed with long flowing hair as a symbol of her virginity. At her feet are depicted breakers of the sea. The mode of attachment was similar to that of Cat 38. Possibly Flemish, early 16th century. D. 32 mm. Drainage coll. Saunders 1986, p 10. *iiE507* **Fig 45**

The Virgin is here depicted as the Star of the Sea, the name by which she was known in, for example, the prayer 'Ave Maria Stella' and the devotional song 'Stella Maris'. Sailors in particular looked up to Mary as a star of comfort.

The remaining badges of the Virgin are believed to be of English origin, beginning with a souvenir of a cult-image that was evidently at London or in its vicinity.

40 Pilgrim badge: the Virgin and Child within the horns of a crescent-moon (*cf.* Cat 38). The Virgin is crowned and sceptred and, though partly concealed by the crescent , she is evidently deemed to be standing. The infant Christ holds an orb (the universe). Late 15th or early 16th century. H. 28 mm. Mitchiner 1986, p 234. *1939/1987* **Fig 46**

One other version of this badge has been found at Salisbury (now in the Blackburn Museum ; illustrated in Seaby 1987, fig V357A). Badges of this type were not connected, as was once suggested (London Museum 1940, p 258), with the famous image of Our Lady of Boulogne (for which see Spencer 1978, p 237; Spencer 1985, p 309; Forgeais 1863, pp 7-27). Still less can they be regarded 'as derivatives of previous Walsingham badges commemorating the Assumption of Our Lady' (Mitchiner, *loc.cit.*) for the Assumption appears to have played no part in the iconography of Walsingham souvenirs. It is significant that no badge of the Virgin in the crescent moon has figured among the many pilgrim souvenirs found in the neighbourhood of Walsingham. In fact, the Salisbury finds and two others from Canterbury are believed to be the only examples to have turned up outside London, where well over three hundred specimens of this badge have been found. Very few of these are matching pairs, underlining the enormous scale of the original ouput, which seems to have been confined to a short period at the end of the fifteenth and beginning of the sixteenth century. Characteristically, five variants of the badge were excavated from a single pit, dated *c.*1520, at the site of Baynard's Castle, Blackfriars, and over thirty have been recorded (1987) from the late fifteenth-century deposits at Butler's Wharf, Bermondsey, and another six (1988) from early sixteenth-century riverine deposits in St Saviour's Dock, Dockhead, Bermondsey. Most badges of this type show the Child in the customary position on the Virgin's left, but about a fifth of them, including the Salisbury find described above (Cat 40), show the infant Christ on her right. In a few instances (e.g. MOL 81.157/1), including one of the badges found at Canterbury, the Virgin and crescent rest on the back of a large stylised bird, perhaps a dove.

A similar bird also appears at the foot of a larger, perhaps slightly earlier type of badge, also remarkably common at London in deposits of the second half of the 15th century, depicting the Virgin and Child standing, but with no crescent moon. Fig 47 illustrates a typical example, recovered (1983) from the Thames near London Bridge (see also London Museum 1940, pl lxix, 16). One of these badges (Fig 48, pc) has been found at Salisbury, too, and is as yet the only example recorded outside London. Among the many variants of this badge found at London, three come from the same mould as the Salisbury find. It seems probable that both this sort of badge and the type represented by Cat 40 commemorated an image or perhaps two images of the Virgin, which for a short period possessed considerable local appeal in or near the capital. Among several possibilities at the turn of the fifteenth century strong candidates would be Our Lady of Willesden, Our Lady of the Pew in the palace of Westminster or even the Lady Chapel (Henry VII's new chapel) at Westminster Abbey, where in 1504 the pope granted to pilgrims the same indulgence as that attached to the immensely popular pilgrimage to the church of Scala Coeli in Rome.

Also rather reminiscent of the cult-figure represented by Cat 40 is another group of pilgrim signs where the subject, the Virgin and Child in a crescent, rests on a panel of trelliswork and is surrounded by an architectural frame. The frame is topped by a crocketed, slightly ogival arch, flanked by pinnacles. Here, too, the crescent is somewhat architectural, almost cornice-like, in appearance (Fig 49; recovered (1987) from spoil removed from a Thames-side site, London). Badges of this type have turned up at many sites on the Thames foreshore at London. The following specimen from Salisbury is the only example yet known to have been found outside the capital:

41 Pilgrim badge: crowned, demi-figure of the Virgin with the Holy Child above a slightly angular 'crescent' which stands above pierced lattice-work and is flanked by pillars supporting a crocketed canopy. 15th century. H. 34 mm. *225t/1987* **Fig 50**

Several other badges depicting standing figures of the Virgin but lacking any distinctive features have also been found at Salisbury. They include the examples illustrated in Figs 51-54 (private collections) and the three following fragmentary badges in the Salisbury Museum's collection:

42 Devotional badge or pilgrim sign: incomplete figure of the Virgin standing, with the Holy Child. 15th century. H. 40 mm. Given by Mr I. Smith. *200d/1987* **Fig 55**

43 Devotional badge or pilgrim sign: incomplete figure of the Virgin standing, with the Holy Child. 15th century. H.34 mm. Given by Mr I. Smith. *200e/1987* **Fig 56**

44 Devotional badge or pilgrim sign: fragment of a figure of the Virgin and Child. 15th century. H. 18 mm. Given by Mr I. Smith. *200f/1987*. **Fig 57**

Our Lady of Eton

In 1440 Henry VI founded Eton College. While the new collegiate chapel was being built, he extended and enriched the existing parish church, which was dedicated to the Virgin of the Assumption and already possessed its own striking cult-figure. The new chapel, in turn, was dedicated to Our Lady of Eton and by the 1480s a superb picture of the Assumption accompanied the painting of the Miracles of the Virgin on its walls. From the outset Henry seems to have been bent on attracting pilgrims to his new foundation. He soon secured substantial indulgences for Eton's clientele and additional inducements for those visiting the college on the Feast of the Assumption and on other festivals of the Virgin; and he granted the college two annual fairs and a weekly market to help cater for pilgrims (Page 1925, pp 262, 268). It can now also be stated that pilgrim signs were adopted as another way of promoting the pilgrimage. Their existence is also an indication of the shrine's popular success, which, in the first phase, lasted till *c.*1460, when the royal founder fell into the hands of the Yorkists. Forty years later, though it ranked far below Our Lady of Walsingham and Our Lady Undercroft at Canterbury in royal esteem, The Blessed Mary of the Assumption at Eton was still included among the thirty-four shrines in southern England and East Anglia specially favoured by Henry VII's queen (Nicolas 1830, pp 3-4). By then Our Lady of Eton had doubtless become a satellite of new cults at Windsor (Cat 114, 123) and older sanctuaries at Reading and Caversham.

45 Pilgrim badge depicting the Assumption of the Virgin. The Virgin and Child, floating on a cloud, are shown above a shield (incomplete) of the royal arms and were originally encompassed by a mandorla or almond-shaped glory, the rays of which were tipped with pellets; one ray survives to the right of the shield. Middle of 15th century. H. 29 mm. Given by Mr M. Green. *142/1978* **Fig 58**

Larger, and probably earlier, versions of this pilgrim sign show the Virgin, crowned and with her hands joined in prayer, supported at the sides by either two (Fig 59, MOL 84.134) or four angels (Fig 60, Museum of Eton Life); at her feet and above the royal arms is a rebus (a letter E and a cask or tun) standing for Eton (Museum of Eton Life *Short Guide* (1985) fig 5; *cf.* the second seal of Eton College, Nichols 1875, fig facing p 102; *cf.* also the wall-painting of the Assumption in Eton College Chapel: Tristram 1929, pl 1). A slightly larger badge (also Museum of Eton Life), retrieved from the Thames foreshore at Vintry House, London, in 1989, shows the Virgin and Child enveloped in a double layer of cloud. The surviving upper part of an even grander specimen shows the Virgin crowned, and, as on the Salisbury find, holding the Child, though here the Child is on her right arm and a sceptre over her left shoulder; like the Salisbury find also, the figures are surrounded by a heraldic cloud instead of angels. A border bears part of an inscription in black letter: . . . *(A) ssumpcione: beate Marie: de Et* . . . (BM M & LA 56,7-1,2069; Smith 1854,p 138). All these badges share the distinctive form of mandorla, its extended rays pearled at the tips. The same applies to simpler badges of Our Lady of Eton, dating from the end of the fifteenth century (e.g. London Museum 1940, pl lxix,19; Mitchiner 1986, p 172, where the badge is wrongly identified as Walsingham, early fifteenth century). Other Eton badges of this period recently found at Canterbury (Figs 61,62) include one where the rays of the mandorla are alternately straight and wavy. A recent find from Butler's Wharf, Bermondsey, London, exemplifies another type of late fifteenth-century Eton badge in which the mandorla has become pear-shaped (Fig 63). Also belonging to the last decade or two of the fifteenth century is a bracteate badge recovered from the Thames foreshore at Trig Stairs, London (1981). Here the figure of Our Lady of Eton supported by three angels is stamped on a lozenge-shaped flan of silver foil (Mitchiner 1986, p 236, classified under Walsingham).

These badges remind us that after the early chapters of the Acts of the Apostles the New Testament says nothing of the closing years of the Virgin Mary. This deficiency was supplied by apocryphal stories, according to which she was warned of her approaching death by the Archangel Michael (Cat 84) and died in the presence of the Apostles. Her soul went to heaven and after three days her body was raised up by angels from its tomb and reunited with her soul. She was then crowned by Christ and enthroned as Queen of Heaven. The Eton pilgrim signs anticipate the coronation by showing her already crowned. Some, like Cat 45, also show her, however inappropriately, with the infant Jesus.

46 Pilgrim badge representing the Assumption of the Virgin. Our Lady crowned and with her hands joined in prayer is surrounded by an aureole (field of radiance) and a circular frame. Perhaps a souvenir from Eton. 15th century. D. 19 mm. *103/1987* **Fig 64**

Our Lady of Poulton

47 Pilgrim sign, incomplete, depicting the Virgin enthroned with a sceptre in her right hand and the infant Christ sitting on her left knee. The subject was probably framed beneath an architectural canopy, only the lower parts of which survive. At the base is a rebus: *pul* in black letter followed by a representation of a cask or tun. 15th century. W. 26 mm. *191d/1987* **Fig 65**

A different badge with the same rebus was found at Brook's Wharf, Upper Thames Street, London (Spencer 1971A, fig xxii,r) and has been variously dated eleventh and thirteenth century and mistakenly associated with St Mary's Abbey, Wilton (Cuming 1868, pp 219-20; Guildhall Museum 1908, p 327). This London find, however, which is complete, depicting both Virgin and Child in tall, arched crowns, must date from the second half of the fifteenth century and, like the Salisbury badge illustrated here, commemorates a pilgrimage to a statue of the Virgin in the parish church of St Mary in the village of Poulton, near Dover, Kent. Another version has been found in the Stour at Canterbury. Apart from these pilgrim signs little else survives to attest what was evidently the wide, though probably short-lived, appeal of this particular statue.

Contrasting sharply with more fashionable Marian pilgrimages enjoying royal patronage, like Our Lady of Eton or Our Lady of Walsingham, Poulton perhaps owed its brief fame to its nearness to Canterbury and its accessibility to pilgrims crossing the Channel. The evidence of wills suggest that by *c.*1515 the cult had subsided and become a matter of purely local interest, appealing to the people of Dover, Folkestone and that neighbourhood (Hussey 1907, pp xviii,251).

Our Lady of Walsingham

It was typical of popular devotion in the fifteenth century that the pilgrimage to Our Lady of Poulton should evidently spring up suddenly, command attention for a short period and then relapse into obscurity and perhaps be replaced by another briefly-popular cult. On the other hand, a miraculous statue of the Virgin had earlier placed another obscure village, Walsingham in Norfolk, among the great sanctuaries of Europe and was to hold it there for three hundred years. From Henry III to Henry VIII all English kings (with the possible exception of

Richard III) were assiduous pilgrims and benefactors to Our Lady of Walsingham. But the cult had a grip on all levels of society. When John Paston fell ill in London in 1443, his young wife, Margaret, hurried off on pilgrimage to Walsingham and his mother-in-law ordered, evidently not for the first time, a wax image of his weight to be sent to Our Lady of Walsingham (Gairdner 1904, II, p 55). The pilgrimage probably reached its peak during the fifteenth and early sixteenth century, when, with Windsor, it clearly overtook Canterbury as the principal English pilgrim resort. On the eve of the dissolution, when educated opinion had turned against pilgrimage, Walsingham alone was still drawing substantial funds from pilgrims, amounting to an income seven times larger than that provided by Canterbury's pilgrims.

Two early sixteenth-century letters epitomise the breadth of Walsingham's appeal. The first was from Elizabeth Newhouse, a poor country widow who had just learned that her son in London had lost his job. She wrote anxiously to him and for his future good luck she sent him a Walsingham badge, for she had just been on pilgrimage there (Gairdner & Brodie 1932, no 29). The second letter was from Sir Edward Howard to Henry VIII reporting that Lord Lisle (the illegitimate son of Edward IV) had been given leave of absence after a naval action off Brest 'for, Sir, when he was in extreme danger and hope gone from hym he called upon Our Lady of Walsingham for help and comfort and made a vow that, an' it pleased God and her to deliver him owt off that peril, he would never eet fleshe nor fyche tyl he had seen heer. Sir I assure you he was in mervelous danger, for it was merveil that the shipp beyng under al her sayls strikyng full but a rok with her stam that she brake not on peces at the first strok.' (Byrne 1981, I, p 158). Another devotee of Our Lady of Walsingham brought back the following souvenir to Salisbury:

48 Pilgrim badge: figure of the Virgin crowned and enthroned, holding a sceptre fleur-de-lys over her right shoulder. The Holy Child, also crowned and wearing a cape, sits to her left. The statue is framed within a gabled canopy, which has pinnacles at the ridge and eaves and knobbly crockets on the top edges and at the sides. First half of the 15th century. H. 50 mm. Mitchiner 1986, p 102. *193e/1987* **Fig 66**

Part of at least one other similar badge has recently been found at Salisbury (pc). Most fifteenth-century badges of Our Lady of Walsingham are small (Spencer 1980, p 11, nos 3-6), but souvenirs of a form and size similar to the Salisbury specimen were also popular in the early part of the century (e.g. Liverpool Museum 8250, Luton Museum BL/1/122/55). Examples with ogival canopies were being produced by the late fourteenth century. In the early fifteenth, embattled canopies, reminiscent of the tops of alabaster panels, were in favour and have occurred among finds from London, Calcot (Berks.) and King's Lynn (Norfolk), (Spencer 1980, p 10; Virgoe 1989, p 182). Smaller versions combined the crenellated top with the crocketed uprights of the Salisbury specimen (Smith 1848, pl xxxi, 4).

Some Walsingham badges show the enthroned statue in the gabled upper storey of a small building (Spencer 1980, p 11, nos 8, 9; never in the lower storeys as suggested in Mitchiner 1986, p 101), thereby celebrating the place in which the image was kept, as well as the image itself. This building was the Holy House, a chapel built about 1130 by Richelde of Fervaques in honour of the Virgin and planned as a replica of the house at Nazareth where Mary had lived at the time of the Annunciation and where Jesus had spent his childhood. The house had been shown to Richelde in a vision and she took note of its appearance and measurements. Eventually Walsingham Priory was built beside this tiny structure, which was preserved intact, within another chapel, until the Reformation. Erasmus, who visited the shrine in 1512, found it small and dark, lit only by sweet-smelling candles, but nevertheless 'meet for saints, so much does it glitter on all sides with jewels, gold and silver'. It was, he said, 'the most frequented place throughout all England' (Nichols 1875, pp 11, 13).

49 Pilgrim badge: the roof from a badge of the Holy House of Walsingham. As on most other badges of the subject the roof is striped diagonally, is topped by three crosses and rises above a clerestory of pierced quatrefoils. Late 14th or early 15th century. W. 15 mm. *10h/1988* **Fig 67**

When complete this Salisbury badge would have been very similar to that in Fig 68 (MOL 88.53; Spencer 1987, p 223). Though badges commemorating the Holy House were made in various sizes and over a long period, they consistently show the roof and clerestory perched on the gable-ends of the upper floor and, under the eaves, depict the ground floor with a central doorway flanked by windows and occasionally candles (Spencer 1980, pp 11-12). Appropriately enough, the actual Holy House at Walsingham contained at least one representation of the Annunciation scene and many badges, like that in Fig 68, have the Annunciation figures in place of the image of Our Lady of Walsingham. In due course the Annunciation scene alone, with the archangel Gabriel giving Mary the news that by the power of the Holy Spirit she would give birth to Jesus, became Walsingham's most popular pilgrim sign, especially after the middle of the fifteenth century (*ibid., loc.cit.*: Streeten 1983, p 111). The connection of most, if not all, of the Annunciation badges with Walsingham Priory is confirmed by examples bearing the name, Walsingham, and by fifteenth-century stone moulds excavated in Walsingham.

50 Pilgrim badge: the left-hand portion from a scene of the Annunciation, depicting the winged figure of Gabriel in the act of speaking (his hand upraised). The Virgin Mary, usually standing, with a flower in a vase between the two figures, would complete the scene. 15th century. H. 29 mm. *205b/1987* **Fig 69**

An identical badge has been found at London, BM M & LA 56, 7-1,2080 (Smith 1854, p 138, no 682).

The precise significance of the tall-stemmed flower (usually a lily) in a vase has not been established. Whether it signified that the Annunciation was the festival of early spring or symbolised the Virgin's innocence, it presented a shape suitable for a range of attractive badges that symbolised the Annunciation and doubtless conveyed to those who wore them the particular association that the Annunciation was believed to have with Walsingham Priory.

51 Pilgrim badge: the Annunciation lily-pot. The vase is narrow-waisted and has bands of dog-tooth ornament at the mouth and base and round the middle. Practically the whole of the flower is missing. A very similar badge, found on the Thames foreshore at the north end of Southwark Bridge, has a pair of handles. Late 14th century. H. 63 mm. *225q/1987* **Fig 70**

52 Pilgrim badge: the Annunciation lily-pot, a two handled vase with the lower parts of a branching flower surviving. A similar badge has been recovered from late 15th-century dumps at Butler's Wharf, Bermondsey. Second half of 15th century. H. 39 mm. *225r/1987* **Fig 71**

On other badges of this subject, the lily is sometimes represented with botanical accuracy and the vase is normally given two handles (*cf.* the vase on the embroidered fifteenth-century altar frontal in the church of St Thomas, Salisbury). The badge shown in Fig 72, also found at Salisbury (pc), presents an interesting pseudo-heraldic development of the subject, whereby the Annunciation lily-pot is flanked by eagles as supporters. The whole composition is then crowned to suggest the outlines of the Virgin's badge, a capital M with a crown over it. The same composition without a crown is to be found on a similar badge recovered at Canterbury. For another badge of the crowned M, found at Salisbury, but of uncertain origin, see Mitchiner 1986, p 104, bottom right.

53 Pilgrim badge: a lily issuing from the centre of a rose. Second half of 15th century. H. 31 mm. *192b/1987* **Fig 73**

The lily from another version of this badge is in Mitchiner 1986, p 243, where it is identified as a mantle. St Bernard described the Virgin as both the lily of purity and the rose of love, but it was not until the later fifteenth century that the association of the Virgin with the rose and the rosary reached its peak in northern Europe. In England at this period, supporters of the Yorkist dynasty, who might wish to indicate their sympathies by wearing a badge of the rose of York (*cf.* Cat 159-62), would doubtless relish the dual symbolism afforded by the device (Tudor-Craig 1973, pp 29-30). Whether or not it had any covert political significance, this Salisbury find and other badges of the same type seem likely to have originated as pilgrim souvenirs from Walsingham, where during the second half of the fifteenth century several varieties of pilgrim signs were introduced depicting the entire Annunciation scene emanating from the centre of a rose (for an example of this sort of Annunciation badge, found at Sandwich, Kent, see Liverpool Museum no 8212; Gatty 1882, p 35).

The lily was the flower of purity and its heraldic form, the fleur-de-lys, was another ubiquitous symbol of the Virgin Mary. Among several badges of the subject found at Salisbury there are two or three which may tentatively be regarded as souvenirs from Walsingham.

54 Pilgrim badge: a fleur-de-lys in a circular frame, from the outer edge of which radiates a series of knobs on stalks. 15th century. D. 28 mm. *190j/1987* **Fig 74**

55 Pilgrim badge: a fleur-de-lys in a setting very similar to Cat 54. 15th century. D. 25 mm. *192e/1987* **Fig 75**

The knobbed decoration was a feature of many pilgrim souvenirs in the second quarter of the fifteenth century and was especially characteristic of certain sorts of badges from Walsingham (Cat 48; Spencer 1968, pl II, 2; Spencer 1980, p 11, nos 5-6; p 13, no 27) and its neighbourhood (Cat 93). The knobs may have been in imitation of the pearls on short stalks of gold, which were used to encircle some contemporary fashionable brooches. Several badges very similar to Cat 54-55 have been found at Salisbury (pc) and London (e.g. MOL 82.144/1).

56 Pilgrim badge: a more impressive version of Cat 54, the heavy frame being ribbed and pearled and the projecting knobs being more widely spaced. 15th century. D. 48 mm. Mitchiner 1986, p 100. *193f/1987* **Fig 76**

Several comparable badges have been found at Canterbury and at London: e.g. three, all from different moulds, in the Canterbury Museum. For a much smaller and a very common type of framed fleur-de-lys badge or brooch, see Figs 283-93.

57 Pilgrim sign or amulet: a fleur-de-lys with the outer edges and the cross-bar pearled. 15th century. H. 45 mm. *191f/1987* **Fig 77**

A pair of very similar badges were found (1987) at Canterbury and among late fifteenth-century material at Butler's Wharf, Bermondsey. This Salisbury find has many other close parallels (e.g. MOL 8713, 82.147/11). Its suggested derivation from Walsingham, however, is far from certain. It may even be a livery badge. Such a badge was worn by members of Sir Thomas Montgomery's contingent on the English expedition to France in 1475 (Barnard 1925, f.2v).

There are also grounds for linking some of the pilgrims' ampullae found at Salisbury with the pilgrimage to Walsingham (Cat 138).

Our Lady of Salisbury

The ordinary folk of Salisbury looked for protection and support as much to the Blessed Virgin, patron of the cathedral, as to its saintly founder, St Osmund (Cat 1-7). Many of the miracles reported by devotees of St Osmund resulted from invocations made jointly to the Virgin Mary and the prelate.

In April 1409, for instance, a girl who was watching a village game at Laverstock, just outside Salisbury, was accidentally struck on the head and seriously injured by an iron quoit, but recovered after bystanders prayed to God, the Blessed Virgin and bishop Osmund. In December 1421, another girl, daughter of a well-to-do Salisbury citizen, fell from a considerable height on to a sharp iron spit, hot from the fire, and was impaled through the abdomen and given up for dead. Here again family and neighbours turned in prayer to the Blessed Virgin and good bishop Osmund and, after the child's miraculous recovery, undertook a pilgrimage to Osmund's tomb to give thanks to Osmund and Our Lady (Malden 1901, pp 60-61; Stroud 1987, pp 108-111).

By the late fourteenth century the fame of Our Lady of Salisbury had spread far beyond the neighbourhood of Salisbury. In parts of the Low Countries, for example, she was reputed to be one of the ten principal objectives for pilgrims destined for England. In the towns and cities of Flanders, Brabant and Hainault it was common practice for courts of law to mete out pilgrimages as punishments for particular crimes. The pilgrimages were assigned from penitential tariffs established by local custom. Most courts gave offenders the further option of buying their way out of the pilgrimage in accordance with a local, graduated price-list. Thus Our Lady of Salisbury is one of a hundred shrines appearing on such a list compiled at Dendremonde (Belgium) at the beginning of the fifteenth century (Beer 1932, pp 59-61). The pilgrimages are there arranged in ascending order of importance, which was assessed partly, perhaps, on popular esteem but mainly on the length and difficulty of the journey. Shrines such as St Servatius of Maastricht, St-Josse (Cat 120), Our Lady of Aachen (Cat 37) or Our Lady of Boulogne were, therefore, placed comparatively low on the list. Rated at twice their value or importance were pilgrimages to the Three Kings at Cologne and to St Thomas of Canterbury. Higher still were St Paul's Cathedral in London and Our Lady of Walsingham. Then in the top group come Our Lady of Salisbury ('Tonser Vrouwen te Salsbri'), alongside St John of Beverley and the long-famous images of the Virgin at Rocamadour and Le Puy in southern France.

Contrasting sharply with, say, the fashionable and somewhat worldly Madonna in Cat 36 are a series of badges depicting stiff, angular figures of the Virgin and Child. Our Lady is crowned and sceptred and stands supporting a puppet-like figure of Jesus, also crowned, against her left hip. The main distinguishing characteristic of these badges is the linear treatment of the Virgin's garments, the folds of which have become crowded stripes of dot-and-circle ornament. This type of badge has been found repeatedly at Salisbury and nowhere else, apart from one example discovered at Canterbury. It seems reasonable to suppose, therefore, that they are Salisbury products made to commemorate the local cult of the Virgin. Below are listed (Cat 58-63) those examples which have so far entered the collections of the Salisbury Museum. Fig 84 illustrates one of several examples which are believed to be in private hands, while Fig 85 (also from Salisbury, pc) is here included as a possible reversed version of the badge.

58 Pilgrim badge: standing figure of the Virgin, crowned, with a sceptre over her right shoulder and the infant Christ, also crowned, supported against her left hip. 15th century. H. 48 mm. *214/1987* **Fig 78**

59 Pilgrim badge: almost identical to Cat 58; the fleur-de-lys terminal of the sceptre survives. H. 49 mm. *225s/1987* **Fig 79**

60 Pilgrim badge: almost identical to Cat 59, but less complete. H. 38 mm. *198a/1987* **Fig 80**

61 Pilgrim badge: a cruder version of Cat 58. The band of metal behind the line of the sceptre appears to be the result of a fault in the mould. H. 39 mm. Given by Mr M. Green. *142/1978* **Fig 81**

62 Pilgrim badge: a cruder version of Cat 58. H. 38 mm. Given by Mr M. Green. *142/1978* **Fig 82**

63 Pilgrim badge: Fragment of a badge from the same mould as Cat 58. H. 20 mm. Given by Mr A.G. Pilson. *107/1987* **Fig 83**

Crosses and holy roods

Another unpretentious type of badge occasionally found at Salisbury also seems likely to be of local make and to celebrate a particular cross, perhaps a churchyard cross, in or near the town:

64 Pilgrim badge of circular medallic form on which is depicted, in a circle, a standing cross with slightly splayed limbs. Probably late 15th or early 16th century. D. 23 mm. Given by Mr W. Wareham. *143/1978* **Fig 86**

65 Pilgrim badge: an incomplete variant of Cat 64. The cross here is modelled slightly, and dots have been added to the border. As with Cat 64, the pin is set far to the right of centre. Probably late 15th or early 16th century. H. 17 mm. Given by Mr A.G. Pilson. *107/1987* **Fig 87**

An even smaller version of this badge (D. 13 mm) is shown in Fig 88 (found at Salisbury, pc). This is more typical of other finds in having the pin and clasp aligned at the centre. One specimen with a pellet on each limb of the cross was retrieved from the Thames foreshore at Vintry House, London, 1984, but this is the only example of the badge so far known outside Salisbury. Also from Salisbury come two pilgrim signs, one small and crude, the other, much larger, portraying in silhouette crosses of similar form to those catalogued above:

66 Pilgrim badge in the form of a cross, the arms splayed, the lower end of the upright missing. 15th century. H. 12 mm. 225v/*1987* **Fig 89**

A complete version, also from Salisbury, is illustrated upside down and consequently misinterpreted in Mitchiner 1986, p 184.

67 Pilgrim badge: a cross on a stepped pedestal. The limbs of the cross are again splayed like those of the heraldic cross patée and each limb has two pellets in the angles. Echoing the hanging figure of Christ is a lily or three-leafed plant, its spiny stem rising from the base of the cross. 14th or 15th century. H. 53 mm. Given by Mr M. Green. *142/1978* **Fig 90**

The concept of the Tree of Life was conveyed in medieval representations of the Cross by the convention of showing foliate shoots protruding from the living wood (Figs 93-94). The unusual and somewhat cryptic iconography of this badge, however, may be open to other interpretations. A palm branch, the emblem of victory, might here represent Christ's triumph over sin and death. A lily, on the other hand, might be an allusion to the belief that the Annunciation and Crucifixion took place on the same date, 25 March (for centuries regarded as the beginning of the year of grace) or to the two events that marked the beginning and end of the Incarnation of Christ (*cf.* the east window of St Mary's, Westwood, Wilts). Whatever the meaning, however, the idiosyncrasies of the badge suggest that it was intended to commemorate a particular wonder-working cross. The stepped base was a regular feature of the churchyard cross, sometimes serving as an outdoor pulpit.

Though they often marked a convenient meeting-place for worship, even before a church existed, relatively few churchyard crosses have survived. Medieval roods, on the other hand, have completely vanished, for all of them were ordered to be destroyed in 1547. Before then every church possessed at least one rood, the great rood, which stood above or within the chancel arch, in full view of the congregation. Some roods, like the Rood of St Saviour in Bermondsey Abbey or the Rood at the North Door of St Paul's Cathedral, grew famous for the miracles they performed. Thus on Holy Rood day, 14 September, 1465, John Paston wrote from Norwich to his wife, 'I pray yow voysyt the Rood of Northedor and Seynt Savyour, at

Barmonsey, amonge whyll ye abyd in London, and lat my sustyr Margery goo with yow to pray to them that sche may have a good hosbond or sche com hom agen' (Gairdner 1904, IV, p 186).

It was inevitable that popular demand would require souvenirs to be made of many such miraculous roods. Unfortunately very few of the resulting pilgrim signs can now be securely identified with a specific place of origin.

68 Pilgrim badge: a rood, complete with the attendant figures of the Virgin Mary and St John, set in a barbed quatrefoil, with a roundel protruding from each point. Late 14th or early 15th century. H. 34 mm. *225c/1987* **Fig 91**

Mary and John are here depicted as statues, in the manner of a formalised rood group. Other versions of the badge, some of them much more elegantly wrought, have been found at London and Canterbury; see especially British Museum M & LA 1904 7-20 5, with which it is interesting to compare a badge of the Virgin and Child enthroned and flanked by candles, from the same workshop (Egan 1986, fig 9 b). The common origin of both badges suggests that they may have been made as devotional trinkets, rather than specifically as pilgrim souvenirs.

Many fourteenth and fifteenth-century badges depict crucifixes of archaic, early medieval or Saxon appearance. Others, including instances found at Salisbury, represent roods with pilgrims kneeling and making offerings at the foot, and there can be little doubt that both kinds of badges were pilgrim signs in the strict sense.

69 Pilgrim badge: Christ, nimbed, hanging on a cross, the upper terminals of which are decorated with paterae and trefoil crockets. The vertical member of the cross, incomplete at both ends, is here restored from an identical copy of the badge found at London. This shows an altar with a diapered frontal at the foot of the cross and with a suppliant to the left of it. 15th century. H. of the Salisbury fragment, 30 mm; of the complete badge, 63 mm. *191g/1987* **Fig 92**

A very similar badge from London has been assigned, without any supporting evidence, to the 'Great Rood' of St Paul's Cathedral; Mitchiner 1986, p 183.

The Rood of Grace, Boxley

A similar arrangement is presented by a larger badge (H. 90 mm), also recently found in Salisbury (Fig 93, pc). Here a pilgrim stands to the right of the altar, clutching a rosary in one hand and with the other placing an offering among the collection of coins and brooches scattered on top of the altar. The cross is of grained wood and its top and transverse limbs end in barbed quatrefoils trimmed with roundels, which are also strewn along the edges of the cross, on Christ's arms and on the oblique label above the head of Christ. Christ is shown nailed through the palm of each hand and with his feet crossed. On the front of the altar in spindly black letter is the word *gras* (grace). Matching badges have been found at London (MOL 8682) and Canterbury (Liverpool Museum, Mayer collection 8191). Many more similar and presumed slightly earlier badges are also known, their main distinguishing characteristic being the trefoils that take the place of the single roundels and the chalice or candles which, in some instances, join the pennies on top of the altar. One example found at Bull Wharf, London (1979), retains some of its original brown and pink paint.

The great regularity with which badges of this type, and of related types described below, have been found points to a shrine of considerable popularity in the late fourteenth and first half of the fifteenth century. The caption on the altar suggests that this was the famous Rood of Grace at Boxley Abbey, Kent, which lay close to the main route of Canterbury's pilgrims. The rood had a life-sized figure of Christ which was denounced as an automaton in 1538; the changes of facial expression with which the image had been credited were then claimed to have been accomplished by 'certain engines and old wires' (Finucane 1977, pp 208-210).

The badges of Chaucer's time showed the Rood of Grace without an altar and therefore with four, instead of three, identical florid terminals. Here again the wood of the cross was depicted as if breaking into leaf or blossom, with trefoils sprouting from its edges. A pilgrim badge of this kind, virtually complete, has been found at Salisbury (Seaby 1987, p 18, pl V350) and is here represented (Fig 94) by means of another badge cast from the same mould (H. 94 mm; MOL 8676). Christ wears a crown with tall fleurons. His feet, turned awkwardly inwards, are held by a single nail. On the upper part of the cross is the title *INRI*, the initial letters being taken from the version given in St John's Gospel (XIX,19) in the Vulgate: *Iesus Nazarenus Rex Iudeorum*.

This badge had many variants and several complete or nearly complete versions have been found at London (e.g. MOL 8674; BM M & LA 56, 9-23,6). All of them are large, ranging from about 90 to 120 mm in height. One example was discovered in a late fourteenth-century deposit in excavations at Swan Lane, while another from the Thames at the southern end of Southwark Bridge (1982) has an added scroll with the inscription *Gode rode of grace* in well-formed black letter. Several fragments of these badges have also been found at Salisbury, including one substantial piece illustrated in Mitchiner 1986, p 88 (no 158) where it is given a London provenance. This badge was officially recorded at the time of its discovery at Salisbury in November, 1984. Among smaller fragments are the following:

70 Pilgrim badge: ornamental terminal and title, *INRI* on a scroll, from the upper limb of a rood. Late 14th century. H. 29 mm. Given by Mr D. Morgan. *198d/1987* **Fig 95**

Part of a badge from the same mould was recovered near the site of Old London Bridge (Southwark, Cuming Museum C1221). From this it can be seen that the heavily moulded terminal (Cat 70), with its interplay of squares and quatrefoils, has lost small trefoils from its edges.

71 Pilgrim badge: upper limb of a rood, with quadrilobe terminal and *INRI* on a scroll. Late 14th or early 15th century. H. 25 mm. *209b/1987* **Fig 96**

72 Pilgrim badge: the lower limb of a rood, its edges and terminal trimmed with trefoils. Late 14th century. H. 20 mm. Given by Mr I. Smith. *200g/1987* **Fig 97**

The form of the terminal is that most commonly encountered on Boxley badges, the inside of the quatrefoil being often decorated with fine lines as here or, in one instance, with red paint.

Relics of the True Cross and Holy Blood

Though the doctrine of the resurrection was incompatible with the existence of any physical remains of Christ, official theological scruples were by and large overcome by popular demand for relics of the Saviour. Relics of Jesus and the multiplication of fragments of the Cross added to the growing number of pilgrim centres associated with Christ and his Passion. Thus, famous pieces of the Cross enshrined at Waltham Abbey (Essex) and Bromholm Priory (Norfolk) gave rise to distinctive pilgrim souvenirs (Spencer 1982, pp 307-9). Other places such as Westminster Abbey or Hailes Abbey (Gloucestershire) gained possession of one of the growing number of relics of Christ's blood, not all of which were claimed to have come from the wounds of Christ. Many were said to have exuded miraculously from statues of Christ or from the eucharistic host. Popular devotion to the Five Wounds of Christ and to the Holy Blood was, however, widespread in fifteenth-century England and the cult appears to have been commemorated by several Salisbury finds.

73 Pilgrim sign or devotional badge of circular medallic form depicting the Fountain of Life. Christ crucified stands in the middle of a circular well or fountain into which his blood streams from the wounds in his side and hands. On either side stand the figures of the Virgin Mary and St John, both nimbed and both apparently bearing vessels, perhaps chalices, to the fountain. A stitching-hole at the rear, like that of Cat 38, evidently proved unsuitable and two extra holes were drilled near the edges of the badge. Probably Flemish, late 15th or early 16th century. Drainage coll. (Brodie). *Sal. Mus. Cat.* 1864, p 56 and 1870, p 11. Saunders 1986, p 10. D. 30 mm. *iiE506* **Fig 98**

This unusual piece of mystical iconography is connected with the late medieval cult of the Five Wounds. The words 'Ye shall draw waters of joy out of the Saviour's fountains' (Isaiah XII,3), used in the Office of the Sacred Heart, caused Christ's wounds to be referred to as fountains or wells in the fifteenth century. A fifteenth-century English finger-ring in the British Museum is engraved with five wells, the wells of pity, mercy, comfort, grace and everlasting life. Especially on the Continent, it was the Fountain of Life (the Sacred Heart) which tended to claim the devotion originally paid to all Five Wounds. Nevertheless the badge follows the inflexible tradition of depicting Christ's wound, not on the side of the heart, but on the right side, symbolically the side of honour and salvation. The only known parallel for the subject of the badge to be found in an English church is in Flemish glass, early sixteenth century, at Marston Bigot (Somerset).

74 Devotional badge or amulet: a four-lobed figure with five roundels or raised dots in circles, one at the junction of each lobe and one at the centre. The badge is enriched with subsidiary dots and pearled decoration. 15th century. H. 22 mm. Given by Mr W. Wareham. *143/1978* **Fig 99**

75 Devotional badge or amulet: another version of Cat 74. H. 19 mm. *195r/1987* **Fig 100**

76 Devotional badge or amulet: fragment of another version of Cat 74. H. 19 mm. Given by Mr I. Smith. *200i/1987* **Fig 101**

The roundels are given more emphasis on some other examples of this badge, some fifty of which are known, all told (e.g. London Museum 1940, pl LXX, 29), at least ten of them having been found at Salisbury. A suggestion that they are Yorkist roses (Mitchiner 1986, pp 205-6) is unconvincing. The badges come from a multiplicity of moulds and when several others of a larger sort are also taken into account (e.g. London Museum 1940, pl LXX, 30), they look like manifestations of a popular cult, most probably the cult of the Five Wounds. The similar geometrical arrangement of the five consecration crosses on medieval altar slabs is likewise best explained as an allusion to the Five Wounds. Such mystical numbers often entered into medieval calculations of piety. John of Gaunt, for instance, bequeathed five nobles to every leper afflicted with 'five maladies' and living within five leagues of London, in honour of the Five Wounds, and he left three nobles to those less afflicted, in honour of the Trinity. For the inclusion of the Five Wounds in medieval charms and for their magical use as an image worn on the person or kept in the home, see Gray 1963.

Other badges relating to Christ

77 Devotional or prophylactic badge: the (incomplete) monogram of Christ, *ihs* or *ihc* in black letter with an abbreviation mark above, being the first three letters of Ihsus or Ihcuc, the name of Jesus in Greek. The presence of the large crown is consistent with the general use of crowns over monograms and initials on seals and signet-rings and, indeed, almost anywhere during the 15th century (*cf.* Cat 78, Fig 270). W. 42 mm. *195i/1987* **Fig 102**

The abbreviation mark is placed between, rather than above, the H and S on another Salisbury find (Mitchiner 1986, p 79). This is a badge of medallic form bearing the inscription + *IHS NAZARENVS* and closely resembling in every other respect a series of mid fourteenth-century badges calling upon St Thomas to intercede for the wearer, *Sancte Thome ora pro me* (e.g. BM M & LA 56,7-1,2039). The badge is also reminiscent of other contemporary circular plaques inscribed with a shortened form of *Ave Maria Gracia Plena* or with the names of the Three Kings (Spencer 1982, p 309). All these stock phrases were well-known in the Middle Ages as magical formulae against sudden death and lesser hazards and were widely recommended to be worn for prophylactic as well as religious reasons (Evans 1922, pp 125-132). It seems likely, therefore, that the whole of this class of badges, including Cat 77, was made for wear as talismans rather than as pilgrim signs.

78 Mould: one section of a stone, two- or three-piece mould for casting pewter roundels bearing the letters *ihc* in black letter (*cf.* Cat 77). The abbreviation mark through the h has been worked into a crown. 15th century. 51 x 49 x 27 mm. Found at King Manor, Clarendon, 24th September, 1887. James & Robinson 1988, fig 95. Given by Dr H.P. Blackmore. *3/1920-21* **Fig 103**

The mould, with its funnel-shaped ingate and pegs for correctly registering the counter-mould, is typical of those used for the production of pilgrim signs and other small objects of pewter (see p 9 above). A badge or brooch of the same form is worn by the Virgin in an early fifteenth-century panel painting known as the *Virgin and Child with the Bean Blossom* in the Wallraf-Richartz-Museum, Cologne. Surviving roundels of this kind appear not to have been designed as pilgrim badges, however. Examples with the *ihs* monogram have turned up at London, Coventry and Bristol, as well as at Salisbury (Salisbury Mus. *100/1987*), and these are fitted with a long rivet, not a pin. One of the London finds was riveted to a piece of wood (MOL 81.134/1), and not to a complete paten, as stated in Mitchiner 1986, p 194. Other examples with central rivets are decorated with figures of saints, the Five Wounds, the vernicle, rose, crown and sunburst. Clearly they cannot be called paten centres (*loc. cit.*), but they may, perhaps, have been made for the thick bases of wooden drinking-bowls, the cheap equivalent of prints from mazer bowls, like the copper alloy print 'enamelled' with a crowned heart containing the sacred monogram on a late fourteenth-century maplewood mazer belonging to St John's Hospital, Canterbury.

Another group of badges found at Salisbury may have been intended to celebrate the Nativity of Christ:

79 Pilgrim badge or amulet in the form of a star with five wavy rays and a tail of straight rays. At the centre is a bordered aperture, recessed behind. Between each wavy ray is a clip, which would normally be bent backwards, out of sight, behind the badge. Probably 14th century. 41 x 63 mm. *225d/1987* **Fig 104**

80 Pilgrim badge or amulet: part of another star similar to Cat 79. 36 x 21 mm. Given by Mr S. Bailey. *201/1987* **Fig 105**

At least one other example of this attractive hat ornament has turned up at Salisbury, while others have appeared as far afield as the Cheshire coast (Spencer 1968, pl IV, 3). All were similarly provided with long clips which were almost certainly intended to hold a tiny convex mirror in the central opening. Somewhat larger mirrors were the central element of some fourteenth-century Canterbury badges and were surrounded, as a rule, by an invocation to St Thomas and by demi-figures of some of his devotees. Convex mirrors also became a regular feature of pilgrim signs made at several continental sanctuaries (Cat 37) in the fifteenth century (see p 11 above). Though one of these was Cologne, the Star of Bethlehem does not appear to have figured among the various sorts of pilgrim signs made to commemorate the famous shrine of the Three Kings there (Meyer-Wurmbach 1964). The star might therefore be connected with a relic of the Nativity of Christ at an English sanctuary, like the portions of the crib kept at Canterbury cathedral or at Peterborough abbey. Whatever its origin, the star and its mirror would have primarily been regarded as magical, capable, through reflection, of capturing, storing and subsequently transmitting some of the spiritual benefits that were thought to radiate from certain relics and images. Another type of badge may fall into the same category:

81 Pilgrim badge or amulet: a star of six wavy rays around a disc that may correspond to the circular mirror originally at the centre of Cat 79. 15th century. W. 29 mm. Given by Mr I. Smith. *200j/1987* **Fig 106**

A few similar badges have been found at Salisbury; for one of them, see Seaby 1987,pl V360A. The pins and clasps with which they were all fitted differentiate them from similar, but purely decorative, plain-backed stars of lead, also found at Salisbury and on medieval sites elsewhere. These leaden stars, which have been wrongly described as Yorkist stud badges (Mitchiner 1986,p 207), were a form of applied ceiling and wainscot ornament, often gilded, and were first recognised during the excavations of the site of Clarendon Palace (Borenius 1943, p 45). For further comment on the use of the six-rayed star as a magical motif on badges see Spencer 1983.

82 Badge: a ray from a much larger star or from the border of a pilgrim sign (*cf.* Spencer 1980, p 15). 14th or 15th century. H. 31 mm. Given Mr M. Green. *142/1978* **Fig 107**

St John the Baptist, Amiens

83 Pilgrim badge: the figure of John the Baptist dressed in a camel skin held in at the waist by a girdle. The skin is from the entire animal. Its hind legs hang stiffly at his sides, while its head and forequarters reach almost to the ground. St John holds the paschal lamb on his left hand and points to it with his right. 15th century. Probably northern French. H. 35 mm. *191e/1987* **Fig 108**

This is a degenerate form of a type of badge more adequately represented by the specimen depicted in Fig 109 (MOL 86.343/2) and by similar examples found at London, Canterbury (Liverpool Museum), Paris (Musée de Cluny) and Rouen (Lamy-Lassalle 1968, fig 14). These are very probably souvenirs connected with the pilgrimage to Amiens cathedral, where a precious relic of St John, a portion of his skull, had arrived from Constantinople in 1206. During the thirteenth and fourteenth centuries, and especially in the early fourteenth century, this relic, the so-called face of John the Baptist depicted as a hemisphere without hair, ears or neck, was the principal feature of Amiens pilgrim signs (Lamy-Lassalle 1973; Spencer 1979; Spencer 1985, pp 310-11).

The Salisbury find, however, emphasises St John's role as prophet and forerunner of Christ. The lamb is an allusion to his remark at the sight of Jesus: 'Behold the Lamb of God, which taketh away the sin of the world' (John I, 29). The entire camel skin is presumably an exaggerated interpretation of the garment of camel hair referred to in the Gospel text. The popularity of the Amiens pilgrimage among English folk was based on the immense appeal of John the Baptist. Nearly five hundred English churches were dedicated to him, a number exceeded only by the Virgin Mary, St Michael, St Peter and St Andrew. He was also one of the most popular patron saints among craft guilds. The wool and cloth trade, leatherworkers, cutlers, needlemakers, chandlers and others all found cause in either the saint's appearance or aspects of his life for regarding him as their special protector.

St Michael, Mont-Saint-Michel

Throughout the Middle Ages St Michael was regarded as the leader of spiritual forces striving for the church against the powers of evil. He was 'one of the chief princes' (Book of David X, 13) of the heavenly host. With this angelic band he 'fought against the dragon . . . And the great danger was cast out, that old serpent, called the Devil, and Satan, which deceiveth the whole world' (Revelation XII, 7-9).

84 Pilgrim badge showing St Michael within a canopied setting, crowned and clad in plate armour. With his lance poised across his body he strikes down the dragon and tramples it. Only a part of the dragon's twisted tail now survives. St Michael's shield, held in his left hand, has also been lost. French, last quarter of 15th century. H. 47 mm. *1909/1987* **Fig 110**

This badge not only symbolised the eternal conflict between Good and Evil; it is a pilgrim sign from St Michael's most famous shrine, Mont-Saint-Michel (Normandy), where an abbey was founded in the tenth century to commemorate an apparition of St Michael. The badge possesses something of the scrawny elegance of many late fifteenth-century badges of north French origin and, more particularly, closely resembles figures of St Michael on Mont-Saint-Michel badges found in France (e.g. Lamy-Lassalle 1969, p 170, pl XXVII, 3; Lamy-Lassalle 1971, pl XXVII, 2, 6).

During the fourteenth and fifteenth centuries the shrine enjoyed the patronage of several French kings. In 1393, for instance, Charles V exempted pilgrim signs from taxation after the local inhabitants complained that the burden of tax was threatening their business. Making signs of St Michael, shells (*cf.* Cat 85), horns (*cf.* Cat 149) and other pewter trinkets for pilgrims was, they claimed, their sole means of livelihood (Secousse 1745, p 590).

The popularity of the shrine coincided almost exactly with the Valois dynasty and therefore with the Hundred Years War, during which Mont-Saint-Michel became famous for its successful resistance to the English conquest of Normandy. The original owner of the Salisbury find is therefore likely to have visited the shrine after the treaty of Picquigny, 1475, and before 1483, for after the death of the last of the Valois, Louis XI, in that year, the pilgrimage rapidly faded.

As noted above, some souvenirs at this shrine took the form of shells which, as a rule, were combined with figures of St Michael (Lamy-Lassalle 1971, pl XXVIII). In the early years of the pilgrimage, in fact, before the growth of a souvenir trade, the monks had encouraged pilgrims to take shells from the beach and wear them as souvenirs. They thereby succeeded in reducing the gradual pillaging of the abbey's stonework by souvenir-hunters (*ibid.*, p 275). The use of the shell as a badge, however, was taken by another major sanctuary, the shrine of St James of Compostela, as an unpardonable infringement of its own copyright.

St James of Compostela

Through the Middle Ages it was accepted almost everywhere that the body of the apostle James the Greater, martyred in AD 42, had been miraculously transported from Jerusalem to Santiago de Compostela in Galicia (in the north-west corner of Spain). From the eleventh century the faithful from every part of Europe journeyed by land or sea to pray at the tomb of St James in far-off Compostela. In 1434 no fewer than 2310 licensed pilgrims set sail from English ports alone and doubtless many more trudged along one of the four recommended routes across France before tackling the immensely difficult way along the north coast of Spain. As a place of pilgrimage, Compostela was consistently regarded as being only second in importance to Rome, which had the bones of two apostles, St Peter (Cat 88-89) and St Paul.

There is literary evidence to show that by the beginning of the twelfth century, the scallop was already well-established as the sign or badge worn by pilgrims who had successfully completed the Compostela pilgrimage.

Compostela shells are now excavated in many countries from early medieval (as well as later) contexts. One example, painted in bright colours and perforated for wearing, was found in a late twelfth-century grave at Keynsham Abbey, near Bristol; another in a thirteenth-century deposit in Lower Brook Street, Winchester (Spencer 1985, nos 173-4). The scallop was indeed the most universally recognised of all pilgrim signs (Spencer 1971A, p 60), and just as St James came to be regarded as the patron saint of pilgrims so, too, did his badge become the generic sign of pilgrimage itself. It is perhaps not so surprising, therefore, that other shrines, much to Compostela's annoyance, incorporated the shell in their own pilgrim signs (Cat 127-37). Other shrines also followed the example set by Compostela and adopted new techniques of multiple production, for, as suggested in the introduction to this catalogue, it was almost certainly from Compostela that the fashion for manufactured pilgrim souvenirs spread to all major sanctuaries. At Compostela itself the souvenir trade became so well-defined that the *concheiros* or scallop-shell makers formed their own guild.

85 Pilgrim badge: the figure of a saint mounted on a scallop-shell. The two components were moulded separately, the figure being provided with a lug at the back. The lug was riveted to the shell by splaying its end with a hot iron, a process that appears to have damaged the corrugations on the front of the shell. The shell is also damaged around the beak. The stub of its broken pin is visible on the left. The headless figure, which stands image-like on a bracket, holds a book at the chest. Late 14th or early 15th century. H. 32 mm. Given by Mr W. Wareham. *143/1978* **Fig 111**

From the beginning of the fourteenth century figures of St James usually show him holding a book (the New Testament) and invariably grasping a pilgrim's staff and wearing a pilgrim's hat. The hat and staff have been broken off the Salisbury find. Often, too, he wears a scrip (the pilgrim's satchel or knapsack) at his side. These attributes, scrip, staff and broad-brimmed hat, are shown on similar badges found at London (London Museum 1940, pl LXX, 28; Spencer 1985, nos 185 and 188). Standing on identical brackets, their figures, however, are cast in one with the shell. On a larger version (MOL 79.403/1), a miniature scallop-shell is depicted on St James's own hat, identifying him as the archetypal pilgrim and natural advocate of his own shrine.

A special rite in the Use of Salisbury made provision for intending pilgrims to have their staves and scrips solemnly blessed at the altar before they set off. Neighbours and fellow guildsmen would give more practical support and a public send-off to pilgrims bound for Compostela or other distant shrines.

86 Pilgrim sign of lead, in the form of a scallop-shell, from the top of which emerges the head and shoulders of St James wearing a voluminous, crumpled cloak and a deep-crowned pilgrim's hat and holding a pilgrim's staff. Tree-rings reproduced on the back of the badge are an unusually clear indication that moulds for pilgrim signs of tin and lead alloys were made of wood as well as stone, *c.*1500. H. 39 mm. Spencer 1985, no 193. *104/1987* **Fig 112**

This Salisbury find is to be distinguished from another form of scallop-badge (e.g. MOL 8883) of English make, where the shell forms the gown, as it were, of a dancing figure, with arms held akimbo. This figure is not St James, as stated in Mitchiner 1986, p 271.

87 Pilgrim sign of copper alloy in the form of a scallop, perforated centrally with a hole as if for the connection of another element. A hook for attachment is fitted at the back. Probably early 16th century. H. 28 mm. *206/1987* **Fig 113**

At Compostela the souvenir trade used various materials beyond lead and pewter. In the fifteenth century and later, the famous *azabacheria* (jet works) produced jet shells with silver mounts and figures of St James in jet. During the second half of the fifteenth century, Compostela badges also took the distinctive form of the pilgrim's staff, which in reality was shoulder-high, and had a knob at the top and another lower down, where the hand rested. Miniature staves or burdons (*bordones*), sometimes in pairs and crossed, were made from bone or ivory or were cast in base metal by the *bordoneros* (Köster 1983A, pp 145-6). A miniature staff may have been fixed to the above Salisbury find (Cat 87). Complete badges of this kind, combining the shell and staff, have been found elsewhere (e.g. Beer 1932, p 127) and are depicted as still-life subjects in late medieval Flemish

Books of Hours (e.g. British Library Add. MS 18852, f 183b; 15677, f 37). They are to be seen as late as 1566 in Pieter Breugel's painting of pilgrims in *The Sermon of St John the Baptist*. St James's staves worn individually, without any other ornament, are also to be seen depicted on the clothing of fifteenth- and sixteenth-century Compostela pilgrims (Kriss-Rettenbeck & Mohler 1984, pl I). A pewter fragment found at Salisbury (Fig 114; pc) is perhaps to be identified as the upper part of such a badge. Care, however, should be taken to differentiate this fragment, with its relatively widely spaced knobs, from similar finds (Cat 192) from Salisbury and elsewhere, which can be positively identified as the hilts of miniature rondel-daggers.

St Peter, Rome

Rome likewise catered for a great concourse of pilgrims, which in jubilee years completely overwhelmed the life of the city. The inducements to this international clientele were priceless relics and prodigious pardons for sins. Nevertheless, because of the difficulties of the journey and the problems of accommodation in Rome, perhaps only a few hundred English pilgrims arrived there in the jubilee year of 1350 (Parks 1954, I, pp 356-7). The following two decades, however, saw the establishment in Rome of an English colony, traders mainly, including some who were involved in the making and selling of religious trinkets. In 1362 this group of English settlers set up a hospice for fellow-countrymen visiting Rome. Margery Kempe, the lachrymose pilgrim from King's Lynn, stayed there in 1416, for example. The hospice's later visitors' books contain the names of several pilgrims from Salisbury: Thomas Marrok and John Style in the summer of 1479, for instance, or Thomas Philip and Walter Lovekyn, priest, a year later. Most pilgrims tended to go to Rome early in the year, especially around Easter. Thus John Hulles, a Salisbury priest, arrived at the hospice on Palm Sunday, 1483 (Venerabile 1962, pp 110, 113, 121).

Pilgrim badges from Rome have been recovered from sites across the whole of Europe (some of these are reviewed in Spencer 1988, pp 43-7). A few of them date from the beginning of the thirteenth century. Rome badges so far found at Salisbury, however, are comparatively late in date:

88 Pilgrim badge: part of a badge depicting the crossed keys of St Peter and a triple-crowned tiara, symbol of the pope's supremacy and in this instance emblem of St Peter as bishop of Rome and founder of the first Christian community there. 15th century. H. 22 mm. *10c/1988*

Fig 115

St Peter was regarded as custodian of heaven's gate after Christ had told him that he would be given 'the keys of the kingdom of heaven' (Matthew XVI, 19). A complete version of the type of badge represented by the Salisbury find has recently been discovered at Canterbury (Fig 116). Here the *infulae*, or pendants at the back of the tiara, are arranged in such a way that the ends appear immediately below the bits of the keys. Among examples recently found at London is a badge from early sixteenth-century deposits at Butler's Wharf, Bermondsey, showing a shield of arms between the bows of the keys (Fig 117). On two closely-related Canterbury finds (Figs 118-19), however, the *infulae* are swept upwards above a face, a representation of the vernicle, which, after the burial-places of St Peter and St Paul, was Rome's principal attraction to pilgrims in the late Middle Ages. The vernicle or *vera icon* was the true image of Christ's countenance left impressed on the kerchief of St Veronica. On some badges (Fig 119), therefore, Christ's crown of thorns is depicted immediately beneath a sumptuous papal tiara. Fifteenth-century pilgrim signs from Rome often combined the vernicle, tiara, keys and the sword of St Paul in the manner of armorial devices (Forgeais 1865, p 140; Heeringen, Koldeweij & Gaalman 1987, p

86), the bows of the keys sometimes being linked together with a tasselled cord, perhaps in reference to Christ's assertion that Peter would have the power of 'binding and loosing'. Badges of the crossed keys seem to have made their appearance around the middle of the fourteenth century and, together with badges celebrating the vernicle (*cf.* the cloth vernicle stitched to the pilgrim's hat in the Frontispiece; see also Spencer in Biddle, forthcoming), to have steadily displaced forms of souvenirs that had long been made at Rome. In his *Vision of Piers the Plowman*, *c.*1370, William Langland identified the vernicle and 'keyes of Rome' among the collection of badges on a pilgrim's hat. The crossed keys continued to be popular well into the sixteenth century. They are depicted, for example, on the hat of a pilgrim in Pieter Breugel's *The Fight between Carnival and Lent*, dated 1559.

89 Pilgrim souvenir or devotional object: lead figure of St Peter, seated with a book in one hand and a key, in the other. Moulded in relatively high relief, the figure has a flat back but no means of attachment to the clothing. Late 15th or early 16th century. H. 30 mm. *195g/1987* **Fig 120**

St Peter, leader of the apostles, came near the top of the heavenly host, which, like medieval society itself, was strictly hierarchical, with God himself supreme. After the Virgin Mary, queen of heaven, came the apostles and evangelists, followed by the multitude of saints who were not in holy writ and were arranged in various ranks down to those whose cult was purely local. In this large group, the two saints who seem to have been most important to Salisbury, St Osmund and St Thomas of Canterbury, have already been given priority in this catalogue.

The catalogue now turns to some of Salisbury's other favourite cults, as revealed, however incompletely, by random finds of medieval pilgrim souvenirs. The arrangement is alphabetical.

St Alban, St Albans

90 Pilgrim badge: fragment of a badge depicting the martyrdom of St Alban. Alban's head hangs from the lower branch of a tree. To the left, and lying in front of the pin, is part of the blade of an upright sword. First half of 15th century. H. 50 mm. *10e/1988* **Fig 121**

The Museum of London possesses a complete example of this badge, recovered from a site at Bankside (Fig 122; MOL 86. 202/17). Several fragments of identical badges and many variants, some of them intact, have also turned up at London (Spencer 1969; Spencer 1987, p 223). It is therefore possible to determine what is missing from this Salisbury find. The scene is invariably framed by two trees, which meet to form an arch. Alban's decapitated body, enveloped in a cloak, sinks to the grass. In this instance the executioner's sword stands symbolically at the centre. To the left of it, the executioner, in full body-armour, raises both hands to catch his own eyes, which are falling out of their sockets.

The badges incorporate all the essential elements of the story of the death of Britain's first martyr. The cloak is the garment that Alban received from the man who converted him to Christianity, a priest later known as St Amphibalus. Alban, who was a legionary at Verulamium, had given his own clothes to the priest so that he could escape a persecution, most probably in *c.*254 under Septimius Severus. Alban was arrested instead, and, after refusing to give up his faith, was taken to the hill on which the church of St Albans Abbey now stands. There his head was tied by the hair to the branch of a tree and then struck off. At the moment the executioner delivered the fatal blow, his eyes fell out so that he should never have the benefit of seeing the virtues that would arise from St Alban's martyrdom.

St Antony, London

91 Pilgrim sign in the form of a boar with a bell round its neck. The badge, worn by a devotee of St Antony, may be the souvenir of a visit to St Antony's Hospital in London. 15th century. W. 30 mm. *191h/1987* **Fig 123**

St Antony, an immensely popular medieval saint, was the patron of swineherds, who customarily vowed to him one pig from each litter. The smallest piglet was consequently known as the tantony. St Antony was often depicted with a pig or boar at his feet. In explanation, the story grew up that wild boar had been his only companions when he went to live in solitude. But the real reason arose from the association of his name and relics with the foundation of an order of Hospitallers at La Motte, in the French province of Dauphiné, *c.*1100. This order of St Antoine de Viennois, with its network of houses in many cities, enjoyed the unusual privilege of being allowed to let pigs loose in the streets to forage at will, provided they wore a bell to distinguish them from strays.

In 1311 the London house, St Antony's Hospital in Threadneedle Street, undertook to put bells on only those pigs which had been given to St Antony's in alms (Riley 1868, p 83). But the city was unable to rid itself of the nuisance until the Hospital was dissolved in 1547. The Elizabethan chronicler, John Stow, could remember seeing St Antony's pigs rootling in London's streets. Once they had been belled by a proctor from St Antony's, he said, 'no man would hurt or take them up, but if any gave to them bread or other feeding, such would they know, watch for and daily follow, whining till they had somewhat given them' (Stow 1908, I, p 184); hence, tantony also stood for a close or obsequious follower. Tantony is also the name given to the smallest in a peal of bells or to a handbell, and derived from the bells carried by the pigs and by collectors seeking alms for St Antony's.

The mother house of the order, the abbey of St Antoine at La Motte, was a famous place of pilgrimage, especially for those who suffered from ergotism, an acutely painful, wasting disease then known as St Antony's fire. During the fifteenth century, the daughter house in London enjoyed a succession of distinguished masters who raised its importance and promoted the cult of St Antony through a confraternity and a body of collectors. Steps were taken in the 1440s to attract more pilgrims to St Antony's Hospital (Graham 1930, pp 363-364), including the production of pewter pilgrim signs and ampullae. Numerous souvenirs in the form of the badge of the order, the Tau-cross or the Tau and bell (*ibid.*, pp 365-368; London Museum 1940, pp 260-1), have been found in fifteenth-century deposits at London. It seems likely that this Salisbury find was another pilgrim souvenir from St Antony's Hospital. The boar is very similar to the animal depicted on the Hospital's seal of *c.*1425 (Graham 1930, pl XIV,6).

St Bridget, Syon Abbey, Isleworth

St Bridget or Birgitta (1303-73), who claimed to have visions about Christ's Passion as well as about future events, spent most of her later life on distant pilgrimages and in the service of pilgrims. Earlier, however, she had founded the monastic order of St Saviour, commonly known as the Brigittines. Beginning with the mother-house at Vadstena, Sweden, the order was eventually established in seventy houses which included Syon Abbey near the river Thames at Isleworth, Middlesex. This famous double house, containing brothers as well as nuns, was founded by Henry V in 1415 as the monastery of St Saviour and St Bridget of Sweden and rapidly became by far the largest and richest nunnery in England. Syon was widely known for the quality of its preaching and for the many privileges it was able to offer pilgrims.

To help stimulate the cult of St Bridget, the pope in 1425 granted pilgrims to Syon the so-called Vincula indulgence (Johnston 1969, p 184; Furnivall 1868, p 19), that is to say, remissions of punishment for sins equivalent to famous pardons obtainable at Rome on the feast of St Peter ad Vincula. A further indulgence, the Pardon of Syon, which St Bridget had first obtained for the mother-house at Vadstena and Henry V had subsequently secured for Syon, was also to be gained by Syon's pilgrims at certain times of the year (Cumming 1929, pp xxxi-xxxvii). A further attraction for pilgrims was the special faculty vested in the brethren at Syon for blessing rosaries and granted by the pope in 1500. This and Syon's proximity to London and Windsor (Cat 45, 114, 123), must have helped to maintain pilgrims' offerings at St Bridget's shrine at an unusually high level during the early sixteenth century (Johnston 1969, p 186). The number and variety of surviving pilgrim signs of St Bridget also underlines the importance of the shrine.

92 Pilgrim badge: St Bridget wearing a puckered wimple and a veil, arranged around the face in a radiating series of waves or ruffles. With her right hand she reaches across to the writing-desk to her left. Mid 15th century. H. 33 mm. *Sal. Mus. Rep.* 1987-8, pl 3c. *213/1987* **Fig 124**

The same subject, with similar distinctive treatment of the veil and with the right arm in comparable attitude, occurs on a number of badges found at London. To this extent the figure is also comparable to pilgrim signs of St Birgitta issued at Vadstena (e.g. Liebgott 1972, pp 310-12; Andersson 1989, pp 30-3; see also a badge re-cast on the surface of a bronze font dated 1437, Liebgott 1973, p 35). Badges commemorating pilgrimages to Syon Abbey, however, took on a wide variety of forms and sizes and some of them, dating probably to the late fifteenth or early sixteenth century, are crudely made. Yet, when complete, they are all consistent in showing the little figure of an angel, who speaks into St Bridget's right ear. This, and occasionally the presence of God the Father above, is presumably a reference to the visions of St Bridget; such a reference is distinctly made on some well-designed Swedish badges (Edgren 1979, fig 1; *cf.* a late fifteenth-century woodcut, Munich 1984, p 121).

Some badges found at London set this scene of St Bridget at her desk within an architectural canopy of moderate (45 mm) height (BM M & LA 56,7-1,2084; Smith 1854, fig on p 139, identified as the temptation of Christ), though several much smaller versions are also known (e.g. Mitchiner 1986, p 178, no 574, described as 'Mother Julian' and *ibid.*, p 191, identified as Our Lady of Doncaster). One example, recovered from the Thames at Brooks Wharf has the caption *sca brigt* in Gothic black letter (Fig 125). Circular frames were also used (MOL 83.348/1), while other more pretentious souvenirs, in crude imitation of the mirror-badges made for Aachen's pilgrims in the middle of the fifteenth century, reserved the circular frame for a mirror and placed the figure of St Bridget and the angel in the superstructure (Fig 126: MOL 84.133; see also Mitchiner *loc.cit.* nos 572-3, also assigned to 'Mother Julian'). The badge from Syon owned by Salisbury's pilgrim (Cat 92) is likely to have taken this form, when complete.

Richard Caister, Norwich

Noted for his piety and learning, Richard Caister was vicar of St Stephen's, Norwich from 1402 until his death in 1420. His considerable output of religious writings included one of the most popular hymns 'Ihesu Lord that madist me.' His tomb was thought to work miracles and the evidence of Norfolk wills and the testimony of Lynn's lugubrious mystic, Margery Kempe, show that it became an object of veneration and pilgrimage between 1420 and *c.*1460 (Meech & Allen 1940, pp 38–40). Caister was typical of many late medieval saints, who, as relatively humble men and women, were proclaimed saints by local people. These badges from Salisbury and others from London and Canterbury, however, show that Caister's reputation for sanctity spread well beyond East Anglia.

93 Pilgrim badge: a priest wearing an academic hood standing in a polygonal pulpit, framed by a scroll arranged as a rough rectangle and edged on the vertical sides with rows of projecting knobs or crockets. The scroll is inscribed in black letter *soli :deo :hoior (honor) et amur (amor) et : :gory (gloria)*. The Holy Ghost in the form of a dove approaches the preacher from the left and above him are the hands and bearded countenance of God the Father. The hands are the open palms of judgment (the right hand is incomplete owing to faulty casting). Surrounding the Father's head is a cross-nimb and a glory. Usually reserved for portrayals of Christ, the cruciform halo is here evidently intended to represent the Second Person of the Trinity. Second quarter of the 15th century. H. 57 mm. Drainage coll. (Brodie). Akerman 1855, p 72 and 1857, pl facing p 94; *Sal. Mus. Cat.* 1864, p 55 and 1870, p 11. Smith 1880, pp 150-151; Saunders 1986, p 10. *iiE503* **Fig 127**

94 Pilgrim badge: head of God the Father from a badge similar to Cat 93. Second quarter of 15th century. H. 26 mm. *225w/1987* **Fig 128**

95 Pilgrim badge: head of God the Father from a badge similar to Cat 93. H. 18 mm. Given by Mr D. Morgan. *198c/1987*. Not illustrated.

Yet another similar fragment from Salisbury, wrongly identified as St John the Baptist, is figured in Mitchiner 1986, p 264. Virtually identical badges have been found at London (e.g. MOL 82.314), while two other less complete versions have been discovered at King's Lynn, Norfolk (Spencer 1980, no 103) and Southwold, Suffolk (Cambridge, University Museum 15.104). Badges of the same form but with an inscription garbled after the first two words have also turned up at London.

96 Pilgrim badge: fragment depicting a priest gesticulating in a pulpit. Second quarter of 15th century. H. 26 mm. Given by Mr D. Morgan. *198b/1987* **Fig 129**

When complete, the figure of Richard Caister would in this case be surrounded by a five-sided scroll, trimmed along its outer edge with projecting knobs and inscribed with the words *MR CAST OF NOUDICHE*. Examples have been found at King's Lynn (*ibid.*, no 102) and at the site of Old London Bridge (BM M & LA 36, 6-10, 48).

97 Pilgrim badge: a priest in a pulpit, framed by a letter R (for Richard), the outer edges of which are ornamented with crockets. At the foot of the pulpit is the caption *Kaster*. Second quarter of 15th century. H. 44 mm. *225a/1987* **Fig 130**

A larger version of this badge from the Thames at Billingsgate (1980) retains the dove (the Holy Spirit) to the preacher's right and shows Caister giving the blessing with his right hand. On a smaller badge from Bankside, London (MOL 86.202/8), Caister grips the front of the pulpit with both hands, the letter R is surrounded by knobbly crockets and covered in scroll-work and the caption reads *r kaste*. Another, perhaps slightly later, badge of this form, found at Canterbury, omits the caption and puts forth small acanthus leaves instead of crockets. But the latter are a characteristic of nearly all Richard Caister badges. They are also a frequent feature of contemporary Walsingham badges (Cat 48), suggesting that the badges commemorating Caister were influenced by Walsingham souvenirs or were even commissioned from the mould-makers of Walsingham by the organisers of the pilgrimage to St Stephen's, Norwich. The Convent of the Holy Trinity, Norwich, which had presented Caister to the living of St Stephen's, and previously to another living, probably took a hand in the promotion of his posthumous cult. The Trinity of the Salisbury badge perhaps alludes to this connection.

The phrase *soli deo honor et gloria* is still the motto of the London Leathersellers' Company, was formerly the motto of the Goldsmiths' and, in the fifteenth and early sixteenth centuries, was favoured as a pious or magical inscription, e.g. on the Campion Cup, 1500 (Victoria and Albert Museum), on jettons and (sometimes with the added word *amor* or *laus*) on purse-frames. The phrase comes from the verse in St Paul's First Epistle to Timothy (Vulgate I, 17) that formed the capitulum or little chapter read at the Office of Prime.

St Dorothy

St Dorothy is thought to have been put to death *c.* A.D. 313 during the persecution of Diocletian. Like St Margaret of Antioch (Cat 121), she was one of several virgin-martyrs who were much revered in the fourteenth and fifteenth centuries. One of her emblems was a basket of apples sent from heaven after her martyrdom in order to convert a young lawyer who had jeered at her prospects of entering Paradise.

98 Devotional badge or amulet: a basket of fruit. Probably 15th century. H. 33 mm. *Sal. Mus. Rep.* 1987-8, pl 3f. *225g/1987* **Fig 131**

Several similar badges are known (e.g. BM M & LA 1904, 7-20, 20). According to the Golden Legend, St Dorothy's final prayer was that any dwelling in which her life was read should be protected from storms, fire and sudden death. Wearing her emblem as a badge might be expected to offer similar benefits to the individual. A badge of St Catherine's spiked wheel has also been found at Salisbury (pc).

St Edith of Wilton

Edith was the illegitimate daughter of Edgar (943-75), king of England and great-grandson of Alfred the Great. In her infancy she was taken by her mother to the famous nunnery at Wilton, near Salisbury, where she was brought up and educated with care, under the guidance of tutors appointed by the king. As the king's daughter she could have enjoyed rapid advancement but she steadfastly refused to be nominated abbess of other convents, preferring to continue a life of contemplation, learning and good works at Wilton. She and her mother (who became abbess) were responsible for securing for Wilton a relic of Christ's Passion, a fragment from the tip of the famous Holy Nail of Trier (Stroud 1984B, p 355). She was only twenty-three when she died at Wilton in 984. Miracles at her tomb helped to establish the pilgrimage. Her name appears in the litany of a service book that once belonged to St Osmund, the first Norman bishop of Salisbury. In later medieval times her cult was doubtless stimulated by pilgrims attracted to Salisbury by Our Lady of Salisbury and St Osmund, especially after Osmund's canonisation in 1456 (Cat 1-7, 58-63). The story of her life was retold in a fifteenth-century verse chronicle.

99 Pilgrim badge: the upper part of the figure of a nun wearing veil and wimple and holding a book. 15th century H. 31 mm. *204a/1987* **Fig 132**

A book would be an appropriate emblem for St Edith, having regard to her concern for books and her ability to copy and decorate them. The library of Salisbury cathedral possesses a psalter that may have belonged to her and that was evidently written at Wilton during her lifetime (*ibid.*, p 353).

Another badge found at Salisbury depicts a similar head and shoulders in a circular frame surrounded by knobs. Mitchiner 1986, p 178 describes this as 'Mother Julian'. There is, however, no evidence that Juliana (who died *c.*1416) was ever a nun before becoming an anchoress in the church of St Julian, Conisford, Norwich. She does not appear to have been an object of pilgrimage and her mystical writings remained unknown for two hundred years after her death.

The discovery of both these badges at Salisbury and the absence of analogies elsewhere strengthen the possibility that they were local products, fifteenth-century souvenirs of St Edith of Wilton.

St Edmund, Bury St Edmunds

Edmund was the king of East Anglia when a Viking army landed there in 869 and took up quarters at Thetford. Edmund was defeated in battle and captured, but refused to give up his kingdom or his Christian faith. Whereupon he was tied to a tree, shot with arrows and beheaded. His head was cast into the bushes where it was guarded from further harm by a wolf. The head was eventually discovered through its ability to call out 'Here, here' to those who were searching for it. St Edmund was soon venerated as a martyr and his remains later enshrined at Bury St Edmunds, where a great Benedictine abbey was founded in 1020. Over sixty English churches are dedicated to St Edmund, one of them being in Salisbury.

100 Pilgrim badge: the body of St Edmund, naked but for his drawers and, when complete, his crown, is shot with arrows. His hands are held behind his back, presumably lashed to the tree, the trunk of which can be seen between his legs. First half of 14th century. H. 48 mm. *190d/1987* **Fig 133**

More complete versions of the badge, one of them from the same mould, show a wolf lying on the grass at the king's feet, looking expectantly up at him (BM M & LA 71, 7-14, 62; Cuming 1868, pl 17, no 12).

The 'braies' or drawers are the sort in fashion between *c.*1250 and *c.*1340; *cf.* the carving of St Edmund's martyrdom at the foot of the mid-thirteenth-century effigy of Bishop Hugh de Northwold, Ely cathedral. On some badges St Edmund's hands are tied across his abdomen and, more often than not, the Y-shaped tree to which he is bound is also depicted in front of him. Somewhat earlier pilgrim signs, following more literally the story of his martyrdom, show him covered in arrows, 'like a thistle covered in prickles' (Spencer 1987, p 223, no 79). These correspond with thirteenth-century representations of St Edmund (e.g. New York, Pierpoint Morgan MS 736, f 14) and appear to antedate a representation of St Edmund's martyrdom in the early fourteenth-century Queen Mary's Psalter, where the iconography closely follows the popular imagery of the badges and, in contrast, depicts St Sebastian being shot with arrows as he lies on the ground fully clothed.

101 Pilgrim badge: St Edmund, robed and crowned (the crown has lost its fleurons), holding his emblem, a large arrow. Early 15th century. H. 56 mm. *205a/1987* **Fig 134**

St Edmund is similarly depicted in several fifteenth-century painted windows and screen-paintings and, most notably of all, in the Wilton Diptych (London, National Gallery), where he and St Edward the Confessor (Cat 103) are shown as the two great royal saints of England and joint-sponsors of the king, Richard II. St Edmund is also occasionally represented with one or more bundles of arrows as distinct from a single arrow.

102 Badge: a 'garb' of arrows held at the middle by a knotted belt. Late 14th or early 15th century. H. 47 mm. Mitchiner 1986, p 176. *193l/1987* **Fig 135**

The badge may be an emblem of St Edmund's martyrdom. On the other hand the purpose of the badge may well have been entirely secular or heraldic (*cf.* Cat 189).

Several similar badges are known, including one other from Salisbury (Mitchiner, *loc. cit.*), all from different moulds. As regards the shape of the buckle or the form of the knot, there is no consistency among them.

St Edward the Confessor, Westminster

Edward (1003-1066), last of the Saxon kings of England, achieved a reputation for sanctity by a life of piety, which centred on the rebuilding of Westminster Abbey, by his generosity to the poor and by his ability to perform miraculous cures. He was canonised in 1161 and, in Westminster Abbey, two years later, his relics were solemnly translated. That day, 13 October, became his principal feast and for Henry III, the most important day of the year, for he took the Confessor as his patron, named his son (Edward I) after him, rebuilt the choir of Westminster Abbey in his honour and translated his relics to another new shrine in 1269. At that period Westminster's pilgrims took away as souvenirs leaden ampullae on which the enthroned figure of the Confessor was depicted.

103 Pilgrim badge: the bust of a king surrounded by a circular frame with pearled edges and close-set dot-and-circle motifs imitating jewels. The king wears a shoulder-tippet with an invected or engrailed lower edge. The king's head is similar to conventional portraits on contemporary coins, with wavy hair framing the face. Late 14th century. D. 22 mm. *194/1987* **Fig 136**

Several other badges of this kind have been found at London (e.g. London Museum 1940, pl lxxi, 36) and King's Lynn (Spencer 1980, p 21, no 82). At London one example was excavated from a waterfront deposit near the site of Baynard's Castle dating from the last quarter of the fourteenth century.

In theory such badges might be linked to one of several royal saints, not excluding Edward II, whose canonisation Richard II was, for largely political reasons, strenuously seeking to obtain in the 1390s. Earlier still, however, Richard had assiduously begun to promote the cult of Edward the Confessor as well as the concept that the Confessor, not William the Conqueror, was the founder of the royal line.

By the late fourteenth century representations of the famous story of St Edward and the Pilgrim were to be found in sculpture, windows, murals and wall-hangings in almost every part of Westminster Palace. By this time, also, St Edward's Day (13 October), falling a fortnight after Michaelmas, the beginning of the medieval financial year, coincided with Westminster's busiest time, when officials and other representatives were drawn there from every corner of the realm. That the pilgrimage to Westminster also enjoyed a spell of popular, as well as official, success at this period is clearly demonstrated by the discovery of pilgrim souvenirs that can be positively identified with Edward the Confessor from their inscriptions or attributes. As on Cat 103, the king's cape is represented with an engrailed edge on some of these, too, most markedly on an attractive and popular type of badge representing St Edward and the Pilgrim (Spencer 1980, p 21). This last-mentioned type should not, however, be identified (as in Mitchiner 1986, p 88), with badges depicting a queen and a young suppliant (*cf.* Smith 1854, p 140).

104 Pilgrim badge similar in most respects to Cat 103, except that the king has long, straight hair swept away from the face. Late 14th century. D. 22 mm. *195d/1987* **Fig 137**

105 Pilgrim badge: a cruder version of Cat 103. The area around the crown was also spoiled by blow-holes in the original casting. Late 14th century. D. 23 mm. Given by Mr R. Davis. *202a/1987* **Fig 138**

A very similar badge has also been found at Salisbury (Fig 139, pc), while on another Salisbury find the king's hair is extended to shoulder-length (Fig 140). The same peculiar hair style, itself a feature of some royal portraits of the 1380s and 90s, appears on versions of this badge found elsewhere (e.g. Smith 1848, pl xxxi, 3; BM M & LA 56,7-1,2072).

106 Pilgrim sign: a crown of fleur-de-lys alternating with smaller trefoils. The side fleurs are represented in true profile, as on English coins after about 1300, and the jewelled circlet is shown in perspective, revealing the hatched lining of the interior. Early 15th century. H. 23 mm. *190k/1987* **Fig 141**

107 Pilgrim sign: another crown, part of its central fleuron missing. W. 27 mm. *225u/1987* **Fig 142**

Probability suggests that these badges, too, are connected with the cult of St Edward at Westminster. Like Cat 103-5, however, crown-badges are capable of other interpretations. They could, for example, be regarded as purely secular livery badges. Attempting to drum up support in 1387, Richard II sent a serjeant-at-arms to hand out badges of silver and gilt crowns to 'the more substantial and influential inhabitants' of Essex, Cambridgeshire, Norfolk and Suffolk on the understanding that they would swear to 'hold with him as their true king' and that 'whenever they were called upon to do so they should join the king, armed and ready'

(Hector & Harvey 1982, p 187). It is therefore possible that pewter crown-badges, in some cases at least, were a less formal or a down-market expression of fealty to Richard or to another king. One Salisbury find that stands a very good chance of falling within this category depicts a crown encircled by a buckled garter (Fig 143; pc).

Many badges from the same or very similar moulds used for the casting of Cat 106-7 have been found at London; several can be seen for instance, in the British Museum, the Canterbury and Liverpool Museums and the Museum of London. Most of these have been recovered from fifteenth-century riverine deposits, though stylistically, the relatively tall proportions of the fleurons suggest that the design could date from the end of the fourteenth century. A somewhat larger and better made badge of identical form has been excavated from a revetment dump at Swan Lane, London, dated by coins to the late 1420s. In a similar and equally popular form of the badge, the hatched interior is replaced by an open hoop (London Museum 1940, pl lxxi, 33; Spencer 1980, p 21, no 83), and the fleurons tend to be lower, suggesting that these may be badges of somewhat later date.

108 Pilgrim badge: Lombardic letter E, originally probably topped by a crown, only a trace of which now survives. Late 14th or early 15th century. H. 25 mm. *192d/1987* **Fig 144**

The crowned letter M (for Maria) was one of the commonest devotional emblems of the Middle Ages. The crowned T (for Thomas) was frequently used as a pilgrim sign at Canterbury (Cat 27-29), and there are similar instances of the use of initial letters at other pilgrim centres like the letter R for Richard Caister (Cat 97). There is therefore a distinct possibility that a crowned E stood for St Edward the Confessor. Some other letters used as badges, however, are more difficult to account for as pilgrim souvenirs or devotional trinkets (Spencer 1982, p 312) and some of these were perhaps simply intended to be identified, like initials used on signet rings, with their wearers' names.

St Etheldreda, Ely

For centuries St Etheldreda (Audrey) was probably the most revered of the Anglo-Saxon female saints. Daughter of a king of East Anglia, she earned this reputation by her piety and good works and by the many miracles attributed to her intercession. She founded the convent of Ely, Cambridgeshire, on the spot where the cathedral was subsequently built and died in 679 as its abbess. Her tomb became an important objective for pilgrims, a regular station in the tours of East Anglian shrines so frequently undertaken by medieval English kings. When Richard II and his queen ordered the court to go on pilgrimage to Ely in 1383 on behalf of one of the royal knights, Sir James Berners, they were witnesses to a miraculous cure. Sir James, who had been struck by lightning and severely disabled, recovered his sight and sanity at St Etheldreda's shrine.

109 Pilgrim badge: standing figure of an abbess holding a book in her right hand and in her left a crosier, its crook trimmed with knobbly crockets. She wears a crown over a loosely-draped veil. Her throat is covered by a pleated wimple, below which a brooch fastens the top of her cloak. The sleeves of her gown are gathered at the cuffs. Late 14th or early 15th century. H. 65 mm. *195c/1987* **Fig 145**

Similar badges have been found at King's Lynn (Spencer 1980, p 23) and at London. One of the latter (BM M & LA 56, 7-1,2086; Smith 1848, pl XXXIII, 15) from the Thames at Fishmongers' Hall has been matched by an identical badge from early fifteenth-century deposits at Stepney. In all instances the royal abbess wears a wimple gathered into vertical pleats and an ornamental brooch. It was another sort of adornment associated with the cult of St Etheldreda, a form of cheap neckwear known as St Audrey's laces, which gave us the word tawdry, meaning showy, without real value.

110 Pilgrim badge: an abbess holding a book in her left hand and a crosier in her right. She wears a crown and a wimple arranged in broad ruffles. Second half of 15th century. H. 45 mm. *190f/1987* **Fig 146**

The list of sainted abbesses who were also queens or princesses is a very long one. Ely alone had two more, St Sexburga and St Ermenilda. The cult of St Etheldreda was incomparably the most important, especially at London, and it is difficult to believe that badges such as these could refer to anyone other than St Etheldreda. There is, however, less certainty about the inclusion here of the next badge:

111 Pilgrim badge: an abbess holding a book and a crosier and wearing a wimple but no crown. 15th century. H. 57 mm. *191b/1987* **Fig 147**

St George

In addition to figures of St Edmund and St Edward, the Wilton Diptych also shows the standard of St George as the emblem of England, and not long after the Diptych had been painted, King Henry V was invoking St George as England's patron at the battle of Agincourt in 1415. Though veneration of this Palestinian soldier-saint had been widespread from early times, his emergence as patron of England and symbol of English nationalism was helped forward by Edward III's foundation (*c.*1348) of the Order of the Garter under St George's patronage, and was further reinforced by the rebuilding of St George's Chapel at Windsor by Edward IV and Henry VII.

112 Pilgrim sign: a tapering, tubular plume-holder, open at the top and sealed at the base. A rectangular stitching-loop is fitted at the back, while, in front, moulded in the round, stands the figure of St George, in full armour and wearing a plume, killing the dragon with his lance. Late 15th century. H. 41 mm. *195f/1987* **Fig 148**

Another plume-holder found at Bankside, London, and designed by the same deft hand, differs in having a crenellated top to the tube (Fig 149; MOL 86.202/21). A larger and even more sophisticated version has a similar tower (Fig 150; MOL 80.150/1; Museum of London 1982, pl 12). Many similar variants show St George in the same attitude, or wielding a sword or mounted on horseback, while similar plume-holders are sometimes attached to entirely different subjects, such as a lily in a pot or a woodwose holding a mask and wielding a club. The use of plume-holders is represented on several fifteenth-century paintings and on a badge depicting a hat (Spencer 1978, fig 4, no 67).

113 Pilgrim badge of square, medallic form, depicting St George and the dragon in a lozenge-shaped field. Late 15th or early 16th century. H. 21 mm. Given by Mr A. Stewart. *197/1987* **Fig 151**

These and a wider variety of late medieval pilgrim souvenirs some of them stamped out on brass foil, confirm a rise in popular interest in St George at the end of the 15th century. The cult was given further stimulus by the arrival in 1505, as a gift to Henry VII, of the relic of a leg of St George. This was borne in procession through London, was the subject of a clause in Henry's will and was further described in 1520 in an inventory of the relics of Westminster Abbey (Thomas & Thornley 1938, pp 328-9; Nicholas 1826, p 31). The Salisbury finds, however, seem more likely to have originated from the pilgrimage to Windsor. Though it was founded primarily for the Knights of the Garter, St George's Chapel possessed an image of St George and associated relics (Bond 1947, pp 148-51, 166-79) that helped to make Windsor a major pilgrim resort (see also Cat 114-8, 123-4). Henry VII's queen made regular offerings to this image (Nicolas 1830, p 42).

King Henry VI, Windsor

After his defeat by Edward IV at Tewkesbury in 1471, Henry VI, the last of the Lancastrian dynasty, was put to death in the Tower of London. Time and again in the Middle Ages popular sanctity was accorded to promiment political figures who died by violence. Thus, within a year of his burial, King Henry began to emerge as almost the last of England's medieval saints. When the Yorkist line came to an end at Bosworth in 1485, the pious followers of Henry VI found all constraints removed and their dead hero flaunted as the sainted ancestor of Henry Tudor. It was then that pilgrims flocked to King Henry's miracle-working tomb in St George's Chapel, Windsor. An abundance of pilgrim signs found in Salisbury and elsewhere confirm that for two or three decades Windsor became perhaps the primary national pilgrim resort (for a more detailed study and catalogue, see Spencer 1978).

114 Pilgrim badge: a king, robed in state, stands above the lion of England. He wears an arched crown of early Tudor form and holds a long sceptre in his right hand and, originally, an orb in his left. The cape, beneath the large neck-roll, has a chequered pattern. *c.*1485–1500. H. 52 mm. *195e/1987* **Fig 152**

Several virtually identical badges have been found at London (e.g. Spencer 1978, p 253, nos 43-4 and MOL 80.82/9) and at King's Lynn (Spencer 1978, p 253, no 45; Spencer 1980, p 22, no 87). More common, however, are badges depicting the king in the same attitude and with the same robes and regalia above a heraldic antelope, powdered with spots, the personal badge of Henry VI.

115 Pilgrim badge: a king, wearing an arched crown and the suggestion of an ermine collar to his cape, holds an orb and cross in his right hand and a sceptre, combining fleur-de-lys and cross, in his left. An antelope lies at his feet. *c.*1485-1500. H. 58 mm. *11b/1988* **Fig 153**

For comparative purposes another version of this badge, from the Thames foreshore at Queenhithe, London, is illustrated in Fig 154. From this it can be more clearly seen that the heraldic antelope, which was derived from bestiaries, not from nature, had a twisting tail, forked towards the end, as well as saw-toothed, forward-pointing horns and a fierce expression. Henry VI had the animal powdered with spots to distinguish it from the badge used by his father, Henry V.

116 Pilgrim badge: a fragment depicting a king robed in state and wearing a purse at this belt. Late 15th century. H. 24 mm. Spencer 1978, p 253, no 48. Given by Mr M. Green. *142/1978* **Fig 155**

More complete versions of this badge, showing the king with a purse, have been found at London; these also depict a lion at the king's feet (*ibid.*, fig 3, nos 46, 47). Another fragment found at Salisbury (Fig 156; pc), however, represents the king with purse standing above a spotted antelope.

117 Pilgrim badge of circular medallic form with pearled edge and diapered ground, on which is depicted the figure of a king, wearing a crown, shoulder tippet and mantle and holding an orb in his right hand and a sceptre over his left shoulder. *c.*1485-1500. D. 25 mm. Spencer 1978, p 251, no 4. Given by Mr W. Wareham. *143/1978* **Fig 157**

Surviving examples of this type of badge are widely distributed. More than forty are known to have been found at London and others come from Marsh Chapel (Lincs.), Sandgate (Kent), Colnbrook (Bucks.), Southampton, Oxford, Ludlow, Bristol and Rouen. Two are from archaeological contexts datable to the last decade of the fifteenth century.

118 Pilgrim badge similar to, and perhaps slightly later than Cat 117. Its mould was more carelessly cut and the king in this instance wears an arched crown of early Tudor form. *c.*1500. D. 24 mm. *105/1987* **Fig 158**

Figures of the king similar to those in Cat 117-8, and sometimes explicitly identified as King Henry, are also depicted on lozenge-shaped badges of medallic form (Spencer 1978, pp 251-3); over fifty of them have been excavated at London alone. Three are known to have been found at Salisbury. The example illustrated in Fig 159 (pc) is one of the crudest yet encountered and demonstrates very clearly the inherent tendency for the design and execution of moulds to degenerate with the passage of time.

The same tendency is demonstrated by

another Salisbury find (Fig 160; pc), the prototype of which depicts a king in splendour astride a richly-caparisoned horse, the king wearing a massive arched crown and holding an orb and cross and a sceptre (Spencer 1978, fig 4, no 57). This type of badge appears to have commemorated Henry VI's return from exile in 1470 and his brief restoration to the throne (*ibid.*, pp 245-6) and may well have been designed in imitation of a once-popular brand of Canterbury badge (*cf.* Cat 10). The example found at Salisbury is one of a series of degenerate representations of the scene, celebrating King Henry's supposedly triumphal return to a martyr's death. None of these badges has survived intact but, taken together, they are seen to represent a king wearing an arched crown and holding an orb and cross and either a sceptre, as in Fig 160, or a sword of state (*ibid.*, fig 4, nos 60-62). Such pilgrim signs are unlikely to have any connection with Richard, earl of Cornwall, and the Holy Blood of Hailes, as proposed in Mitchiner 1986, p 190.

St Hubert

St Hubert was bishop of Maastricht and then of Liège in the early eighth century. From the fourteenth century onwards he was perhaps chiefly famous for the story of his conversion (which, in turn, was borrowed from the life of St Eustace). He was said to have been converted when hunting on Good Friday as the result of the appearance before him of a white stag bearing a shining crucifix between its antlers. Some badges commemorate this vision by depicting simply the stag's head with its antlers bridged by an image of the crucified Christ. Others depict the entire scene. Thus a pilgrim sign in the British Museum (M & LA CRS 5202) shows St Hubert on horseback, his hunting-horn upraised, being confronted by the stag; the surrounding inscription reads *sanct hubert dardenne*, a reference to St Hubert's shrine at Saint-Hubert-en-Ardenne (Belgium).

Commoner still are badges in the form of St Hubert's emblem, the hunting-horn. It seems probable that of the horn-badges found in the Low Countries, the majority originated as pilgrim souvenirs from Saint-Hubert in the Ardennes. But the remainder were evidently made elsewhere for use as amulets (Heeringen, Koldeweij & Gaalman 1987, p 71). Many horn-badges have been found in England also (including Cat 119, from Salisbury), but their forms, though similar to those found on the continent, are sufficiently distinctive for them to be assigned to an English manifestation of the cult of St Hubert, the patron saint of huntsmen.

119 Devotional badge or amulet in the form of a hunting-horn, fitted with mounts and straps; the main loop of the shoulder- strap is missing. 15th century. W. 29 mm. *191t/1987* **Fig 161**

For a very similar, virtually complete example, see London Museum 1940, pl LXX, no 27. In several other instances the ends of the straps are likewise united by a circular or rectangular tiret, from the base of which often hangs a tassel (Spencer 1968, pl III, 8). Perhaps such badges were worn for luck in hunting, a favourite medieval pastime, which was celebrated by various other sorts of badges (Cat 194-6).

St Jos, Saint-Josse-sur-Mer

120 Pilgrim badge: A saint in monk's habit, equipped for pilgrimage with cloak and with hood drawn over his head. He holds a book in his left hand, and, when complete, would have leaned with his right on a long staff, decorated with a zoomorphic top. Third quarter of 14th century. H. 71 mm. *190e/1987* **Fig 162**

An identical badge is in the collection of the Society of Antiquaries of London. Others from the same mould have been excavated from the mid to late fourteenth-century silt of 'Baynard's Castle' dock, London, and from the Thames foreshore at Vintry (1989). Another example, virtually identical except for the addition of a pendent belt-end, comes from the Thames at Queenhithe (wrongly identified as St Etheldreda; Mitchiner 1986, p 106). Other versions of the badge show him bearded and holding a rosary instead of the book (e.g. BM M & LA 56, 7-1, 2090 and *ibid.*, p 262); one of these was recovered intact at Swan Lane, London (illustrated on the front covers of *Popular Archaeology* V, 4 (1983) and *The London Archaeologist* IV, 11 (1983)).

The source of these badges is not entirely certain. The closest attributable analogies, pilgrim signs of St Jos or Jodocus (d. *c.*668), are a century later. These, too, show a man dressed for holy travel and holding a staff, book and rosary and also carrying a scrip. One such badge, captioned *josse*, was reproduced on the surface of a bell at Niederburg (W. Germany) dated 1477 (Köster 1957, pl V, 30 and pp 85-6) and actual contemporary badges with similar captions have been dredged from the Dyle at Malines, Belgium (Vandenberghe 1976, fig 1, no 6) and from the Weser at Bremen (Rydbeck 1958, p 211, fig 2). Son of a king of Brittany, Jos renounced his wealth and went on pilgrimage to Rome and then chose the life of a hermit, living thereafter in a monastery in the place that was later called after him, Saint-Josse-sur-Mer (Pas de Calais). After his death, his hermitage soon became a hospice for English pilgrims. His cult in England was given further stimulus when refugees from Saint-Josse brought his bones to Winchester, where they were enshrined at the beginning of the 10th century. In 977 rival relics were discovered at Saint-Josse and they became the main focus of his cult. The celebration of the quincentenary in 1477 prompted interest among pilgrims from many countries (*ibid.*, p 214) and the badge used in 1477 when moulding the Niederburg bell was perhaps made for that very anniversary. Could it be that the Salisbury find belonged to the centenary celebrations of 1377? Chaucer caused his Wife of Bath to swear 'by Seynt Joce'. Having also sent her three times on pilgrimage to Our Lady of Boulogne, he must surely have taken it for granted that she would also have paid her respects at Saint-Josse nearby.

St Margaret of Antioch

It is doubtful if St Margaret ever existed, yet she was one of the most popular saints of the later Middle Ages. The legend was that, having been discovered to be a Christian convert in the time of the Roman emperor Diocletian, she was seized and subjected to various ordeals. She was even swallowed by a dragon. When she made the sign of the cross, however, the dragon burst asunder, leaving her unharmed. That, according to a fifteenth century commentator John Mirk, was why she was generally 'painted or carven with a dragon under her feet and a cross in her hand, showing how, by virtue of the cross she gat victory of the fiend.' Nevertheless, she was ultimately beheaded for her faith.

121 Pilgrim sign or devotional badge: St Margaret of Antioch standing on a dragon. A spear surmounted by a cross is crooked in her right arm and a book held in her left hand. She wears a mantle and a belted, full-skirted gown with baggy sleeves. Her crown or coronet signifies her supposed noble ancestry. The dragon's head, which would have been transfixed by the spear of the long cross, is now missing but the dragon's upturned body is clearly visible, with a scaly wing, a leg and a claw and a twisting tail reaching as high as St Margaret's waist. Early 15th century. H. 54 mm. *190c/1987* **Fig 163**

A similar badge has been found at Canterbury while others have turned up at Roche Abbey, Yorks., and on the site of a deserted medieval village at Ketsby, Lincs. The cult of St Margaret was particularly strong in the East Midlands. Of the two hundred or more English churches that were dedicated to her, over a quarter lay in Norfolk. Late fifteenth or early sixteenth-century pewter medallions with St Margaret on one side and the monogram of Christ or the Crucifixion on the other have been found nearer to the focus of the cult. As compared with the Salisbury find, these were probably designed specifically as amulets, perhaps made for the benefit of women in labour. No fewer than eight have been found at Ketsby, including one with an unused, unperforated suspension-loop; two more have come from other Lincolnshire sites (for one of them, see Mitchiner 1986, p 174) and one from Norfolk. Mitchiner (*loc. cit.*) claims that medallions of this type 'can be attributed to St Margaret's at Lynn with some accuracy', but they were at least as likely to have been associated with the former church of St Margaret at Ketsby, where an image of St Margaret was still attracting notable offerings in 1529.

St Quirinus of Neuss

St Quirinus was a military tribune who was put to death in Rome for his Christian beliefs in about A.D.130. His relics eventually reached Neuss (near Dusseldorf) where he was adopted as the town's patron. The rise of his cult to international fame during the fifteenth century followed from Neuss's nearness to the cluster of great and long-established pilgrim centres on or near the Rhine and Maas, such as Cologne, Aachen, Maastricht, Kornelimünster and Trier. Though, up to 1984, the discovery of only thirteen original pilgrim badges of St Quirinus had been recorded on the continent, many more badges were known from the evidence of bells. Having been carried home by pilgrims as far north as Sweden and as far south as Yugoslavia, a few of the badges from Neuss were incorporated by bell founders in the moulds of bells in well over a hundred different localities between 1424 and 1532 (Köster 1984B, pp 212-4). Most badges depict Quirinus as a knight in armour, holding a lance with a flag hanging from it in his right hand and his shield-of-arms in his left and standing astride a label bearing his name. Fragments of badges of this sort have recently been found at London and Canterbury. Another type, known from a painting on an altarpiece of *c.*1485-90, shows this figure in an oval frame fitted with stitching-loops. Finally, at the end of the fifteenth century and during the early sixteenth, there emerged a much smaller badge of medallic form with a cabled rim cast in pewter. The smallest badge worn by the pilgrim in the Frontispiece is of this kind. These badges again show Quirinus as a knight with lance, flag and shield. To this scene, however, were also added two subsidiary coats-of-arms which the German emperor had given to the town of Neuss after successfully resisting an eleven-month siege by Charles the Bold and the Burgundian army in 1475 (Köster 1984A, pp 19-21; Heeringen, Koldeweij and Gaalman 1987,p 75; Bergen op Zoom 1987, p 62). It is a badge of this type, albeit cruder than the few other examples discovered abroad, that has recently been found at Salisbury:

122 Pilgrim badge of polygonal, medallic form, and cast very thin in an open mould, depicting a knight in armour holding a lance with a flag in his right hand and a shield in his left. In the background are two smaller shields and the whole scene is surrounded by a circular cabled border. Early 16th century. H. 28 mm. *195h/1987*

Fig 164

John Schorn, North Marston & Windsor

Schorn was vicar of North Marston, Bucks, from 1290 until his death in 1314. There, his knees grew horny through long devotions. His main claim to fame, however, rested on his success as an exorcist, for he was believed to have conjured the Devil into a boot. His tomb and health-giving well at North Marston became such a draw to pilgrims that in 1478 the bishop of Salisbury, Richard Beauchamp, secured papal dispensation to translate Schorn's body to the new St George's Chapel, then under construction at Windsor. The relics were duly moved into the first complete portion of the chapel, where they evidently attracted a large clientele. The cult appealed especially to those who sought protection against the ague and other feverish ailments, drowning, toothache and blindness and to 'unhappy boys who are in sadness.' The popular success of John Schorn and his boot at Windsor, as well as at North

Marston, is attested by more than fifty pilgrim signs found at London (Spencer 1978, pp 249, 257-8) and at Canterbury and by the following badges discovered in Salisbury:

123 Pilgrim badge: a priest wearing the long cape of an academic hood and with a nimbus round his head. In his left hand he holds a book and with his right he squeezes the top of a long-toed boot, out of which appears the horned, winged figure of the Devil. Late 15th century. H. 41 mm. *216/1987* **Fig 165**

The boot is usually depicted with a long, pointed toe but a badge found at Butler's Wharf, Bermondsey (1987) has a massive boot of the duck-bill variety fashionable at the beginning of the sixteenth century. The same theme, Schorn holding his famous devil-trap, occurs in an astonishing variety of designs, some simply containing his portrait with a boot. Others show him in a pulpit (Fig 166: Canterbury Museum), thrusting the devil into the boot. Beside the pulpit there also stands a flower-spike in a pot, perhaps an allusion to a miracle of his, which led to the sudden appearance at North Marston of a spring of thaumaturgic water. A stone mould for casting badges of this description (though nearly three times the size of Cat 124) was found (1987) at Edelsborough, Beds., near North Marston.

124 Pilgrim badge: a fragment showing Schorn's tonsured head and, to the left, the devil's tail emerging from the upper part of a boot, together with much of the badge's canopied frame. Second half of 15th century. H.27 mm. Given by Mr A.A.Allen. *199/1987* **Fig 167**

St Werburga, Chester

St Werburga was the daughter of a king of Mercia and became a nun at Ely under her great-aunt Etheldreda (Cat 109-111). She was later chosen to supervise some of the monastic foundations in the Midlands and, after her death in *c.*700, was buried in one of them at Hanbury (Staffs.), where she performed posthumous miracles. Because of the threat from Danish raiders, her body was moved during the first half of the tenth century to the safety of Chester. Her shrine remained an object of pilgrimage until the Reformation. Part of the shrine still survives in Chester cathedral.

125 Pilgrim badge: five geese inside a wattle enclosure, four looking left and the last looking right. 15th century. W. 44 mm. *Sal. Mus. Rep.* 1987-88, pl 3f. *225b/1987* **Fig 168**

126 Pilgrim badge: a fragment of a badge similar to Cat. 125. *190l/1987* **Fig 169**

Most examples of this badge, including one from a fifteenth-century deposit at Bankside, London, are almost identical, though one (BM M & LA 1904, 7-20, 16) reverses the geese so that four look right and the one at the rear looks left.

The badge probably illustrates one of St Werburga's miracles, which is also the subject of one of the misericords in Chester cathedral. A flock of geese was devouring the crops at her abbey of Weedon (Northants.). Werburga told her servant to put a fence around them and punish them for their misdeeds. The servant protested that the geese would simply fly away, but St Werburga repeated the instruction and the geese followed the servant and obediently remained penned overnight. The following day they were brought before St Werburga. They expressed their sorrow to her with a wailing sound, were forgiven and flew away. But they soon returned as one goose was missing. St Werburga discovered that the goose had been killed, roasted and eaten the previous day, so she took up the bones and restored the goose to life. It was reunited with the flock, which flew off and never returned.

Ampullae

Ampullae or miniature phials were another important kind of pilgrim souvenir. Generally flask-shaped, but with a narrow, flattish section, they were designed to contain a dose of the thaumaturgic water that was dispensed to pilgrims at many shrines and holy wells.

Like pilgrim badges, ampullae, too, were normally made of tin or lead or tin-lead alloy and were provided with a pair of handles or loops so that they could be conveniently suspended from a cord or chain around the wearer's neck. Coming into use in the last quarter of the twelfth century, they were, in England, almost the only kind of pilgrim souvenir to be had during the thirteenth century. They were nevertheless available at a number of shrines and, thanks to returning pilgrims or to local entrepreneurs, probably featured as secondary relics in virtually every thirteenth-century English parish church. Until the early fourteenth century, ampullae took various forms, were frequently inscribed and usually bore representations of the cult-figure or relic that they were intended to commemorate (Spencer 1971B; 1975; 1981; 1982, pp 305-9; 1984 and 1988).

Pilgrim badges had also been in use at some continental sanctuaries since the second half of the twelfth century, and a remarkably large number of these badges from far-off places have been recovered in recent years from English thirteenth-century sites. It was not until the early fourteenth century, however, that pilgrim badges were introduced at English shrines and it was to this more flexible medium that the picturesque, iconographical elements of the ampullae were then transferred. Thereafter ampullae grew more functional, more stereotyped, less elaborate and less informative, and by the second half of the fourteenth century all of them were small enough to be worn, if so desired, on the hat, like pilgrim badges.

The possession and use of water that had in some way been in touch with a relic was one of the most popular means of achieving contact with a chosen saint. Thus, St Cuthbert afforded miraculous cures away from his shrine at Durham through the agency of water in which his body had been washed or through a mixture of water and dust removed from his tomb (Raine 1835, pp 90-91). Similarly, devotees of St Godric of Finchale (Co. Durham) were sometimes cured by drinking water into which relics of St Godric had been dipped (Stevenson 1847, pp 368-70). At Norwich a devotee of St William managed to obtain a piece of stone from his tomb. This she gradually reduced to a powder which she mixed in water and gave to her family as medicine when required (Jessopp and James 1896, pp 135-6). Ampullae were a less destructive way of setting aside relic-water for future emergencies. This form of prophylactic could be comfortably kept on the person or easily hung up in the home or be suspended, for the benefit of livestock, in the stable or cowshed or on the beehive. Ampullae were often donated to the neighbourhood, to be hung up in the parish church. Almost as a matter of course, churches throughout thirteenth-century England secured possession of Canterbury ampullae containing what was perhaps the most famous of all elixirs, the water of St Thomas, water tinged with the martyr's miracle-working blood.

Ampullae, particularly those cast in lead during the fourteenth or fifteenth century, are robust vessels and have a relatively higher rate of survival than the more fragile badges. In consequence, they are found more widely than pilgrim badges, often on the sites of medieval hamlets and farmsteads in all parts of the country. As often as not they are found unopened. At Salisbury at least twenty-two ampullae have been discovered. They are difficult to date individually, but all are presumed to fall within the late medieval period, *c.*1350-*c.*1530. They are decorated, generally both on the (more rounded) obverse and the (flatter) reverse, with simple, cryptic and, therefore, often enigmatic emblems, the like of which have been considered more fully elsewhere (Spencer 1971A).

A few have a flower on one side, but half of the Salisbury finds are decorated on the obverse with a scallop-shell. The scallop, besides being the badge of St James of Compostela, was the emblem of pilgrimage itself. Canterbury, therefore, took the instantly and universally recognisable scallop-shell as the decoration for the fronts of some of its earliest ampullae (Spencer 1974), and the same motif was later adopted at other shrines, including, probably, Walsingham, with its well or wells of healing water. The shell motifs on the Salisbury finds, as on finds nationally, are of two sorts. Type I (e.g. Fig 170) resembles the true scallop, its bold, radiating ribs producing a corrugated surface, notched edges and well-defined shoulders. Type II (Fig 179) more nearly resembles the common cockle, with fine grooves and smooth edges. At Salisbury type I predominates, though throughout the country as a whole the two types are found in about equal numbers. It is as yet uncertain, however, whether the difference between the two types has any bearing on either the place or the date of manufacture.

127 Ampulla: obv. scallop-shell motif, type I; rev. the cross on a shield. H. 30 mm. *11a/1988* **Fig 170**

It is unlikely that basic shields-of-arms, such as the cross and others listed below, could have had any true heraldic significance. Affirming, rather, their purely decorative purpose, some wide-bodied ampullae, shaped to resemble contemporary pottery costrels (travellers' water-bottles), have as many as six different shields of ordinaries applied to their fronts and backs.

128 Ampulla: obv. scallop-shell, type I; rev. the chevron on a shield, on a lozengy ground. H. 62 mm. *Sal. Mus. Rep.* 1987-88, pl 3e. *225e/1987* **Fig 171**

A very similar ampulla was recovered from the sea-shore at Moels, Cheshire (Grosvenor Museum, Chester) and a cruder version has been found at Great Bircham, Norfolk. Others which differ only by depicting the chevron in a circle have turned up in Old Pullover, Sutton-on-Sea, Lincs., and in Caistor, Lincs. (Spencer 1971A, fig XXI, a,b).

129 Ampulla: obv. scallop-shell, type I; rev. the bend on a shield, in two concentric circles. H. 54 mm. Mitchiner 1986, p 150. *193g/1987* **Fig 172**

Very similar ampullae have been recovered from the Thames near Cannon Street Station (MOL 8815) and the Stour at Canterbury. A variant, with the bend sinister, has been discovered at Kirmington, Lincs.

130 Ampulla: obv. scallop-shell, type I; rev. the arms of Mortimer (barry with the chief paly and the corners gyronny and with a scutcheon) on a lozengy ground; alternate hatching on the arms suggests the tinctures, or and azure. H. 50 mm. Drainage coll. (Brodie). *Sal. Mus. Cat.* 1864, p 55 and 1870, p 11; Spencer 1971A, fig XXI, g; Saunders 1986, p 10. *iiE502* **Fig 173**

This is one of few instances where the arms on an ampulla are identifiable and were presumably intended to be more than simple ornamental clichés. Such an ampulla may have been part of a special order. Household accounts occasionally include payments at sanctuaries for pilgrim signs commissioned for a nobleman and his followers. As regards this ampulla, the same mould, with an altered heraldic device, appears to have been used for casting an ampulla found at Moels, Cheshire (Grosvenor Museum, Chester).

131 Ampulla: obv. scallop-shell, type I; rev. a large letter W on a shield, within three concentric circles. H. 46 mm. *Sal. Mus. Rep.* 1987–88, pl 3e. *225f/1987* **Fig 174**

An identical ampulla was found on the site of Bull Wharf, Upper Thames Street, London (MOL 86.202/27). Another, from the Thames at Three Cranes Wharf (1981), combines the W with the bend sinister. The letter W sometimes appears on the obverse, above a scallop-shell of type II, the reverse being decorated with a crown in a roundel; identical specimens of this type come from Great Linford, Milton Keynes, Bucks., Dunwich, Suffolk (Southwold Museum) and Ipswich (Ipswich Museum 1935.65.55). The possible significance of the letter W is discussed below (Cat 138).

132 Ampulla: obv. scallop-shell type I; rev. a heart within three concentric circles, at the centre of which the mould-cutter's compass-point has left its mark. H. 52 mm. *191w/1987* **Fig 175**

The heart is hatched and faintly crowned on otherwise similar ampullae found at London and Maltby Springs, near Louth, Lincs. Another ampulla, found at Brandon, Suffolk, has an identical crowned heart on the reverse, but the obverse bears a crown similar to that on Cat 140-2. Another ampulla found at Salisbury (Fig 186; pc) depicts the same crowned heart on the reverse, but has a different obverse, mentioned again below.

133 Ampulla: obv. scallop-shell, type I; rev. a six-petalled flower. H. 45 mm. Mitchiner 1986, p 152. *193h/1987* **Fig 176**

An identical ampulla was found (1978) in the Thames at Queenhithe, London (MOL 79.135/2).

134 Ampulla: obv. scallop-shell, type I; rev. the saltire on a shield, within three concentric circles, the outer pair hatched. H. 53 mm. *195j/1987* **Fig 177**

135 Ampulla: fragment from an ampulla similar to Cat 134. *203b/1987*. Not illustrated.

An ampulla with a type I scallop-shell on the obverse and a blank reverse has also been found in Salisbury and, though not recorded, is thought to be very similar to examples found at Burghclere, Hants., and Cavenham, Suffolk.

136 Ampulla: obv. scallop-shell, a form intermediate between types I and II; rev. a Greek cross with splayed ends. H. 37 mm. *1900/1987* **Fig 178**

A virtually identical ampulla has been recovered from the Thames foreshore at Billingsgate, London.

137 Ampulla: obv. scallop-shell, type II; rev. a reversed letter S, perhaps once crowned, on a hatched ground. H. 54 mm. *191i/1987* **Fig 179**

Similar ampullae come from Ipswich (Ipswich Museum 939-23) Witnesham, Suffolk, and Kettleby Thorpe, Lincs. The crowned S (Spencer 1971A, p 64) also appears on ampullae with obverses bearing a four-leaf motif similar to that depicted in Fig 182; identical specimens have come from a moated site at Old Park, Devizes, Wilts., and from the site of Whitehall Manor, Botany Hill, Billericay, Essex.

An ampulla with a type II scallop-shell on the front and a crowned W on the reverse has also been found in Salisbury, though not officially recorded. Fortunately, identical finds have occurred at several other spots, such as Milston, Wilts. (Salisbury Mus. *2/1989*), Dunwich, Suffolk, Cirencester, Glos., Old Park, Devizes and on the site of the priory, Portchester, Hants (Cunliffe 1977, pl xlii, e). The crowned W also appears on the following find from Salisbury:

138 Ampulla: obv. a crown on a hatched ground; rev. a crowned W on a hatched ground. H. 52 mm. Given by Mr M. Green. *142/1978* **Fig 180**

An identical ampulla was found at Huntingdon (1981) and others with the same combination of motifs were found at Cobham, Kent (1982) and near Norwich (1984). Both the crown and crowned W occur separately on many other ampullae. In addition to those listed in Spencer 1971A and to those mentioned above, further examples of the crowned W have turned up at Walsingham, Harling (Norfolk), London (three), Boxley (Kent) and Wantage (Berks.), and of the crown at Bury St Edmunds, Norwich, Brandon (Suffolk), Waltham Abbey, Newington (Kent), Langley Burrell (Wilts), Bradwell Bury moated manor (Milton Keynes, Bucks), and Abingdon (Berks). More examples of the crown motif on ampullae found at Salisbury are catalogued below.

Ampullae bearing the crowned letter W have been tentatively associated with the cult of Our Lady of Walsingham (Spencer 1971A, pp 63-4). The relatively large number and wide distribution of the ampullae involved point to a shrine of major importance, such as Walsingham. The crown can be accepted as the emblem of the Virgin as Queen of Heaven and while there is a good case for regarding the W as standing for Walsingham, the letter may also have had a more general meaning as double V (Virgo Virginium) and M for Maria when inverted.

139 Ampulla: obv. a large crown on a hatched ground; rev. a wheel-like device. H. 52 mm. Mitchiner 1986, p 139. *193i/1987* **Fig 181**

Owing to a faulty casting, the handles are not perforated. That the ampulla was nevertheless put to use is shown by the usual crimping at the mouth. The perforations are present on an identical ampulla found (1986) at Hunts Hill, Swindon, Wilts. A reverse similarly divided into eight segments, is combined with a scallop-shell type I on an ampulla found (1979) at New Romney, Kent.

140 Ampulla: obv. a flower, comprising four large pointed petals or leaves with midribs and lobed markings, and with four more leaves in the interstices; rev. a crown, the lining of which is hatched. H. 46 mm. *190n/1987* **Fig 182**

141 Ampulla: identical to Cat 140. At least one other identical specimen has also been found in Salisbury. See also Cat 142. H. 49 mm. *207/1987* **Fig 183**

142 Ampulla: a waster from the same mould as Cat 140-1. The ampulla has unduly thick walls, uncharacteristically rough on the inside. This added thickness and granular interior surface is evidently the result of over-prolonging the process of slush-casting. An air-lock in the mould also rendered one handle incomplete. H. 50 mm. *217/1987* **Fig 184**

Another thick-walled waster from the same mould has also been unearthed at Salisbury. Neither this nor Cat 142 appear to have been used, their necks being too rigid to be squeezed flat manually before being sealed by crimping, the procedure adopted for correctly-cast versions, Cat 140-1, and, indeed, most other ampullae catalogued here. The occurrence at Salisbury of at least five ampullae, two of them apparently wasters, from the same mould suggests very strongly that these are local products. Only one other identical example has been discovered outside Salisbury, on the Thames foreshore at Billingsgate (1984), though several further ampullae have a very similar combination of motifs, among them finds from Langley Burrell, Wilts., Winterbourne Whitchurch, Dorset, Wolverley, Worcs., King's Hill Farm, near Dursley, Glos., Ipswich, Aby Church Field, near Louth, Lincs., Canterbury and Marske-on-Sea, Yorks (Spencer 1968, Fig 1, e,f) while others have crowns of this particular downward-curving form combined, on the obverse, with a pseudo-shield of arms with crown above (Aylesby, Lincs., and St Richard's Friary, Pontefract, Yorks.).

143 Ampulla: obv. a figure made up of four petals or leaves, decorated with veins and spots; rev. the cross on a shield. H. 37 mm. *190p/1987* **Fig 185**

The same four-leaf motif, possibly deriving from either the four-leaf clover or the true-love (Herb Paris, *paris quadrifolia*), is depicted in the simplest possible form on another Salisbury find already referred to (Fig 186; *cf.* also Cat 29).

Cat 143 is a good example of an ampulla which has been opened by using a knife or shears to slice off the top of the neck, just below the crimped seal. In this instance, however, the ampulla was subsequently re-sealed by pinching and turning over what was left of the neck, partly blocking the loops of the handles in the process. The re-use of empty ampullae is also occasionally recorded. Some pilgrims took 'old' ampullae back to Canterbury for a refill of St Thomas's water, for example, while at Oxford a pilgrim used an empty Canterbury ampulla to take away a drop of water blessed at the shrine of St Frideswide. It should on the other hand, be noted that a surprisingly large proportion of ampullae were lost or discarded with their original seals intact and contents unused, emphasising, perhaps, the role of the ampulla as a prophylactic, the equivalent for the ordinary person of the reliquary-pendants owned by the well-to-do.

144 Ampulla: obv. a compass-drawn flower surrounded by a running ziz-zag border, alternately hatched and cross-hatched; rev. a crowned letter I on a shield within a roundel, the ground partly hatched and cross-hatched. H. 43 mm. Mitchiner 1986, p 144. *193j/1987* **Fig 187**

A very similar ampulla was found during the excavation of a moated site at Arnold, near Beverley, Yorks: this differs only in having the crown above the shield, instead of over the I (Humberside Field Archaeology Unit). The letter I, sometimes crowned, occurs on the reverse side of several other ampullae. Here the obverses include the scallop-shell type I (Wootton Bassett, Wilts, 1981), type II (Outer Moat, Sandal Castle, Wakefield, Yorks; Mayes & Butler 1983, pp 232-4) and intermediate type I-II (Thames, Queenhithe, London, 1980). On the latter sort the I stands above a shield with the saltire cross.

It has been suggested above that the letter W and W crowned on ampullae may stand for Our Lady of Walsingham. Following the same line of argument, the letter I or the crowned I might therefore be expected to allude to another well-known attraction to fifteenth-century pilgrims, Our Lady of Ipswich. There is, however, the further possibility that the letter I is the initial, not of a place, but of a saint's name, just as letters T or the crowned T were used on ampullae as well as badges to signify St Thomas of Canterbury. This might bring St Ives into the reckoning. His cult at Ramsey Abbey (Hunts) was partly based on the repute of thaumaturgic water. St John of Beverley (to mention but one St John) might also be considered. Another possible candidate would be St James, whose hand was the principal relic of Reading Abbey. Here pilgrims were invited to look upon St James as heavenly doctor and were given doses of water in which the hand had been dipped. There are indeed many possible options, though the identification of the I with Jesus (Mitchiner 1986, pp 143-4) is unlikely to be one of them, and further speculation about them would not be likely to lead to any certain conclusions.

145 Ampulla: obv. the pile inverted and cross-hatched on a shield, which is shown suspended; rev. a large, star-like flower with pointed petals. H. 52 mm. *195k/1987* **Fig 188**

146 Ampulla: obv. a simple geometric device resembling an archer's target: rev. blank. H. 49 mm. Given by Mr W. Wareham. *143/1978* **Fig 189**

Though the significance of the device is not understood, a similar target is combined with a large arrow on a fifteenth-century badge mould that is likely to have been connected with the souvenir trade at Walsingham (Spencer 1980, p 15, no 35). A pewter badge from a similar mould has been found at London (MOL 85.435/1).

Whistles and rattles

Feast days, anniversaries, public showings of relics, reports of miracles, all brought forth parties of pilgrims, groups very often made up of people from the same parishes or towns. At the same time, a common interest in pilgrimage or in a specific shrine often lay at the root of much of the social and spiritual life of a locality and led to the foundation of parish guilds, made up of people who had accomplished a particular pilgrimage or who wished to help others to do so. The sense of solidarity of such parties and their occasional exuberance on pilgrimage, which must in many ways have resembled the boisterous good humour of works' outings or excursions of football supporters today, evidently found expression in the creation of noise. The wish to draw attention to themselves and to the occasion they were helping to celebrate was partly satisfied at some shrines by the sale of bells. The bells worn as souvenirs by Canterbury's pilgrims were sufficiently distracting in numbers for one observer to complain that they constituted a general nuisance (Cat 34). Little bells were popular, too, with fifteenth-century pilgrims to the Holy Land. The bells were dipped, according to custom, in the miracle-working waters of the Jordan in the belief that their jingling would thereafter protect their owners and wearers from storms (Faber 1896, IX, p 20; see above p 11). From the fourteenth-century the pilgrim-trade at Aachen and Cologne was supplied by the pottery industry at Langerwehe with earthenware horns and trumpets. Other shrines, such as Saint-Nicolas-de-Port, near Nancy, followed suit. The horns were blown in processions and at the exhibition of relics and, according to contemporary observers, made a deafening noise (Meckseper 1985, I pp 408-9; Heeringen, Koldeweij & Gaalman 1987, p 10). Examples of these instruments have been found at various sites in England. An unusually small earthenware horn, recovered from the Thames foreshore at the northern end of Southwark Bridge in 1982, is illustrated (half actual size) in Fig 190 (pc, but stolen in 1988).

Other pilgrim resorts manufactured whistles for their clients. A Walsingham whistle, presumably a whistle sold to pilgrims at Walsingham, is referred to as if it were an item of common knowledge in 'Mankind', a popular miracle play written *c.* 1465-70. One of the characters says, 'I kan pype in a Walsyngham wystyll,' and goes on to imply that such a whistle was a trifle of negligible worth (Eccles 1969, pp 168, 221). Whistles associated with the pilgrimage to Rocamadour were likewise scoffed at as products of little monetary value (Gay 1928, s.v. 'sifflet de pèlerinage'). Indeed, the prevalence of whistles as cheap trinkets in the later fifteenth century is perhaps the implication of phrases like 'not worth a whistle' which had by this time passed into the general currency of speech (Whiting 1968, W223 and 224). Many surviving whistles of tin or tin-lead alloy can be reasonably regarded as pilgrim souvenirs, though none can be positively identified with Walsingham or any other sanctuary. They can, however, be classified into three main types, and, of these, two are well represented in the Salisbury Museum's collection.

One type is in the form of the traditional boatswain's whistle, a pipe with a hollow, often elliptical bulb at one end, the sound being produced when air is blown across the hole in the base of the bulb. The use of the verb 'to pipe' in conjunction with the Walsingham whistle mentioned above suggests that this was an instrument of this type. Like true boatswain's whistles (Lawson, 1986), which to judge from fifteenth and sixteenth-century specimens found at London were usually of brass or silver, pewter whistles were made in two sizes, one being small enough to be held between the teeth, leaving both hands free. On the small whistles the bulb is normally decorated, often with a human head.

147 Whistle of boatswain's type, with a short pipe and a bulb in the form of a man's head with a pudding-bowl hairstyle characteristic of the second quarter of the 15th century. A suspension loop on top of the head retains an S-link and was perhaps primarily intended for use with a brooch (Cat 208-9), but the provision of a second loop meant that the whistle could also be worn suspended round the neck. L. 29 mm. *223/1987*

Fig 191

148 Whistle similar in size to Cat 147, but the man wears a moustache and forked beard and his hair is brushed back from the forehead and covers the ears. Early 15th century. L. 34 mm. *1959/1987*

Fig 192

This was a long-lived type, several examples of which have also been encountered at London. A few of them can be dated both on stylistic and archaeological evidence to the late thirteenth or early fourteenth century. Other examples have turned up in the Low Countries, at Bruges (Vandenberghe 1988, p 199), for example, and at Oud-Krabbendijke.

Another series of pewter whistles of

boatswain's type are 70-90 mm long, much nearer to the size of comparable naval issue today. These normally have two loops with a strip of cresting or tracery running between them along the top edge of the pipe (Fig 193; found on the Thames foreshore at the northern end of Southwark Bridge, 1985). One example from the Thames at London (1848) retains its pewter chain (Fig 194; Cuming Museum, Southwark, C4750), with links of mainly elongated form so typical of English and continental pilgrim souvenirs and of late medieval pewter jewellery (*cf.* Fig 298).

Another popular sort of whistle took the shape of a hunting-horn. The horns were hollow-cast and invariably designed to be worn suspended round the neck.

149 Whistle, horn-shaped, of hexagonal section and fitted with two suspension loops. The front bears an injunction in black letter to *be meri*, preceded by a crown; the back has a running scroll. Late 14th or early 15th century. W. 76 mm. Mitchiner 1986, p 33, where the whistle is wrongly dated 13th century and its inscription misread. *193p/1987* **Fig 195**

Another whistle identical to Cat 149 has also been found at Salisbury. This type of whistle was blown through the larger 'bell' end of the horn, into which the block or fipple of the whistle was soldered. The cutting-out of the side-hole was also a separate operation. Fig 196 shows a comparable whistle, found at St Katherine's Wharf, London (1987), still with much of its neck-chain attached. This bears the instruction *bla (blow) me,* which, with the jovial message on the Salisbury finds, contrasts sharply with the *ave maria* on other versions (e.g. BM M & LA 56, 7-1, 2137). Other, contemporary horn- whistles of similar size are more realistically round in section; these, too, sometimes retain portions of neck-chain.

Spheres of radiating, often reticulated pewter tracery encasing two or three cockle-shells, may also belong to the category of noise-making pilgrim souvenirs. Their place of origin is uncertain, though Walsingham has been suggested as a possibility (Spencer 1971, p 61; Spencer 1980, p 17). The intact specimen illustrated in Fig 197 (MOL 84.241) shows that they were products of considerable skill and delicacy. They were cast in separate halves. These were then soldered together, sealing in the contents, which remained loose within the openwork, and therefore both visible and audible, when shaken. Several complete examples have been recovered from fourteenth-century deposits at London, while portions of many more have been found at King's Lynn, Norf. Parts of others have been found at Hull, Yorks. (in a late fourteenth-century deposit at Monkgate), Chester and, in the case of the following example, at Salisbury:

150 Pilgrim souvenir: fragment from a sphere of reticulated tracery which would originally have contained cockle-shells. 14th century. Given by Mr A.G.Pilson. *107/1987* **Fig 198**

It is possible that such shell containers were regarded in some sense as reliquaries and were carried as prophylactics, worn perhaps, like later pomanders, on the end of a chain or cord (on the more general significance of the scallop-shell in the imagery of the medieval pilgrim, see Spencer 1971A).

There are also grounds, however, for suggesting that these objects were intended to rattle and even to be used as rattles. Examples recently recovered from fourteenth-century deposits at London contained not only shells but pea-sized pebbles and small, spherical bells of copper-alloy and, in one case, of pewter. In a few other instances, the lower half of the sphere is still attached to, and in some cases cast in one piece with, a short, straight handle, which is either tubular (Fig 199) or composed of four strands. Finally, broadly the same design, with a smaller openwork sphere and a more slender stem appears to have been used for babies' pewter rattles in the sixteenth century, judging from the evidence of recently excavated examples.

List of Figures of Pilgrim Souvenirs

* An asterisk denotes an item deposited on loan to the Museum

Fig No	Cat No	Provenance	Accession No	Page
49	—	London	pc	28
50	41	Salisbury	225t/1987*	28
51	—	Salisbury	pc	28
52	—	Salisbury	pc	28
53	—	Salisbury	pc	28
54	—	Salisbury	pc	28
55	42	Salisbury	200d/1987	29
56	43	Salisbury	200e/1987	29
57	44	Salisbury	200f/1987	29
58	45	Salisbury	142/1978	29
59	—	London	MOL	29
60	—	London	Museum of Eton Life	29
61	—	Canterbury	pc	30
62	—	Canterbury	pc	30
63	—	London	pc	30
64	46	Salisbury	103/1987	30
65	47	Salisbury	191d/1987*	30
66	48	Salisbury	193e/1987*	31
67	49	Salisbury	10h/1988	32
68	—	London	MOL	32
69	50	Salisbury	205b/1987	32
70	51	Salisbury	225q/1987*	32
71	52	Salisbury	225r/1987*	32
72	—	Salisbury	pc	32
73	53	Salisbury	192b/1987*	33
74	54	Salisbury	190j/1987*	33
75	55	Salisbury	192e/1987*	33
76	56	Salisbury	193f/1987*	33
77	57	Salisbury	191f/1987*	33
78	58	Salisbury	214/1987	34
79	59	Salisbury	225s/1987*	34
80	60	Salisbury	198a/1987	34
81	61	Salisbury	142/1978	34
82	62	Salisbury	142/1978	35
83	63	Salisbury	107/1987	35
84	—	Salisbury	pc	34
85	—	Salisbury	pc	34
86	64	Salisbury	143/1978	35
87	65	Salisbury	107/1987	35
88	—	Salisbury	pc	35
89	66	Salisbury	225v/1987*	35
90	67	Salisbury	142/1978	35
91	68	Salisbury	225c/1987*	36
92	69	Salisbury	191g/1987*	36
93	—	Salisbury	pc	36
94	—	London	MOL	37
95	70	Salisbury	198d/1987	37
96	71	Salisbury	209b/1987	37
97	72	Salisbury	200g/1987	37
98	73	Salisbury	iiE506	38

Fig No	Cat No	Provenance	Accession No	Page
99	74	Salisbury	143/1978	38
100	75	Salisbury	195r/1987*	38
101	76	Salisbury	200i/1987	38
102	77	Salisbury	195i/1987*	38
103	78	Clarendon	3/1920–21	39
104	79	Salisbury	225d/1987*	39
105	80	Salisbury	201/1987	39
106	81	Salisbury	200j/1987	40
107	82	Salisbury	142/1978	40
108	83	Salisbury	191e/1987*	40
109	—	London	MOL	40
110	84	Salisbury	190g/1987*	41
111	85	Salisbury	143/1978	42
112	86	Salisbury	104/1987	42
113	87	Salisbury	206/1987	42
114	—	Salisbury	pc	43
115	88	Salisbury	10c/1988	43
116	—	Canterbury	pc	43
117	—	London	pc	43
118	—	Canterbury	pc	43
119	—	Canterbury	pc	43
120	89	Salisbury	195g/1987*	44
121	90	Salisbury	10e/1988	44
122	—	London	MOL	44
123	91	Salisbury	191h/1987*	44
124	92	Salisbury	213/1987	46
125	—	London	pc	46
126	—	London	MOL	46
127	93	Salisbury	iiE503	46
128	94	Salisbury	225w/1987*	47
129	96	Salisbury	198b/1987	47
130	97	Salisbury	225a/1987*	47
131	98	Salisbury	225g/1987*	48
132	99	Salisbury	204a/1987	48
133	100	Salisbury	190d/1987*	49
134	101	Salisbury	205a/1987	49
135	102	Salisbury	193l/1987*	49
136	103	Salisbury	194/1987*	50
137	104	Salisbury	195d/1987*	50
138	105	Salisbury	202a/1987	50
139	—	Salisbury	pc	50
140	—	Salisbury	pc	50
141	106	Salisbury	190k/1987*	50
142	107	Salisbury	225u/1987*	50
143	—	Salisbury	pc	51
144	108	Salisbury	192d/1987*	51
145	109	Salisbury	195c/1987*	51
146	110	Salisbury	190f/1987*	51
147	111	Salisbury	191b/1987*	52
148	112	Salisbury	195f/1987*	52
149	—	London	MOL	52

Fig No	**Cat No**	**Provenance**	**Accession No**	**Page**
150	–	London	MOL	52
151	113	Salisbury	197/1987	52
152	114	Salisbury	195e/1987*	53
153	115	Salisbury	11b/1988*	53
154	–	London	pc	53
155	116	Salisbury	142/1978	53
156	–	Salisbury	pc	53
157	117	Salisbury	143/1978	53
158	118	Salisbury	105/1987	53
159	–	Salisbury	pc	53
160	–	Salisbury	pc	54
161	119	Salisbury	191t/1987*	54
162	120	Salisbury	190e/1987*	54
163	121	Salisbury	190c/1987*	55
164	122	Salisbury	195h/1987*	56
165	123	Salisbury	216/1987	57
166	–	London	Canterbury Museum	57
167	124	Salisbury	199/1987	57
168	125	Salisbury	225b/1987*	57
169	126	Salisbury	190l/1987*	57
170	127	Salisbury	11a/1988*	59
171	128	Salisbury	225e/1987*	59
172	129	Salisbury	193g/1987*	59
173	130	Salisbury	iiE502	59
174	131	Salisbury	225f/1987*	59
175	132	Salisbury	191w/1987*	60
176	133	Salisbury	193h/1987*	60
177	134	Salisbury	195j/1987*	60
178	136	Salisbury	190o/1987*	60
179	137	Salisbury	191i/1987*	60
180	138	Salisbury	142/1978	60
181	139	Salisbury	193i/1987*	61
182	140	Salisbury	190n/1987*	61
183	141	Salisbury	207/1987	61
184	142	Salisbury	217/1987	61
185	143	Salisbury	190p/1987*	61
186	–	Salisbury	pc	61
187	144	Salisbury	193j/1987*	62
188	145	Salisbury	195k/1987*	62
189	146	Salisbury	143/1978	62
190	–	London	pc	63
191	147	Salisbury	223/1987	63
192	148	Salisbury	195q/1987*	63
193	–	London	pc	64
194	–	London	Cuming Museum	64
195	149	Salisbury	193p/1987*	64
196	–	London	pc	64
197	–	London	MOL	64
198	150	Salisbury	107/1987	64
199	–	London	pc	64

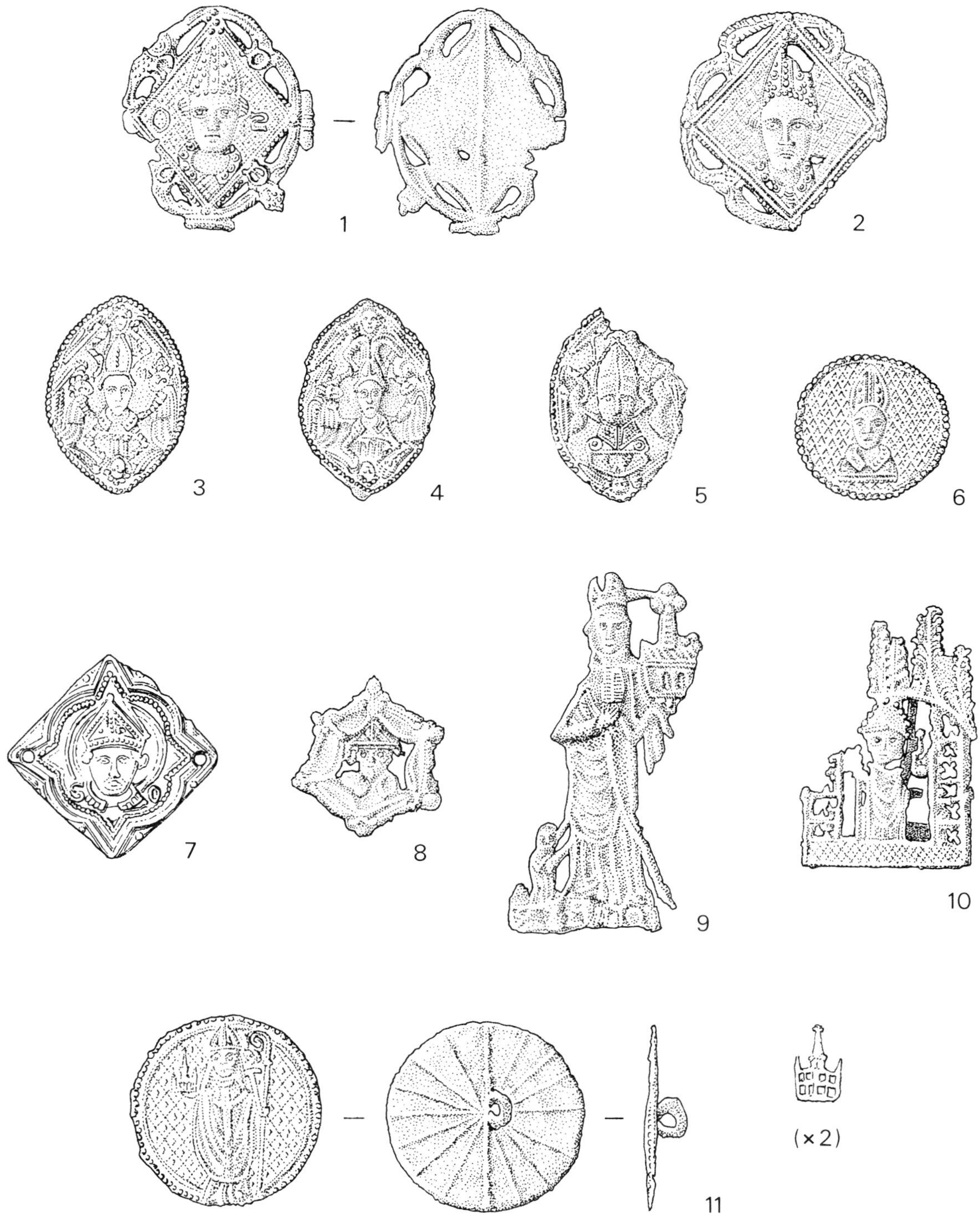

Pilgrim souvenirs. Figs 1-11. Scale 1:1, detail 2:1

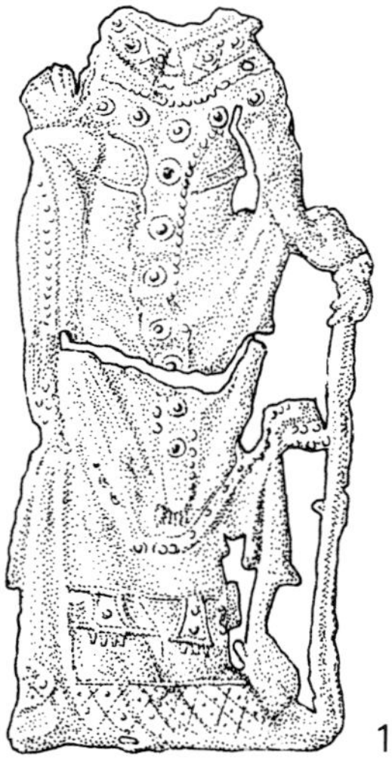

12

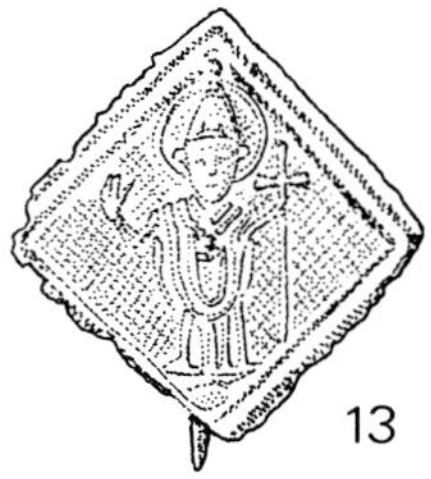

13

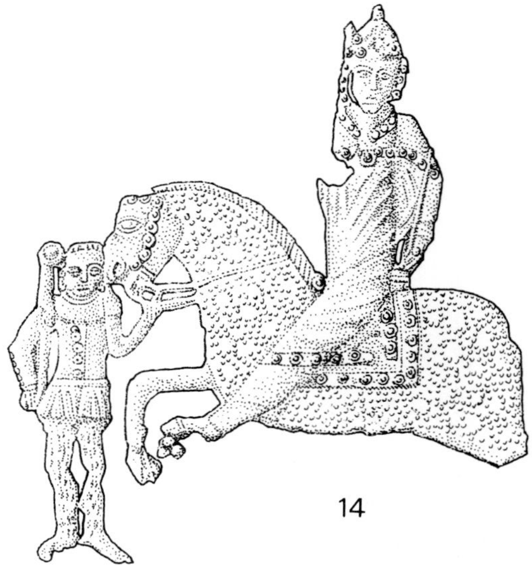

14

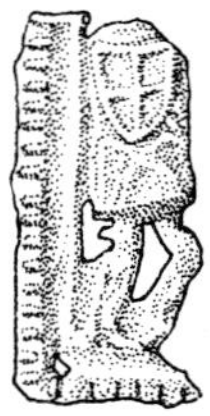

17

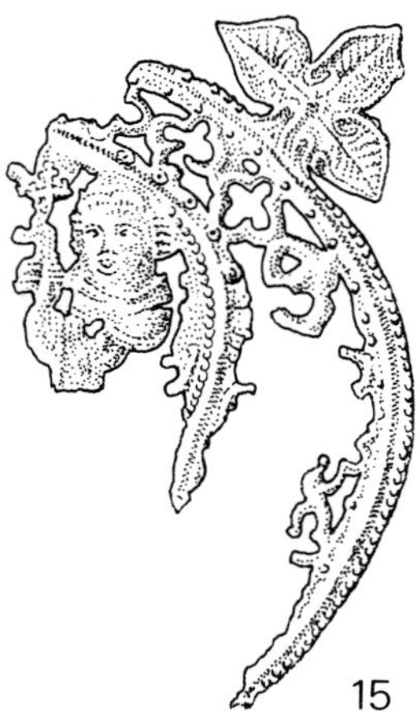

15

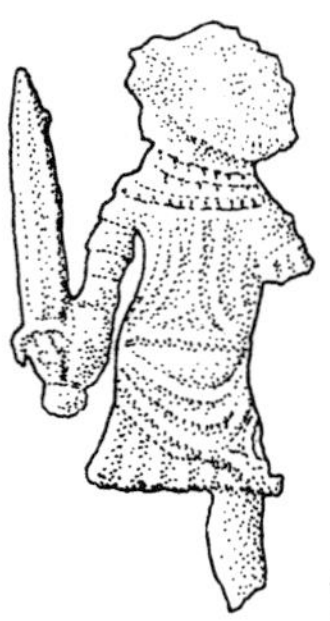

16

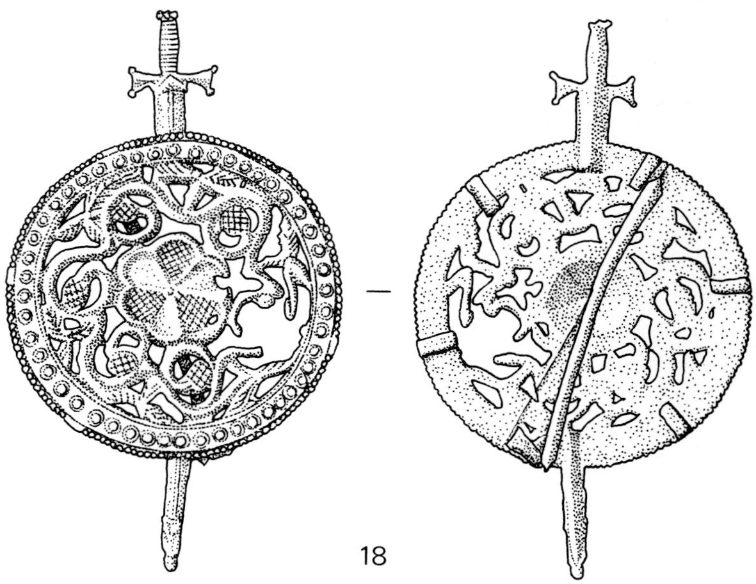

18

Pilgrim souvenirs. Figs 12-18. Scale 1:1

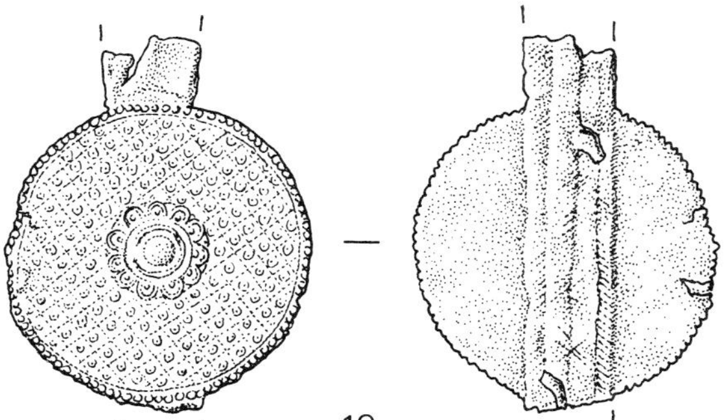

19

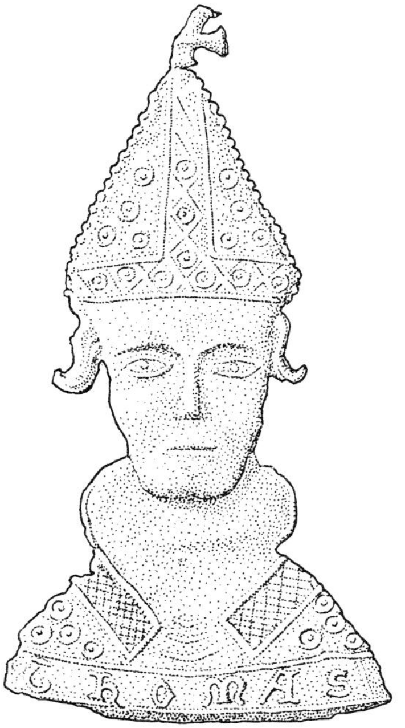

20

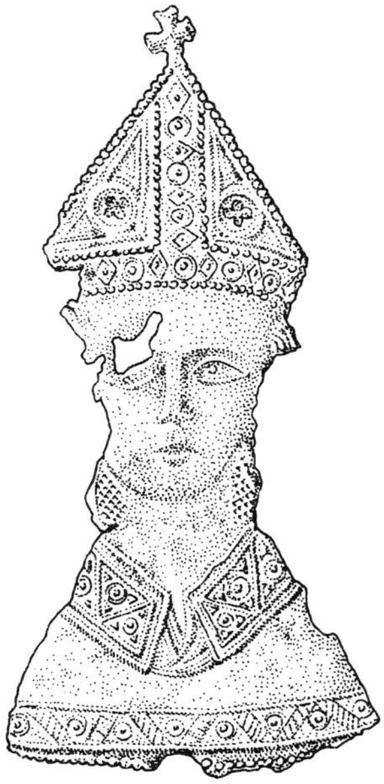

21

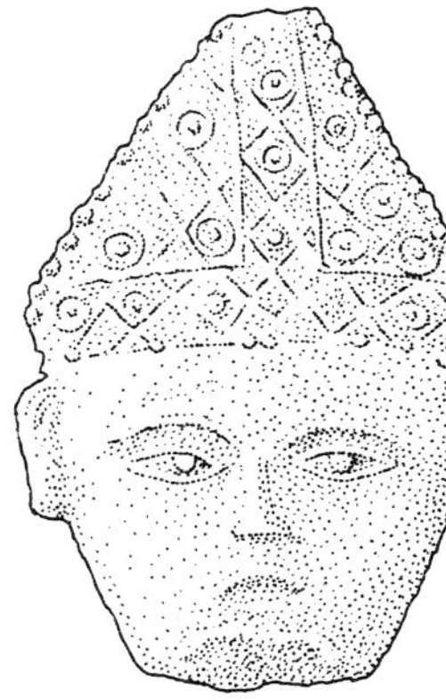

22

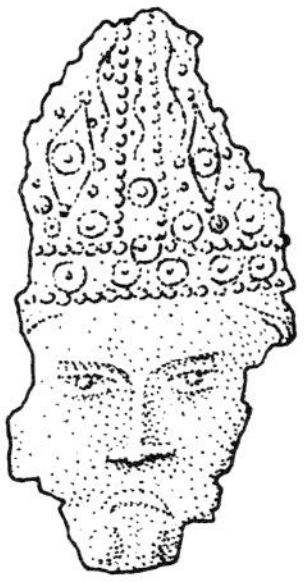

23

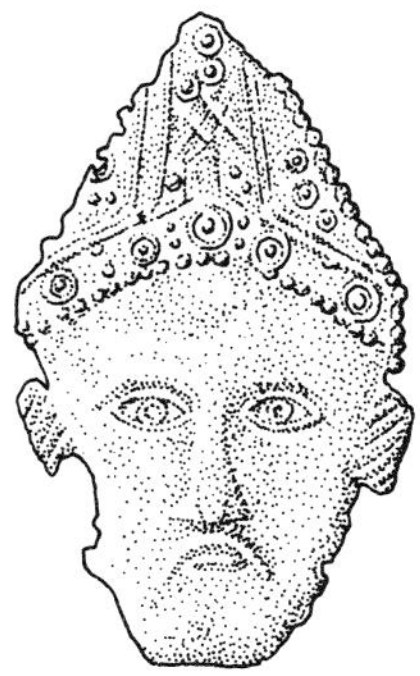

24

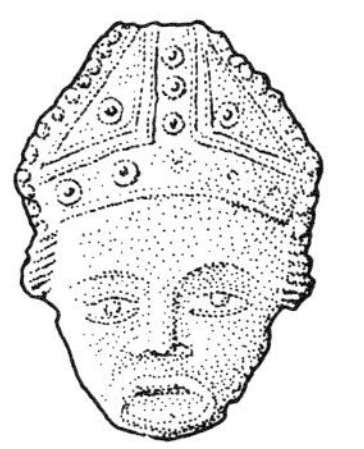

25

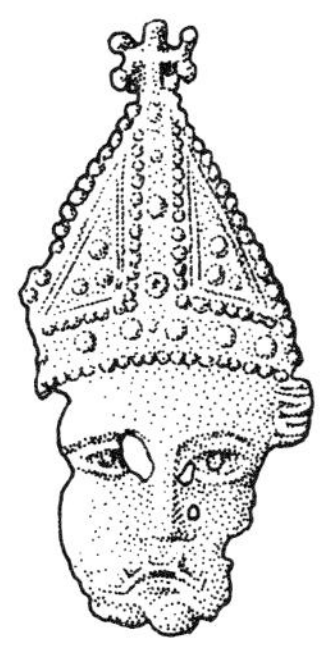

26

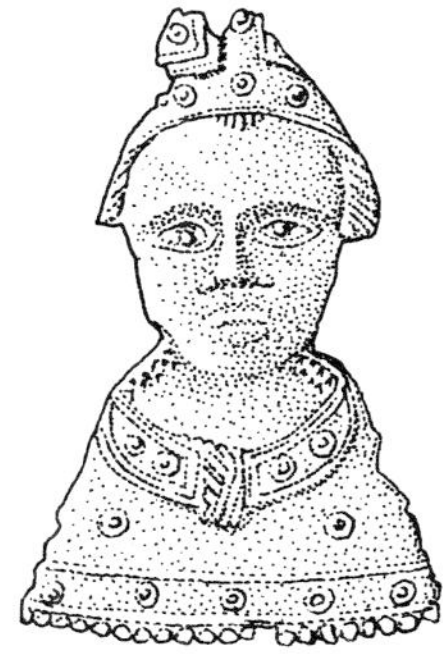

27

Pilgrim souvenirs. Figs 19-27. Scale 1 : 1

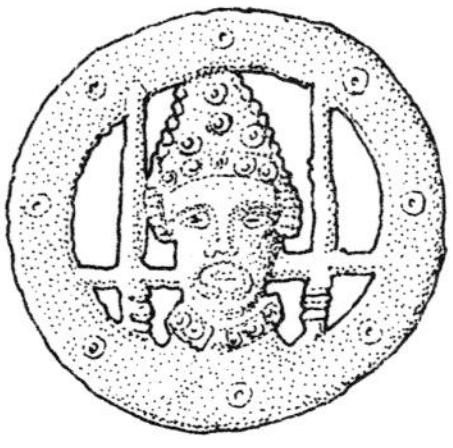

28

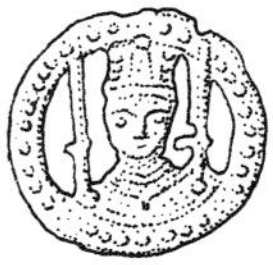

29

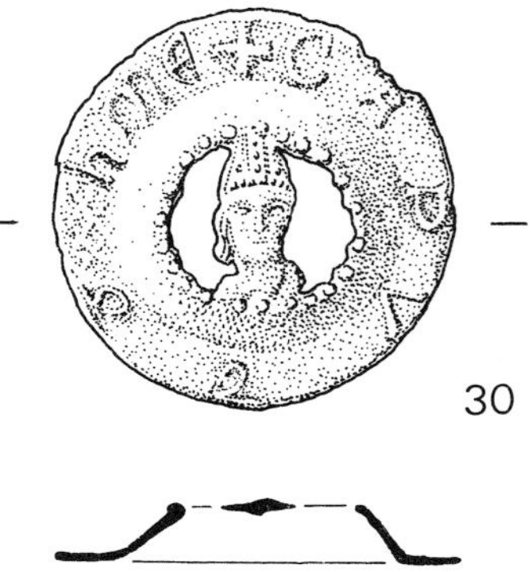

30

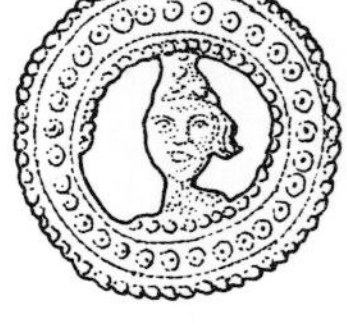

31

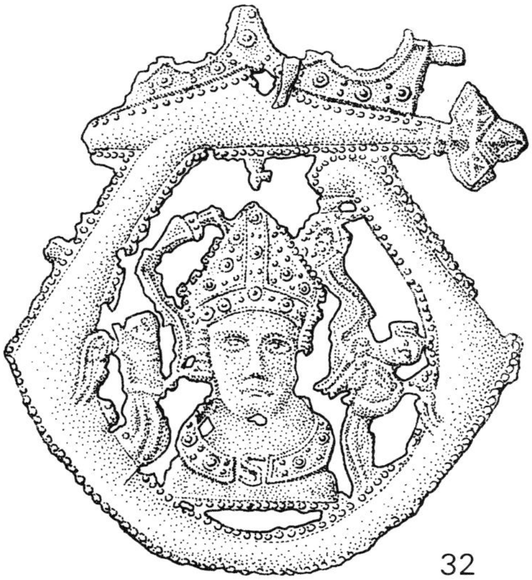

32

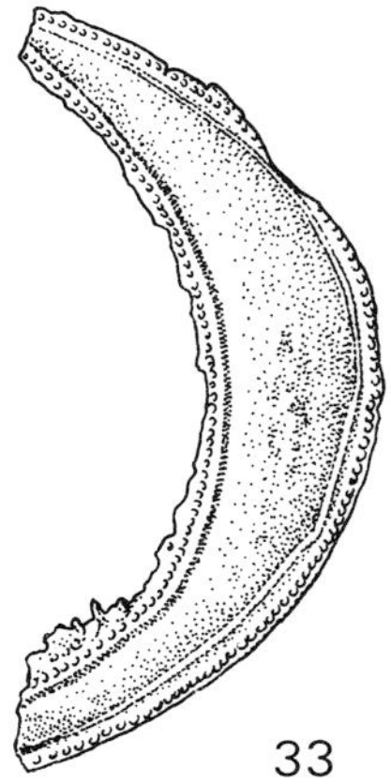

33

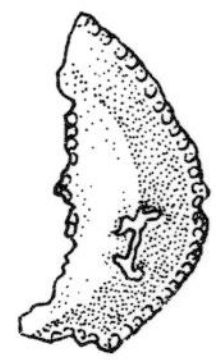

34

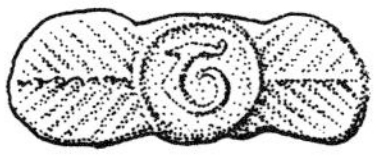

35

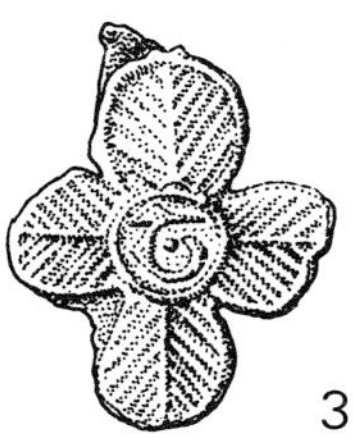

36

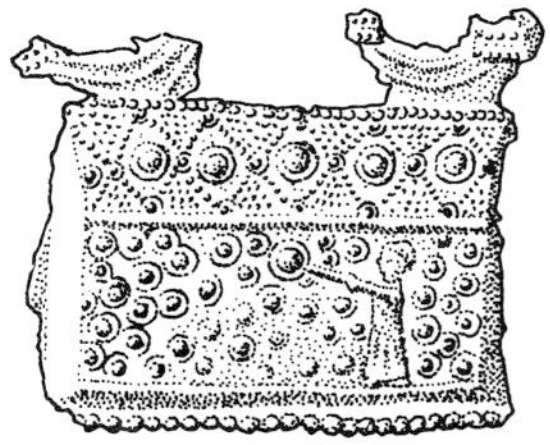

37

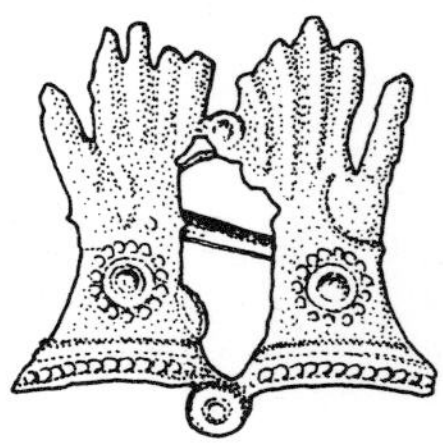

38

Pilgrim souvenirs. Figs 28-38. Scale 1 : 1

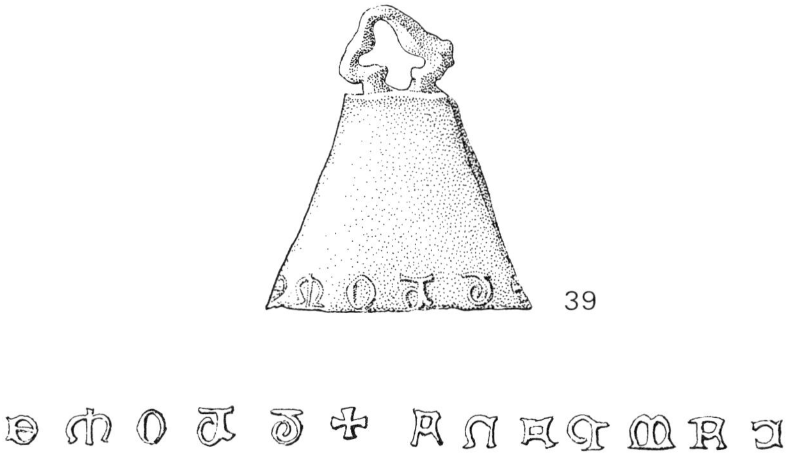

39

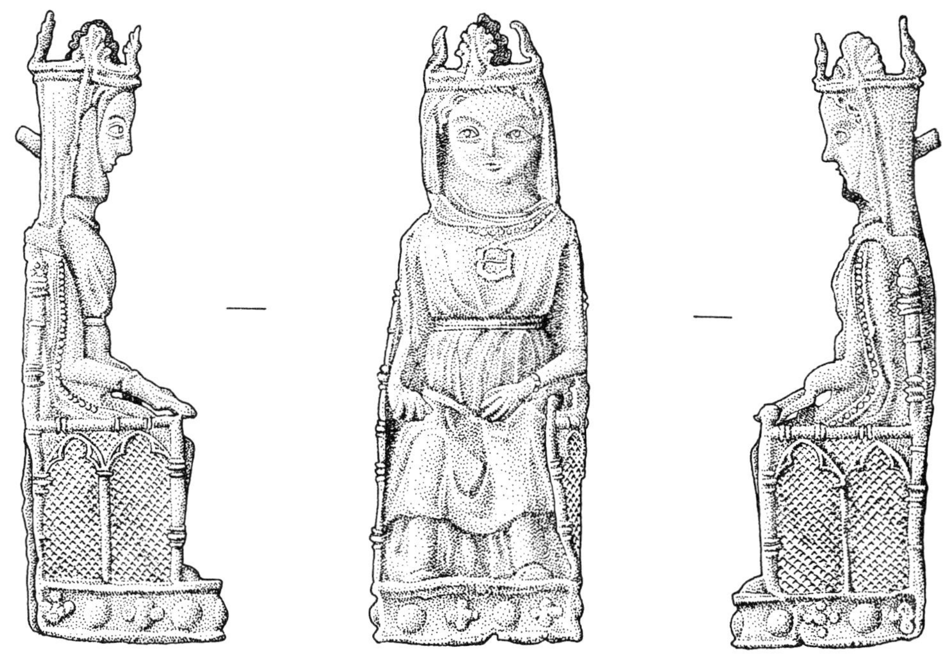

40

Pilgrim souvenirs. Figs 39-40. Scale 1 : 1

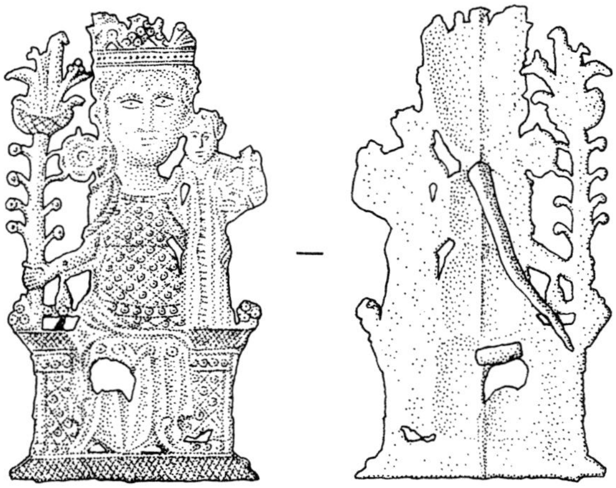

41

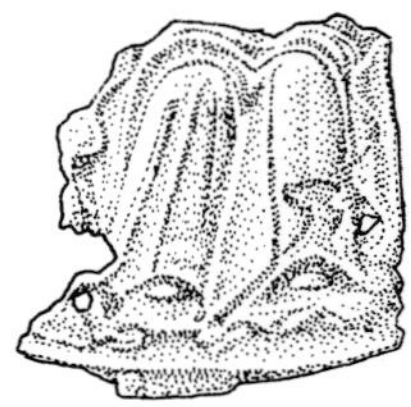

42

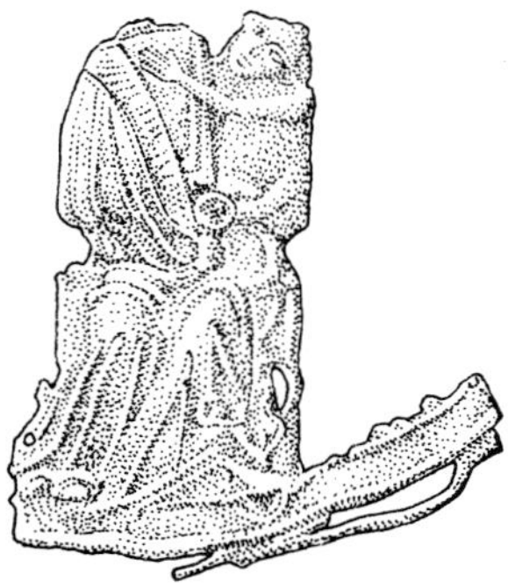

43

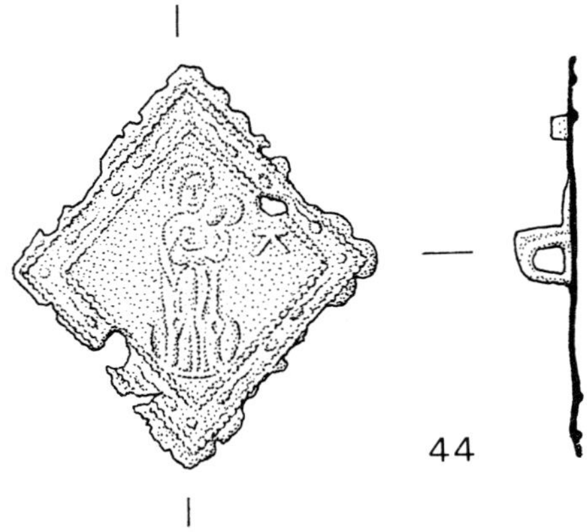

44

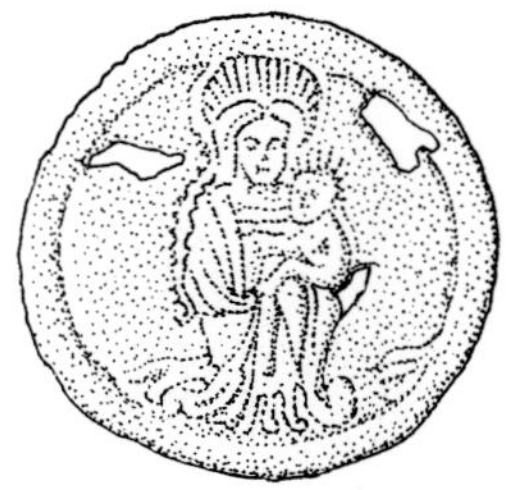

45

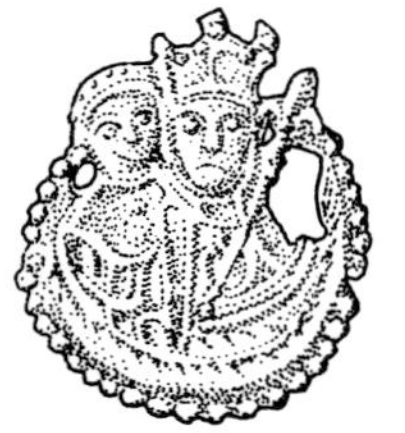

46

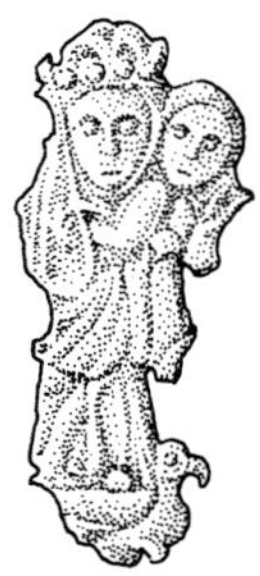

47

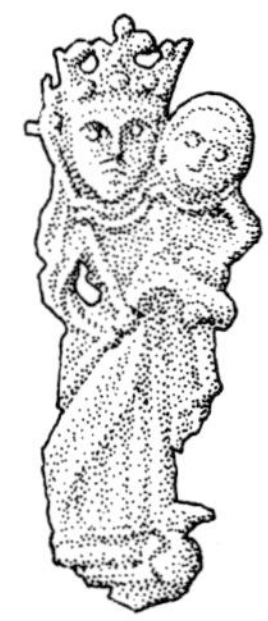

48

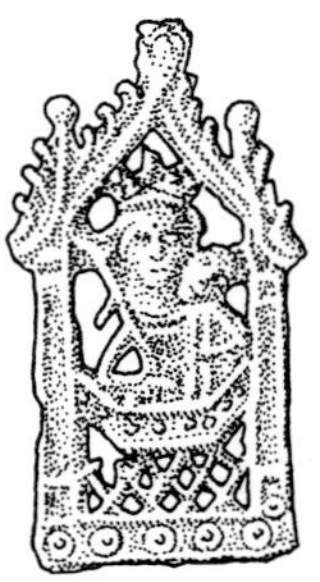

49

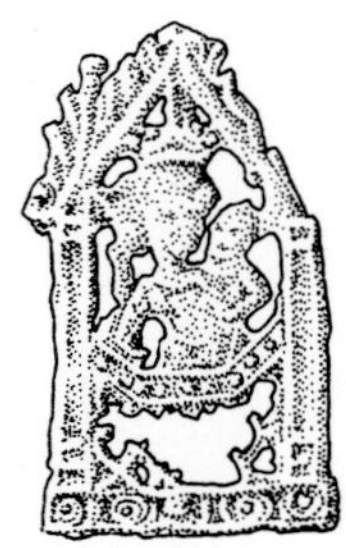

50

Pilgrim souvenirs. Figs 41-50. Scale 1 : 1

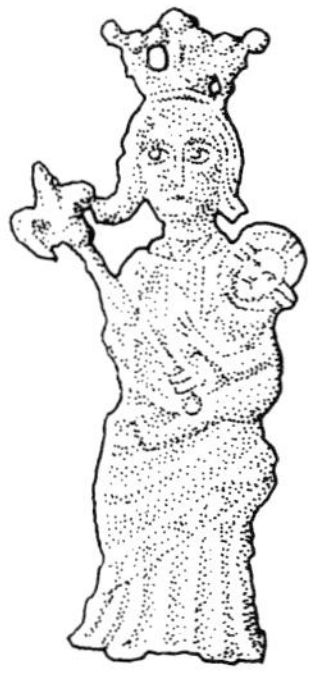
51

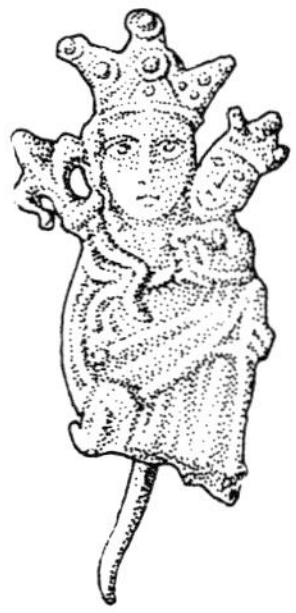
52

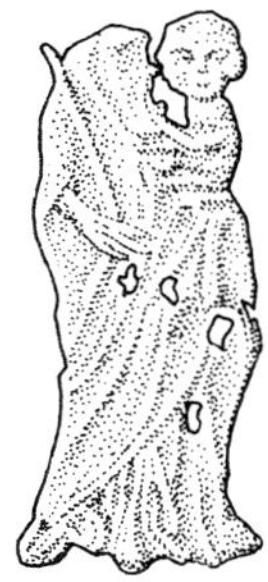
53

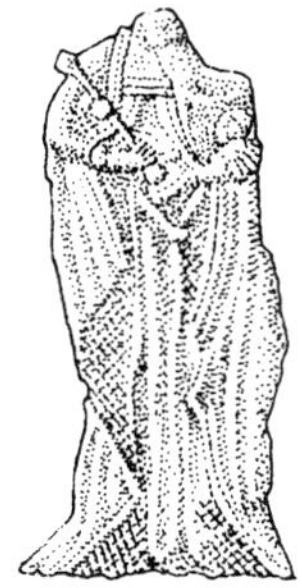
54

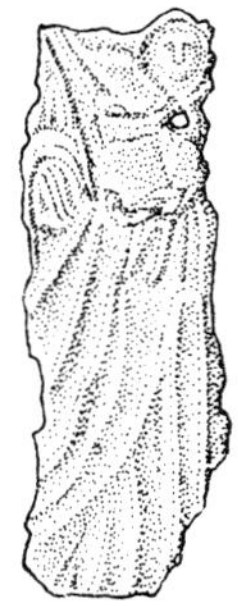
55

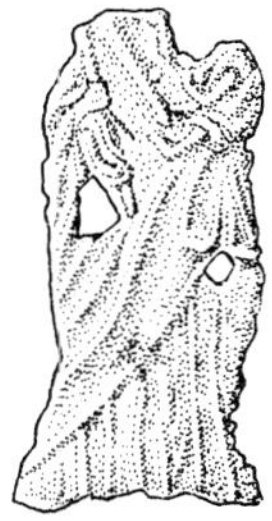
56

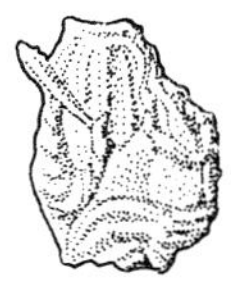
57

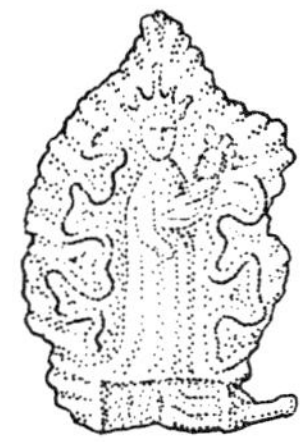
58

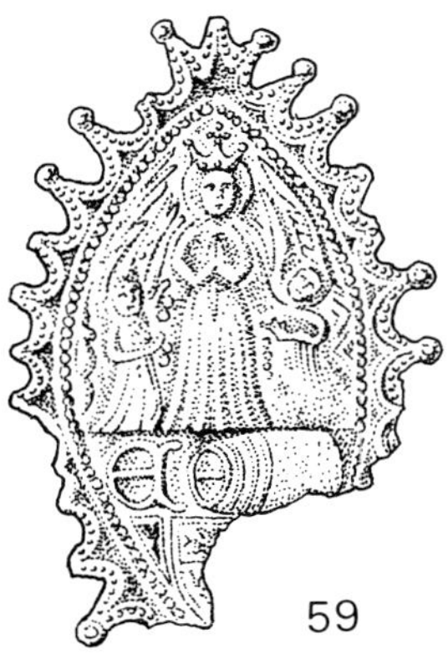
59

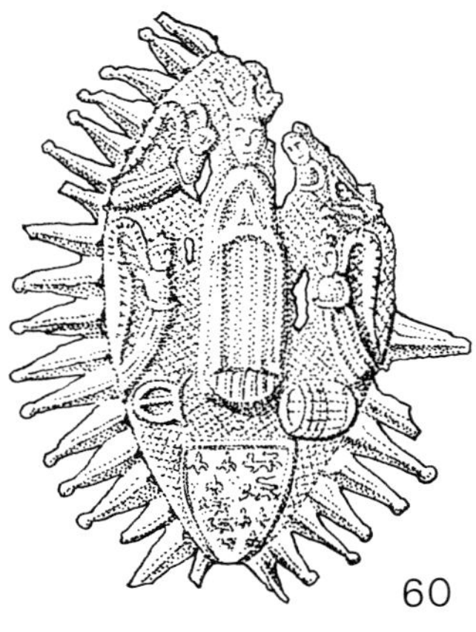
60

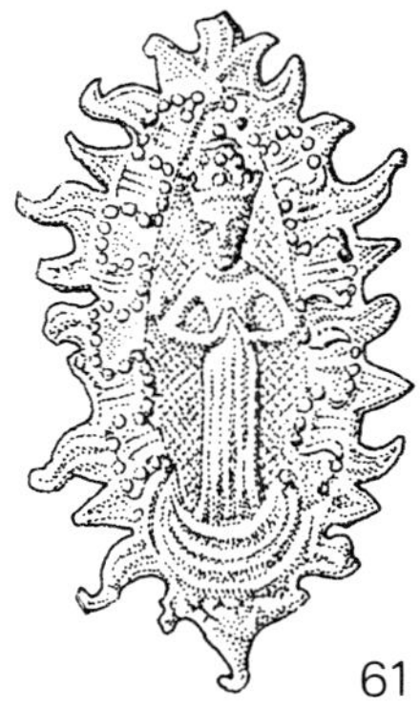
61

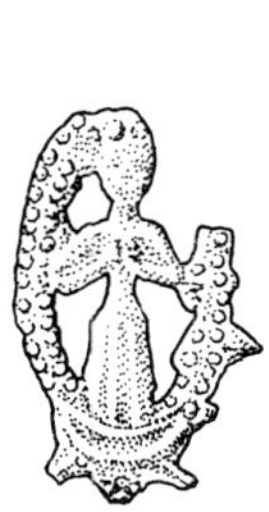
62

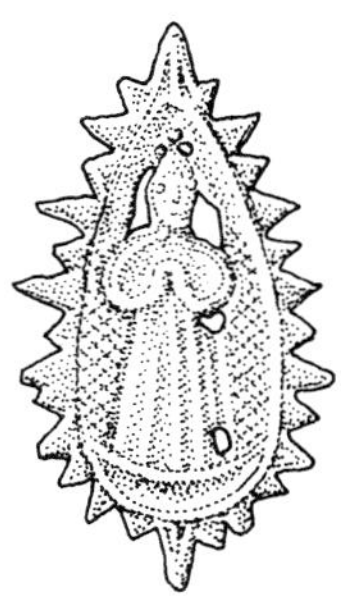
63

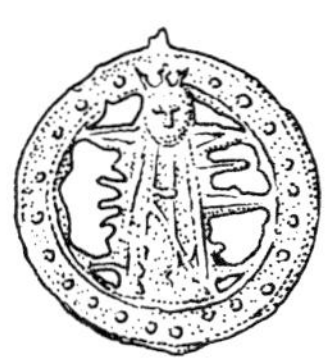
64

Pilgrim souvenirs. Figs 51-64. Scale 1 : 1

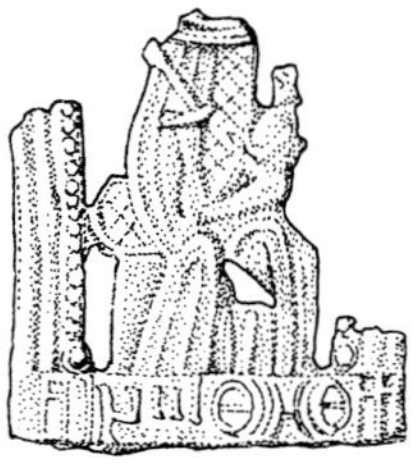

65

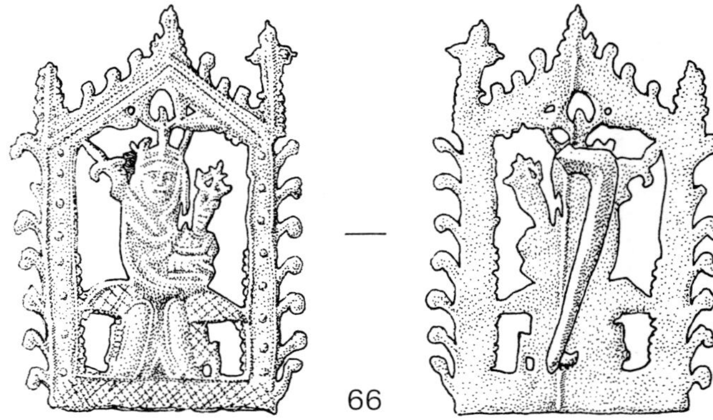

66

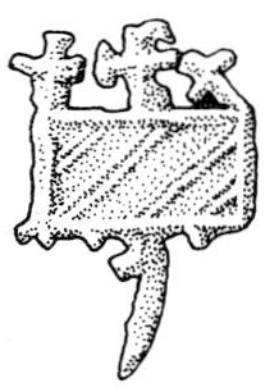

67

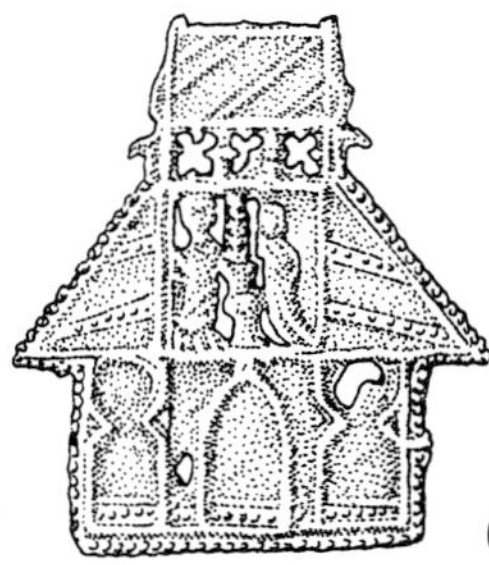

68

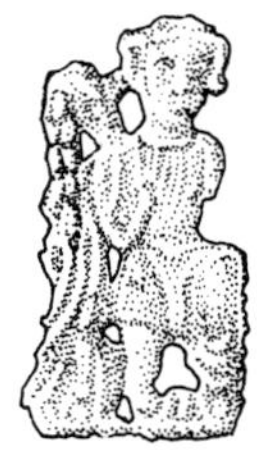

69

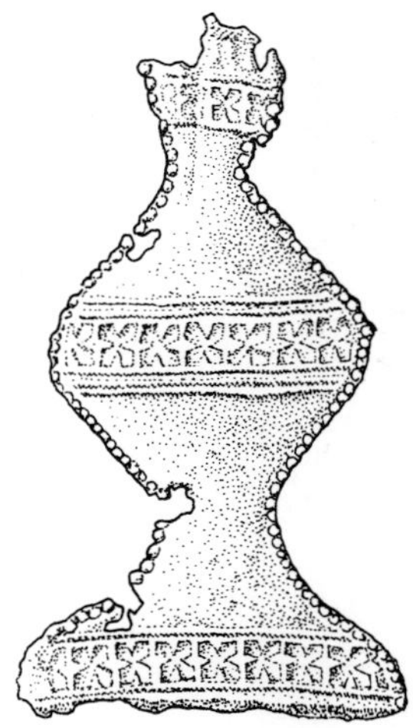

70

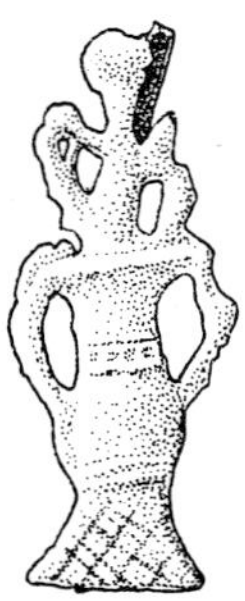

71

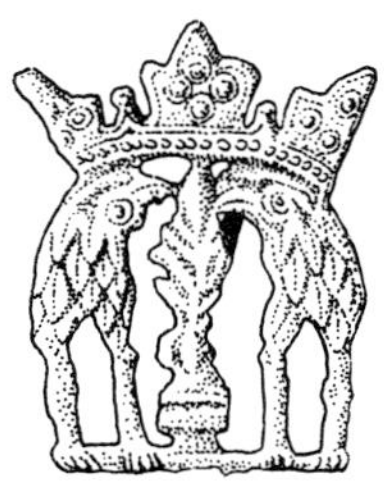

72

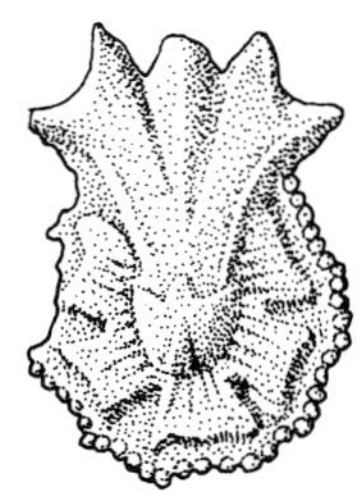

73

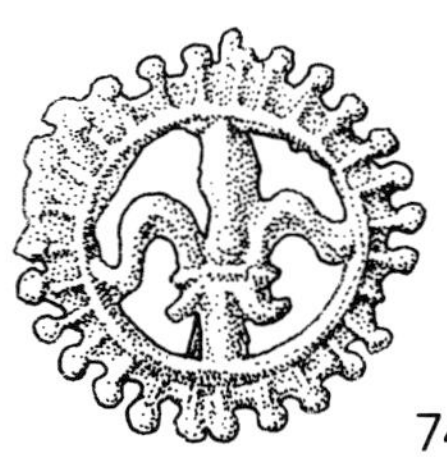

74

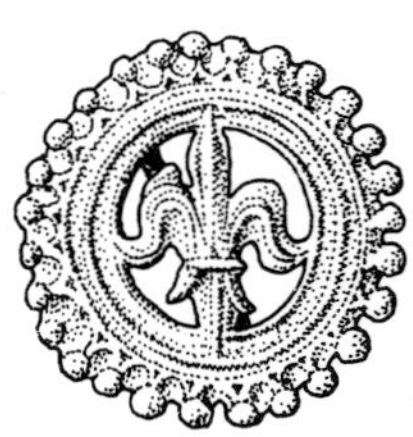

75

Pilgrim souvenirs. Figs 65-75. Scale 1 : 1

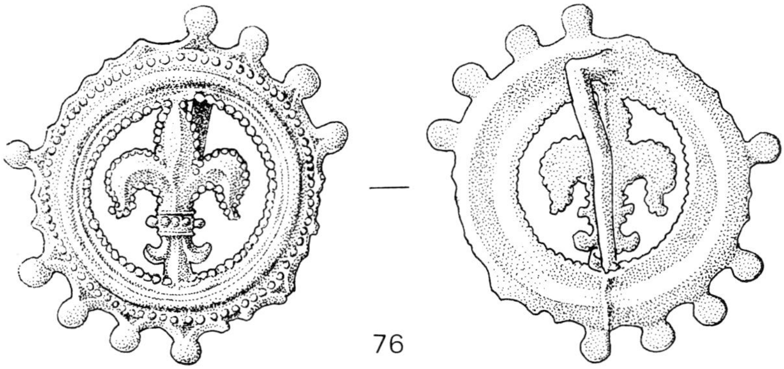

76

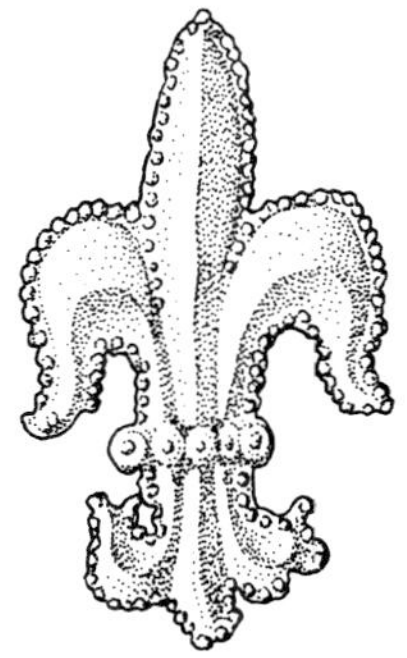

77

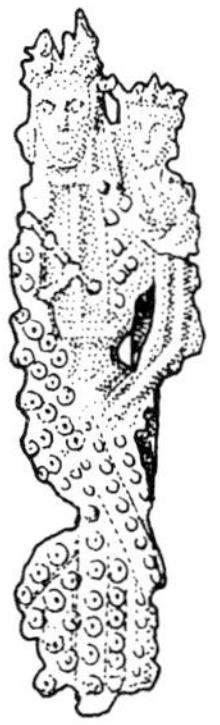

78

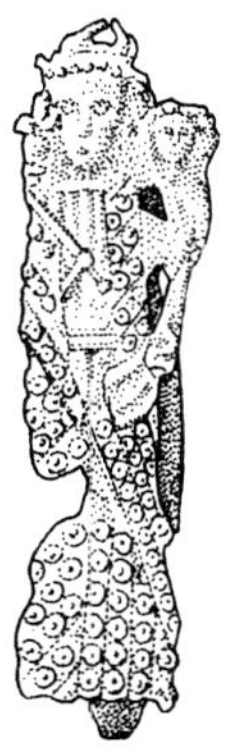

79

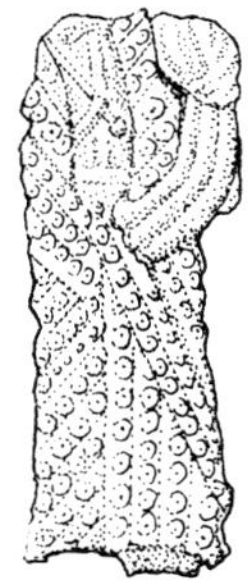

80

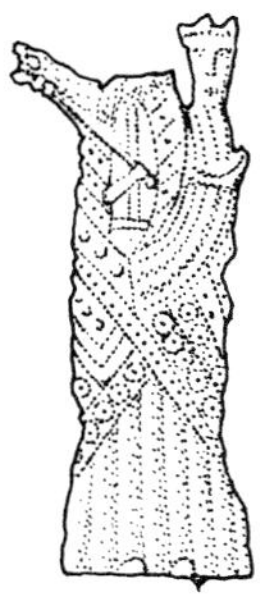

81

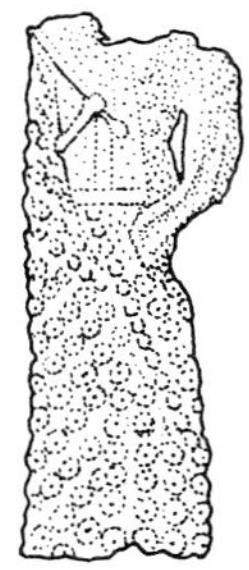

82

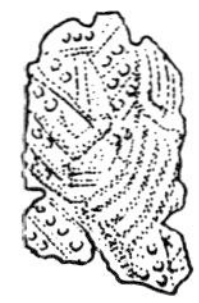

83

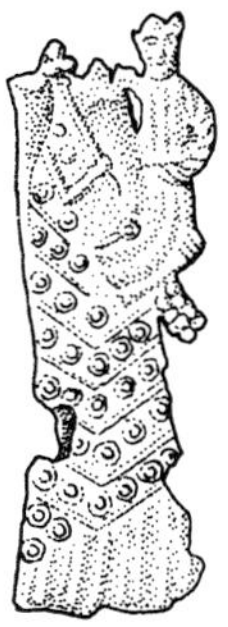

84

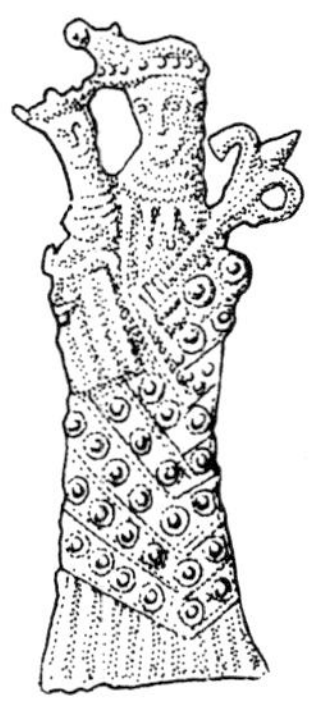

85

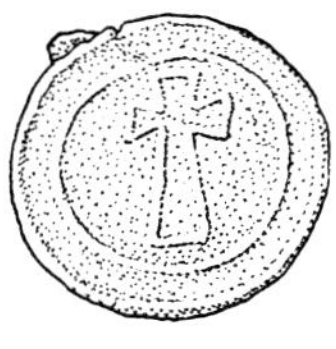

86

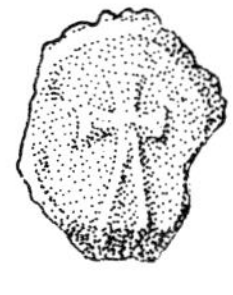

87

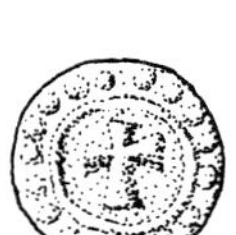

88

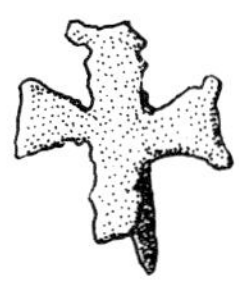

89

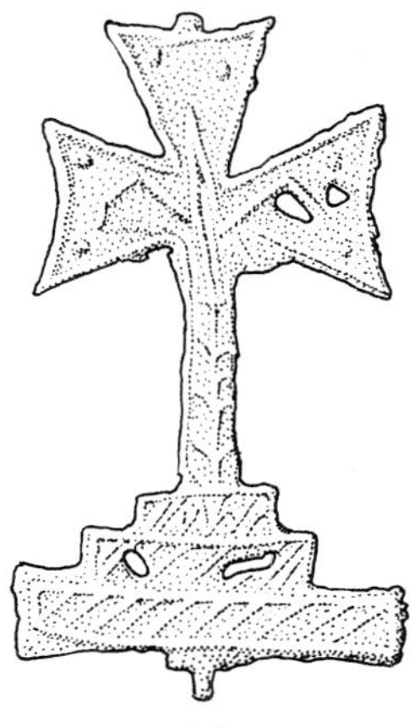

90

Pilgrim souvenirs. Figs 76-90. Scale 1 : 1

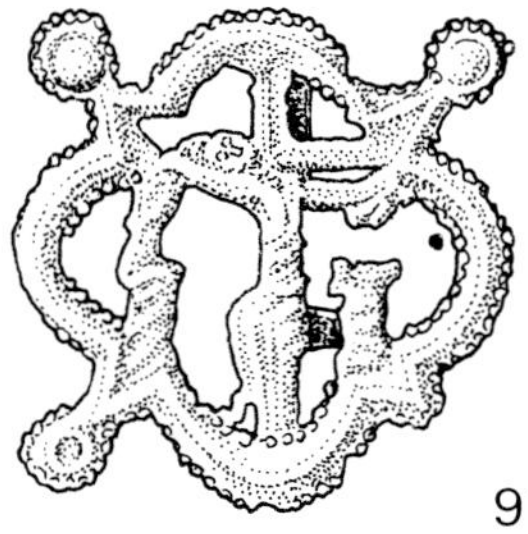

91

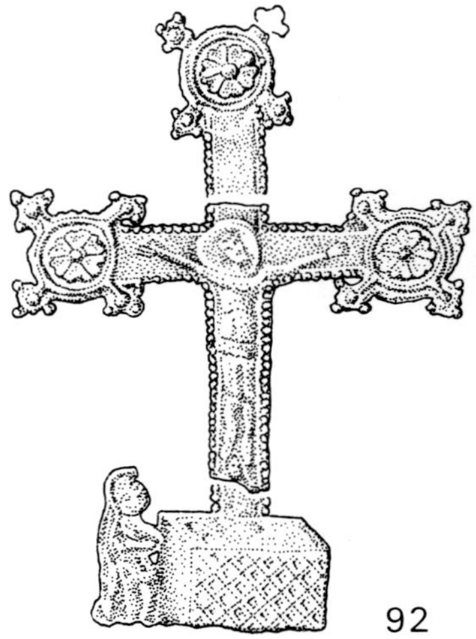

92

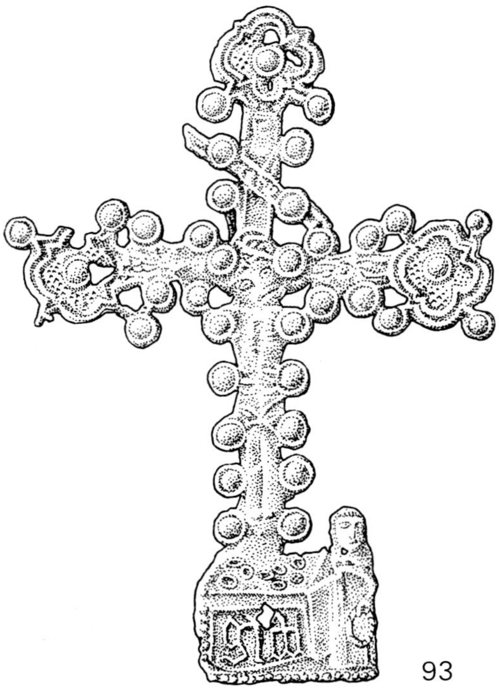

93

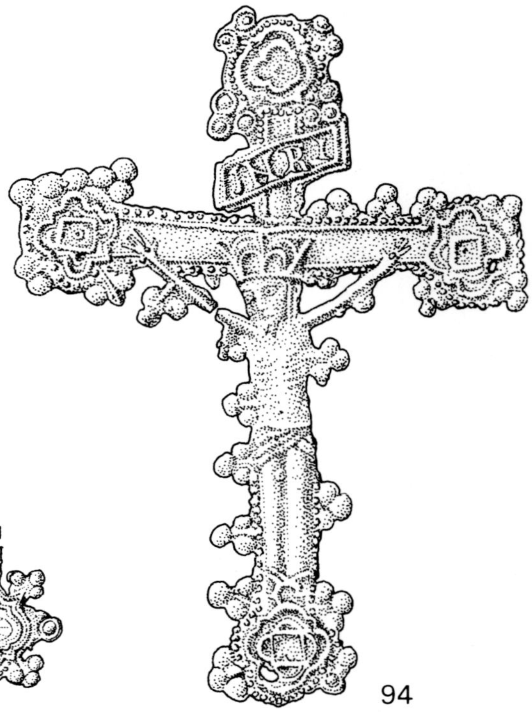

94

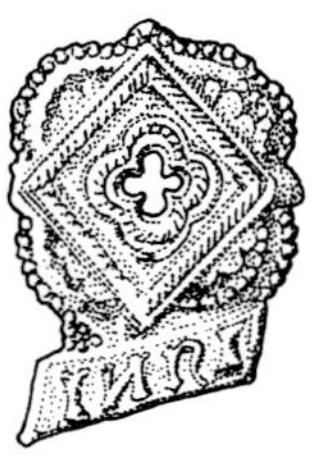

95

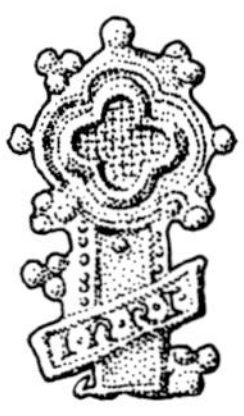

96

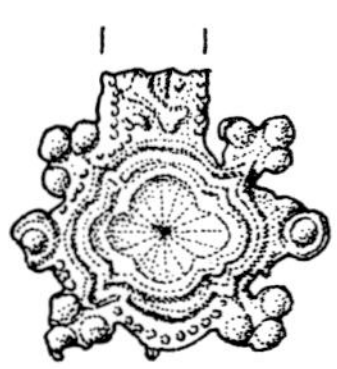

97

Pilgrim souvenirs. Figs 91-97. Scale 1 : 1

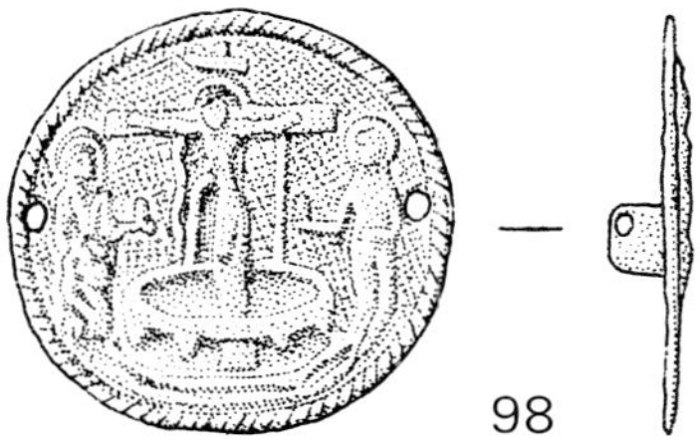
98

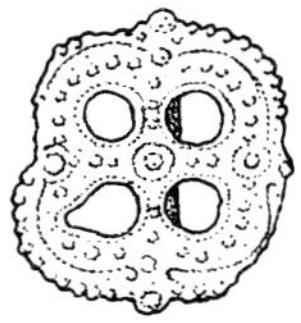
99

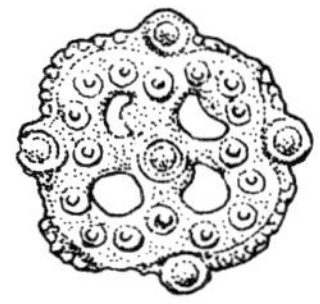
100

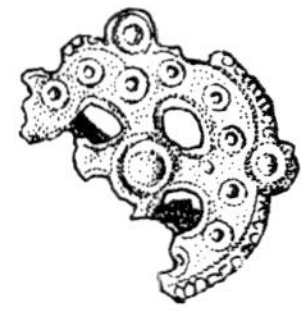
101

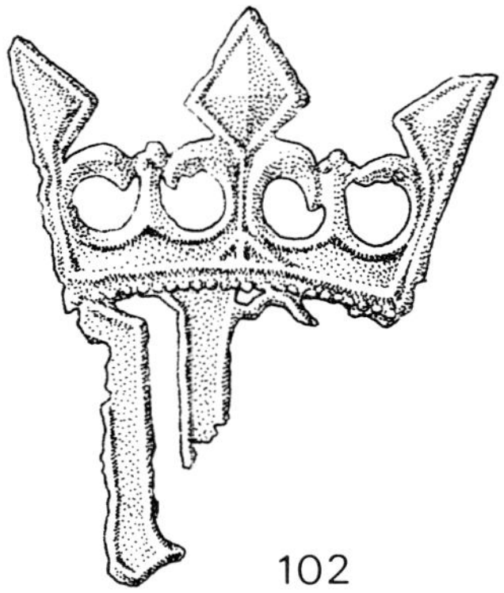
102

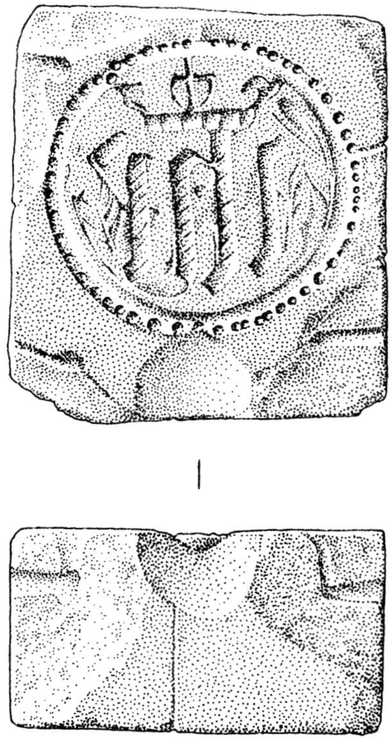
103

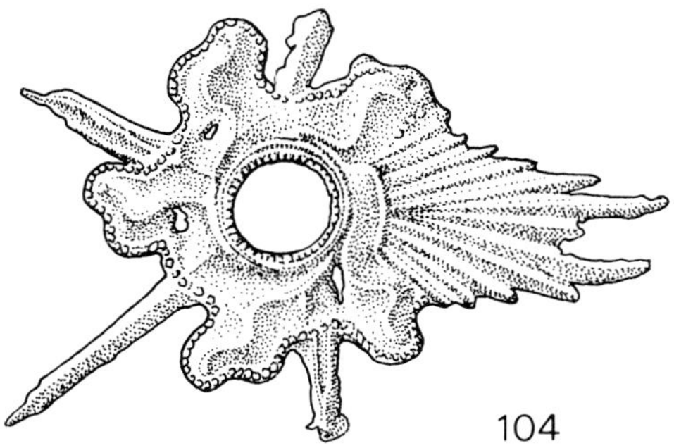
104

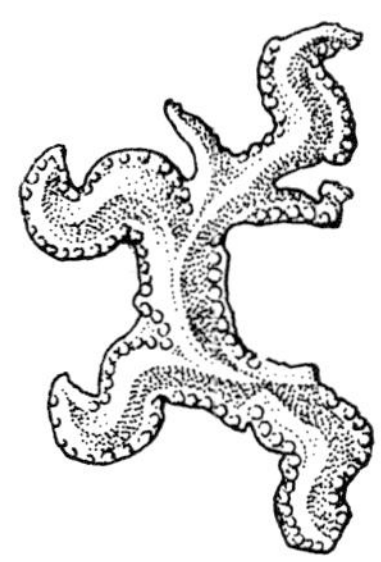
105

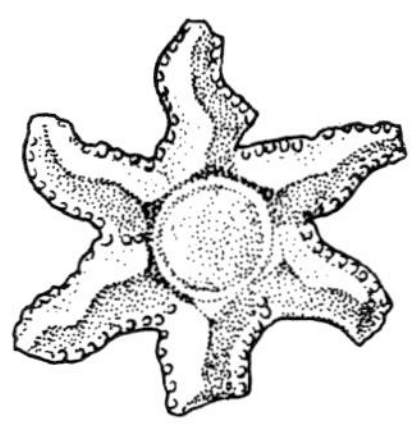
106

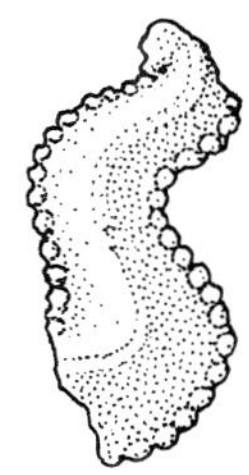
107

Pilgrim souvenirs and stone mould. Figs 98-107. Scale 1 : 1

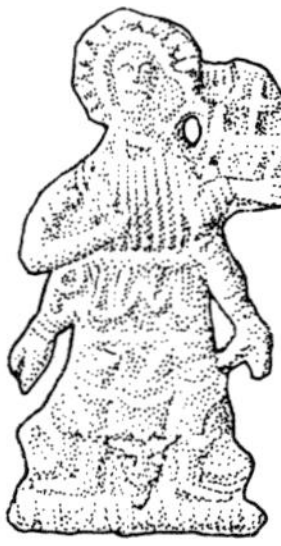
108

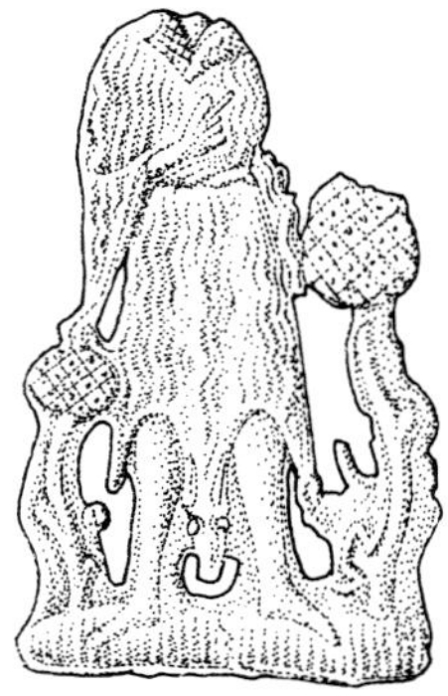
109

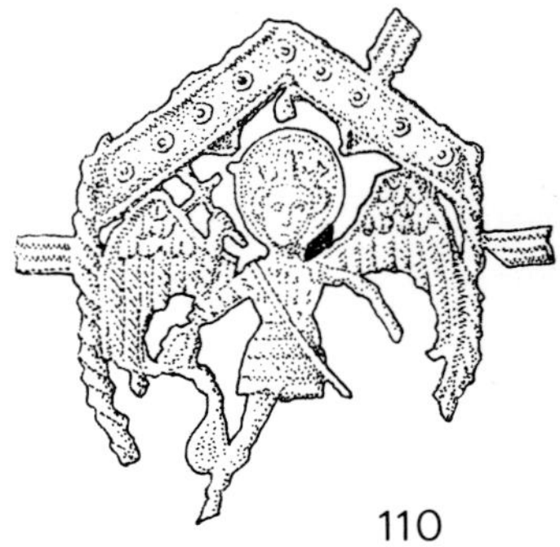
110

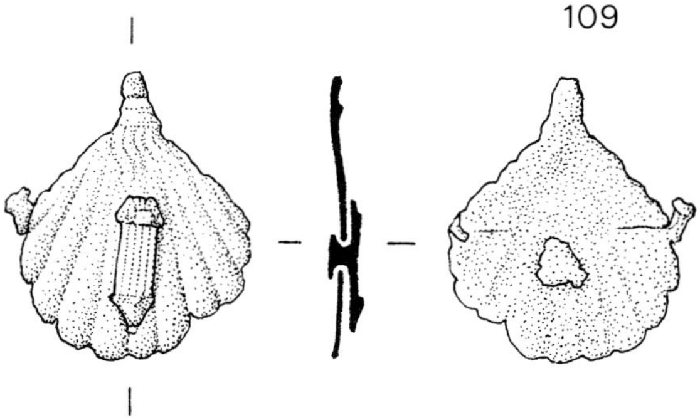
111

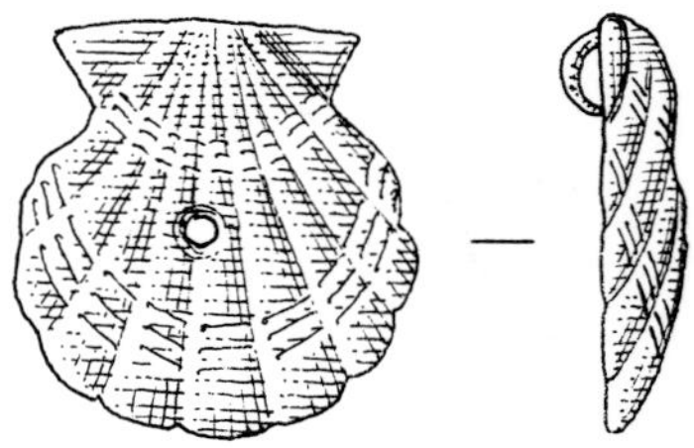
113

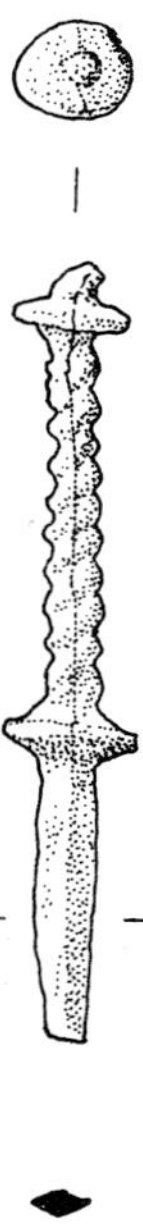
114

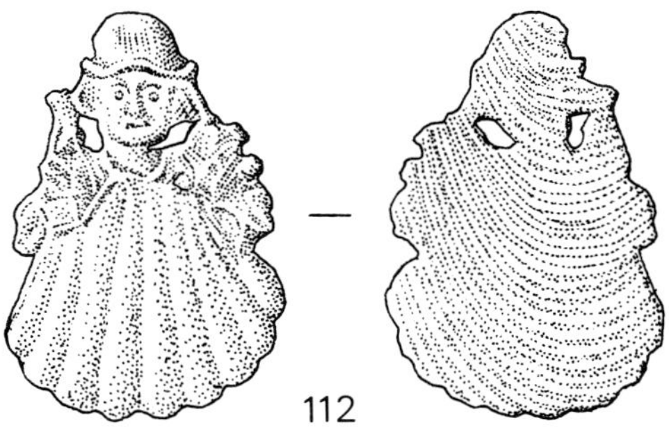
112

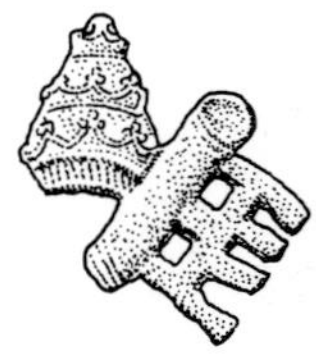
115

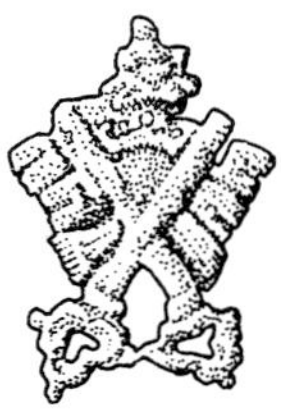
116

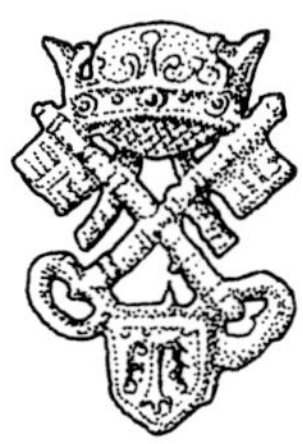
117

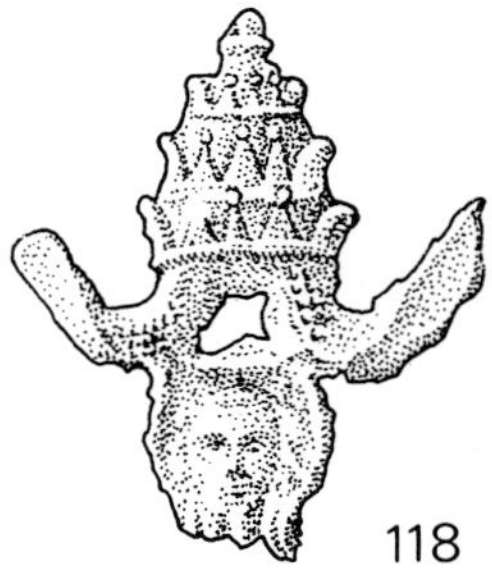
118

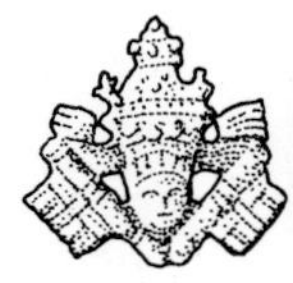
119

Pilgrim souvenirs. Figs 108-119. Scale 1 : 1

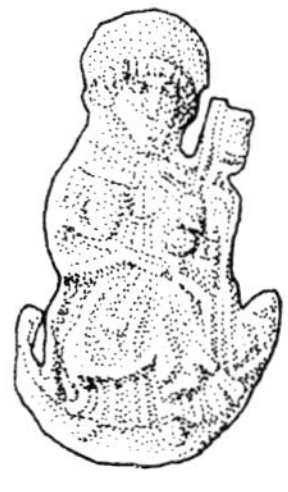
120

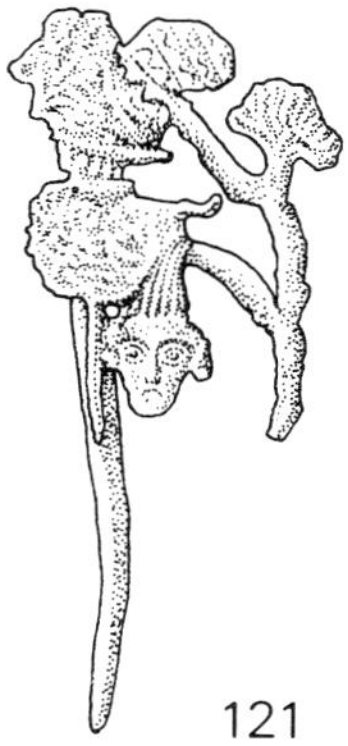
121

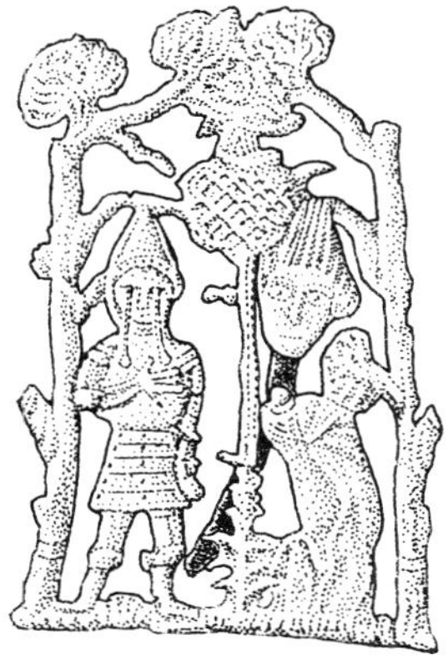
122

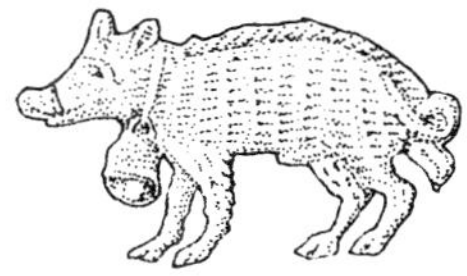
123

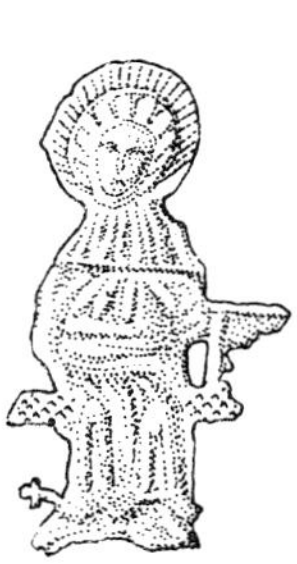
124

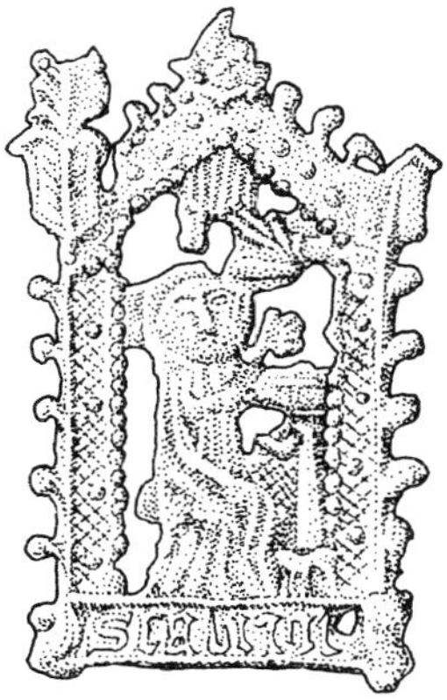
125

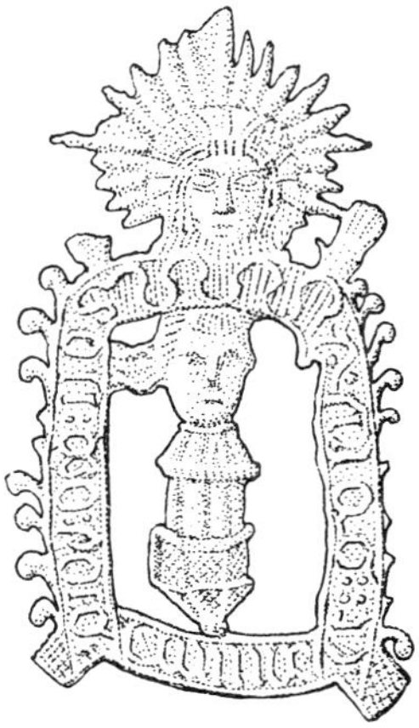
127

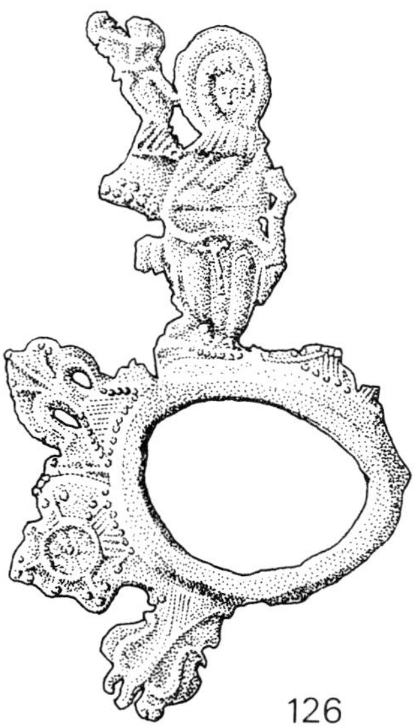
126

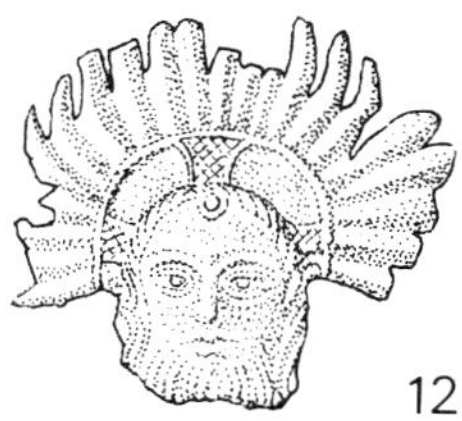
128

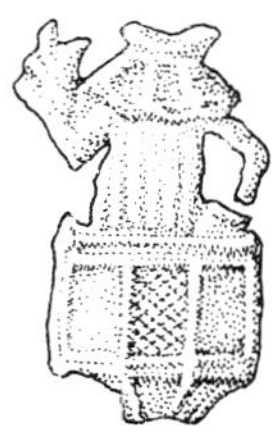
129

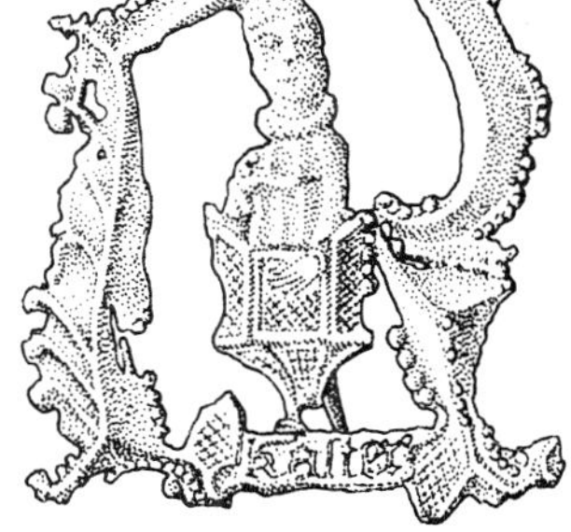
130

Pilgrim souvenirs. Figs 120-130. Scale 1:1

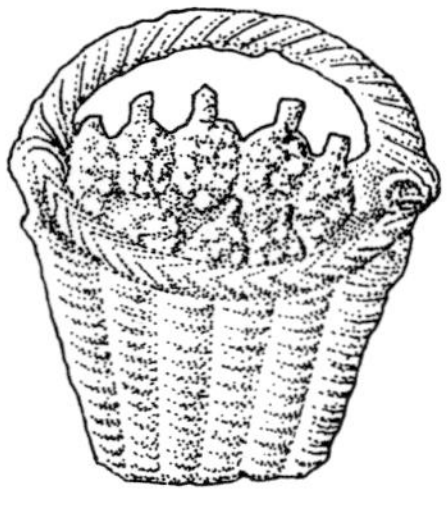

131

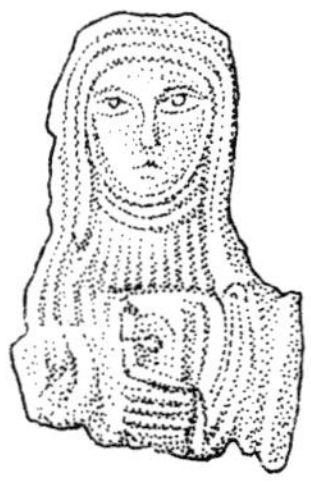

132

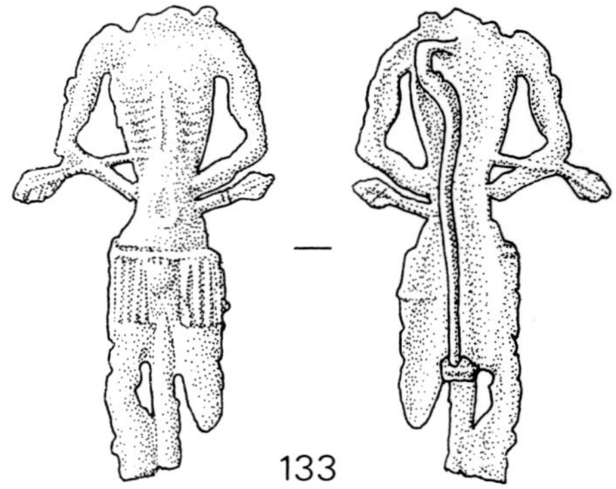

133

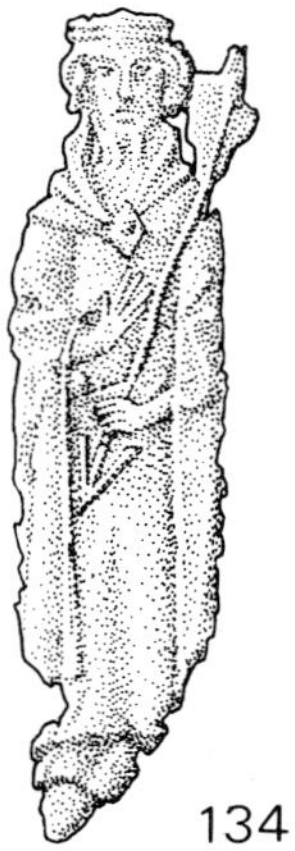

134

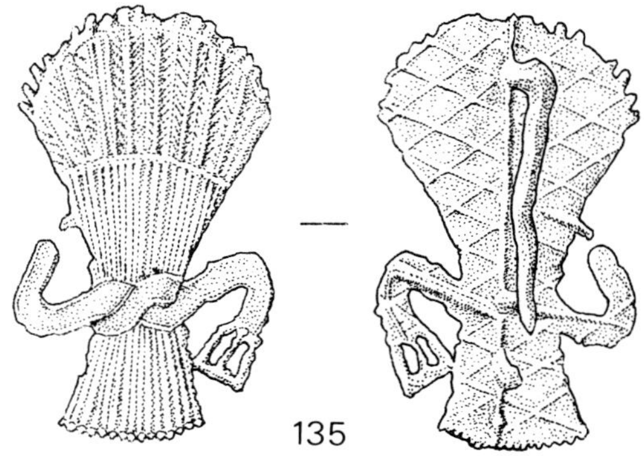

135

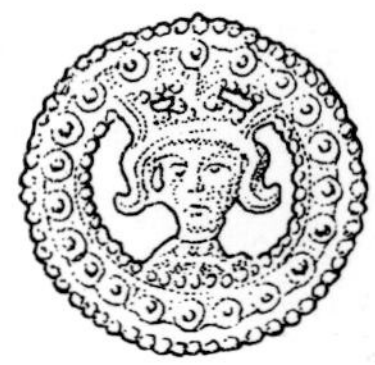

136

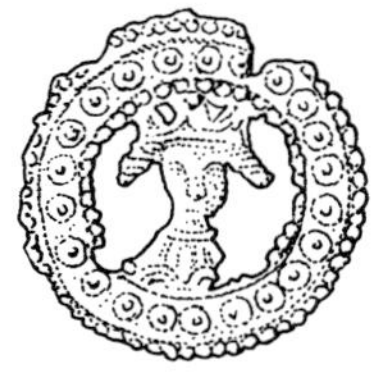

137

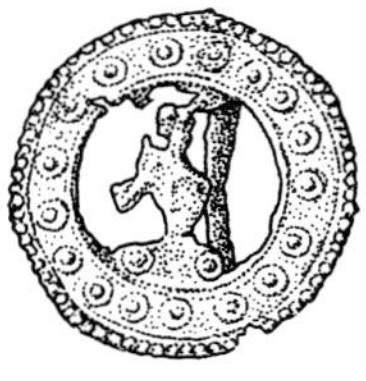

138

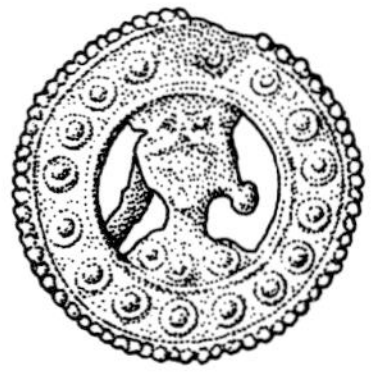

139

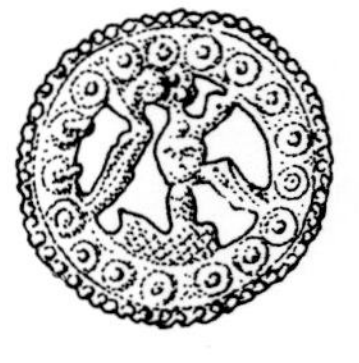

140

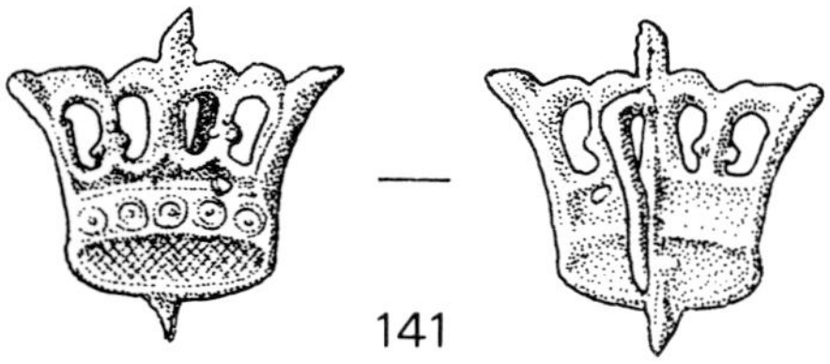

141

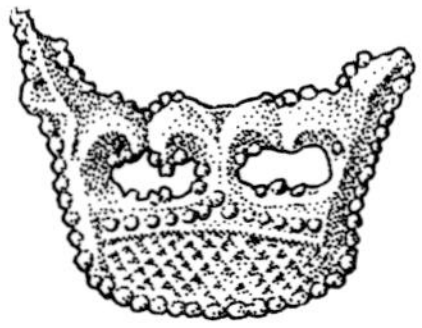

142

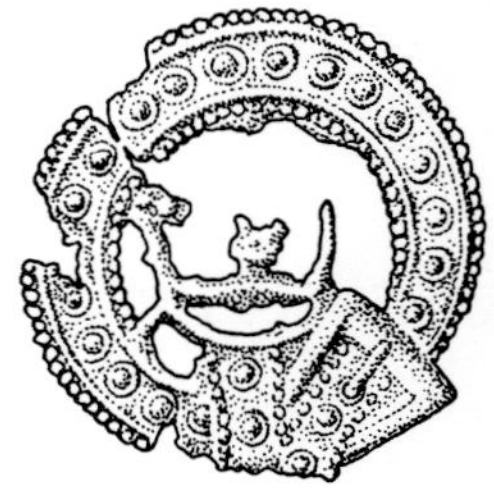

143

Pilgrim souvenirs. Figs 131-143. Scale 1 : 1

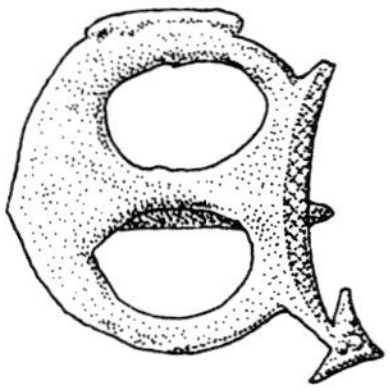

144

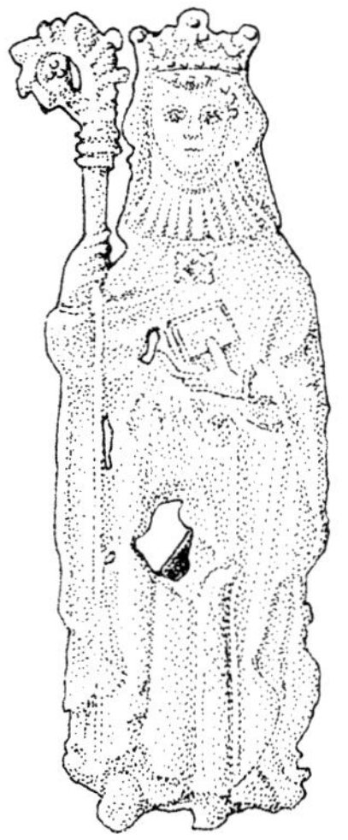

145

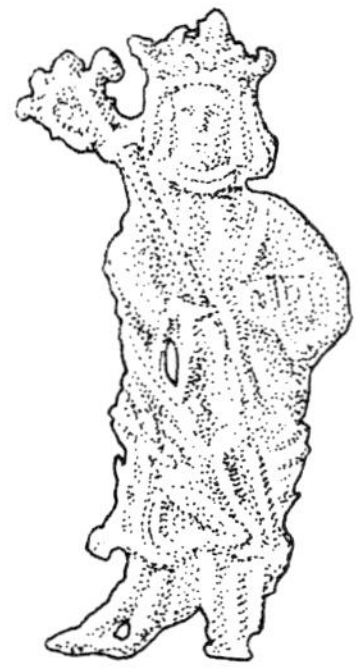

146

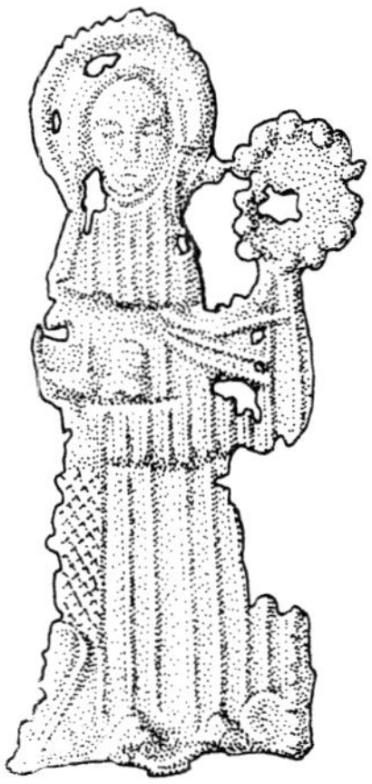

147

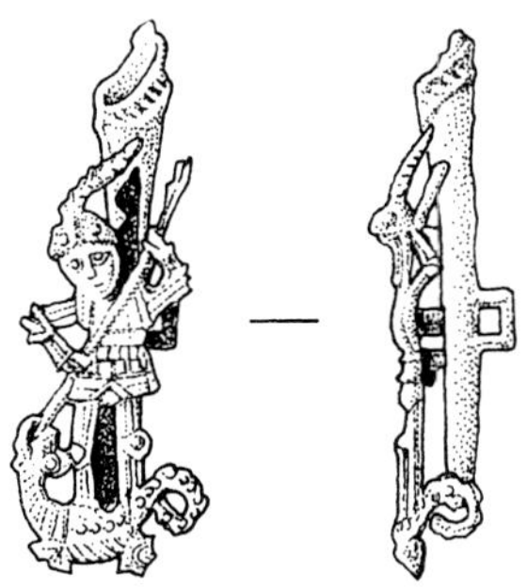

148

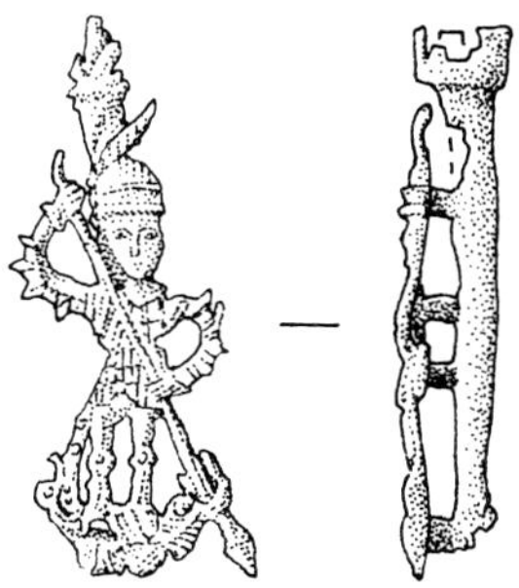

149

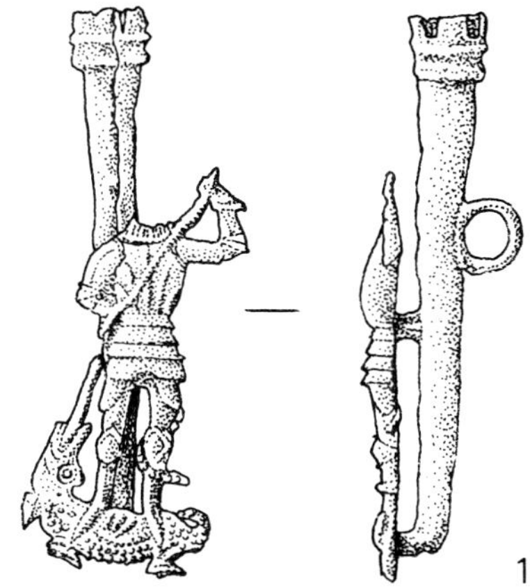

150

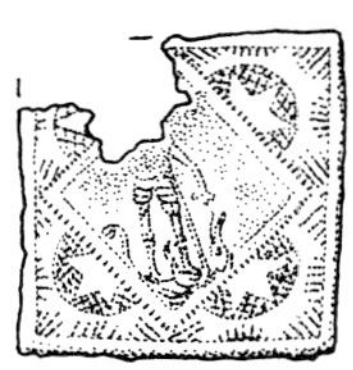

151

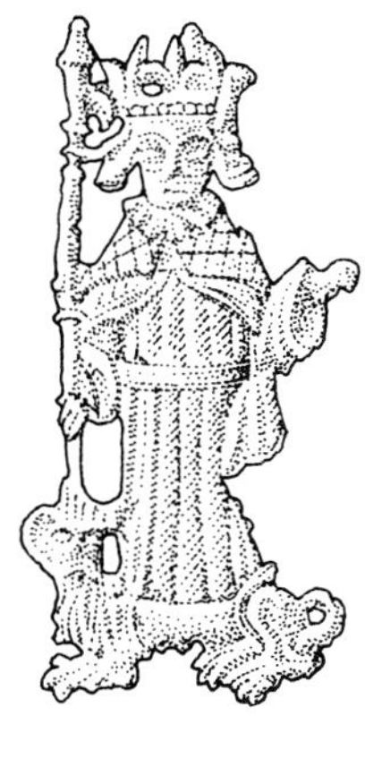

152

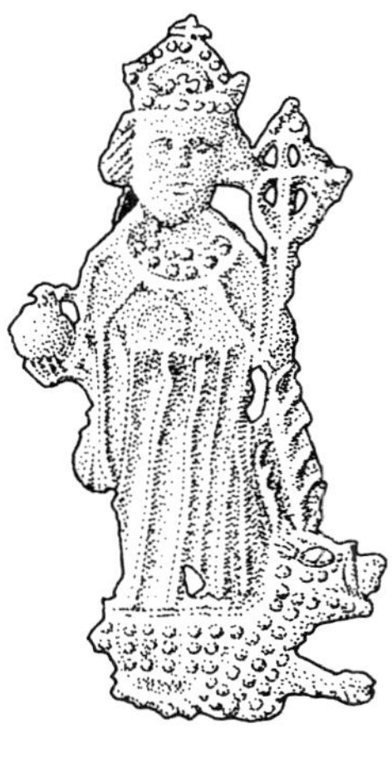

153

Pilgrim souvenirs. Figs 144-153. Scale 1 : 1

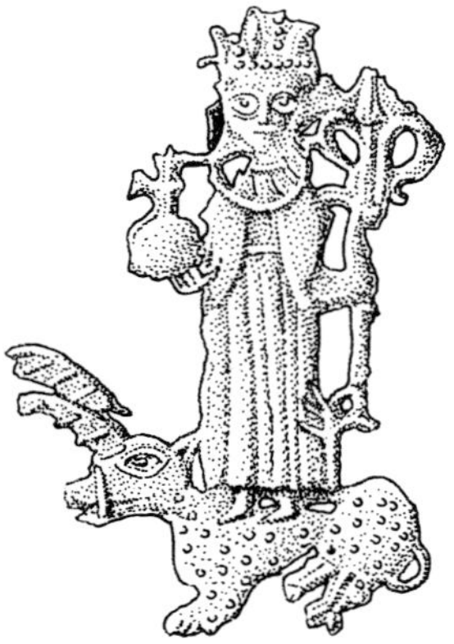
154

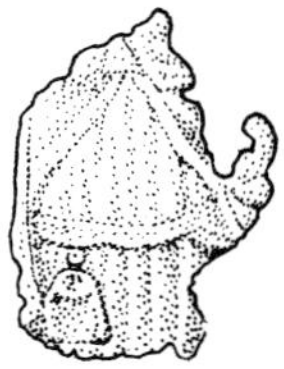
155

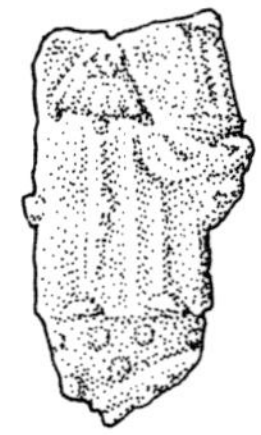
156

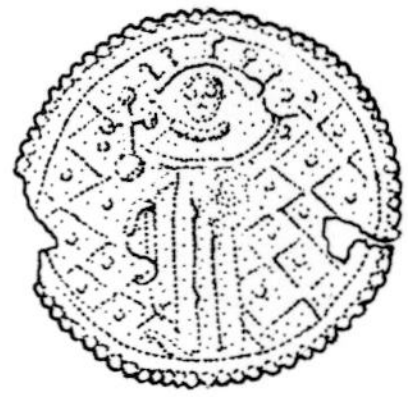
157

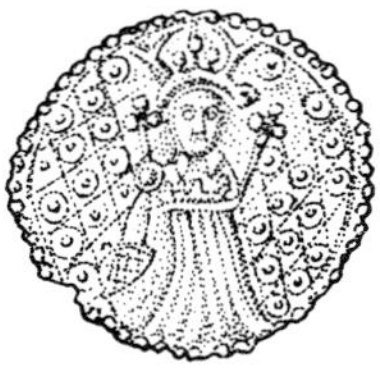
158

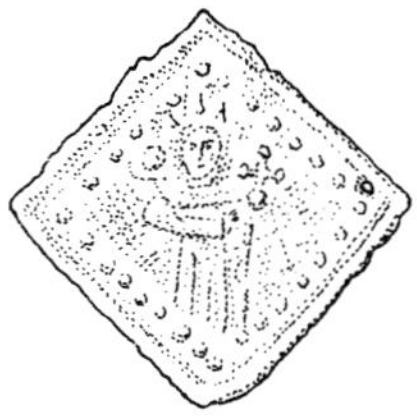
159

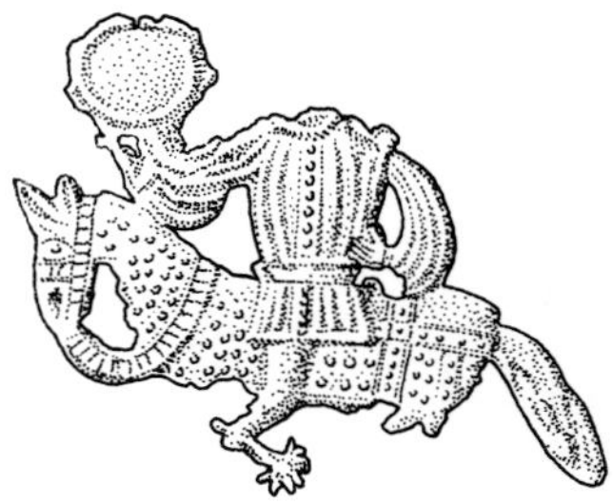
160

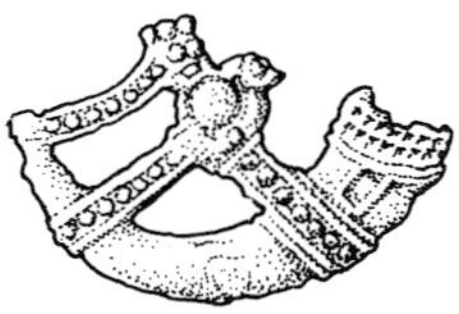
161

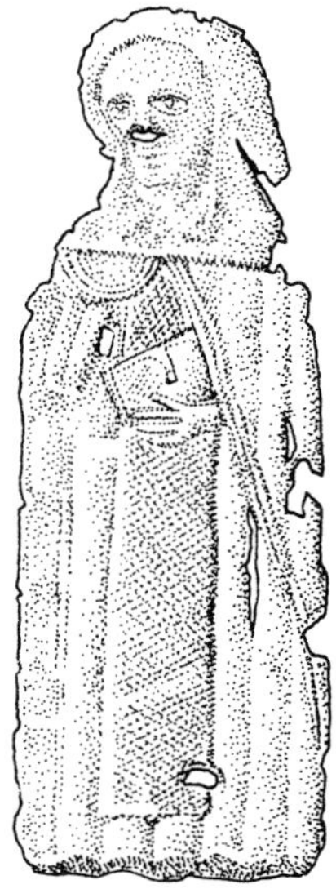
162

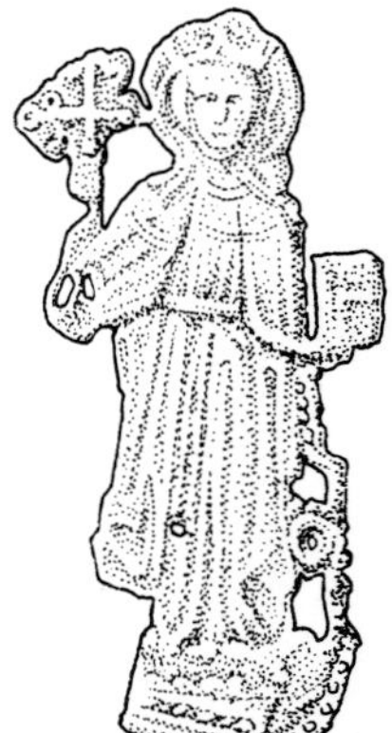
163

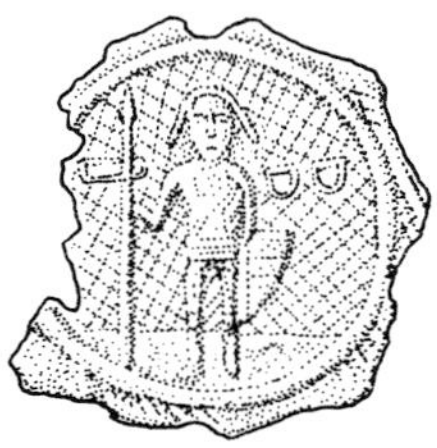
164

Pilgrim souvenirs. Figs 154-164. Scale 1 : 1

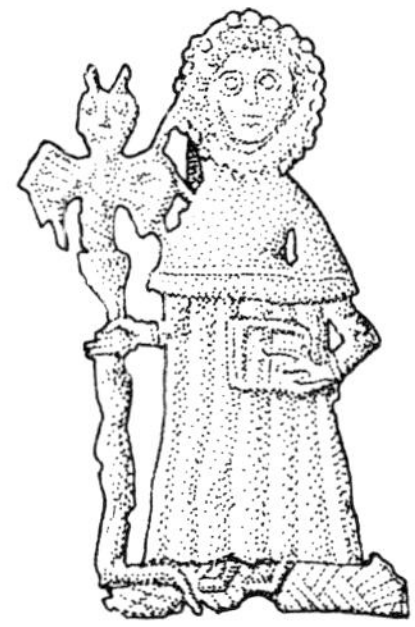

165

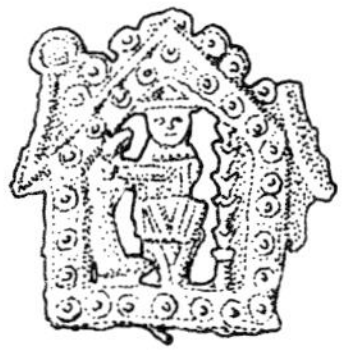

166

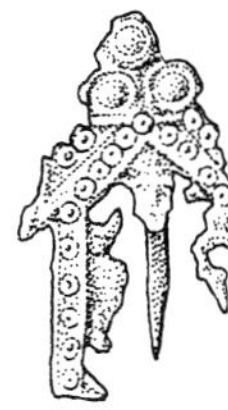

167

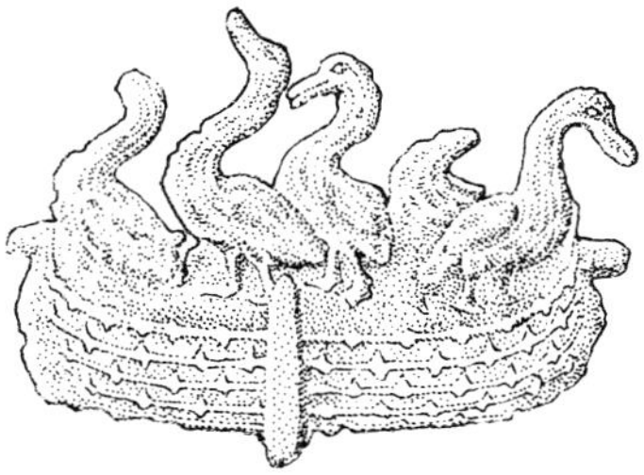

168

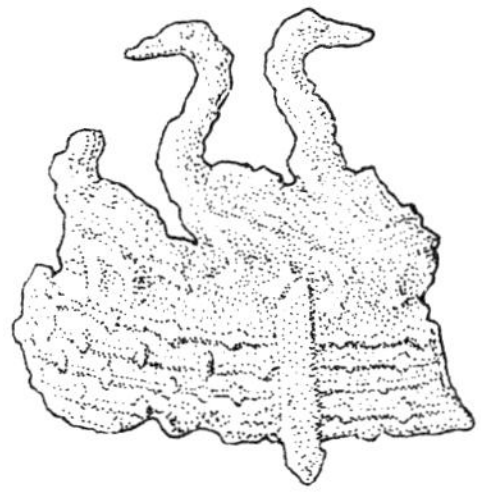

169

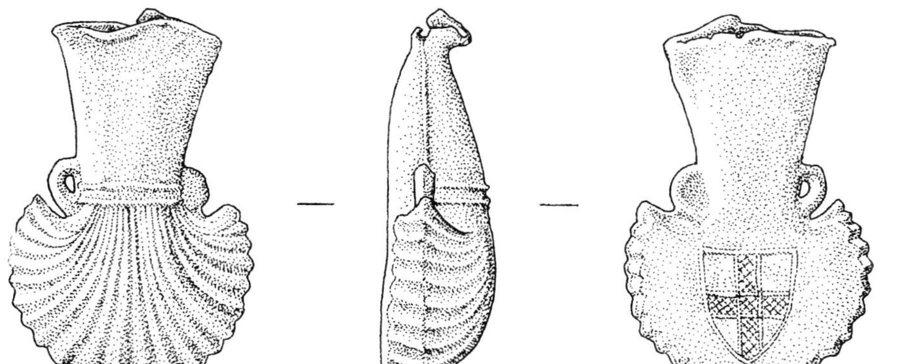

170

Pilgrim souvenirs. Figs 165-170. Scale 1 : 1

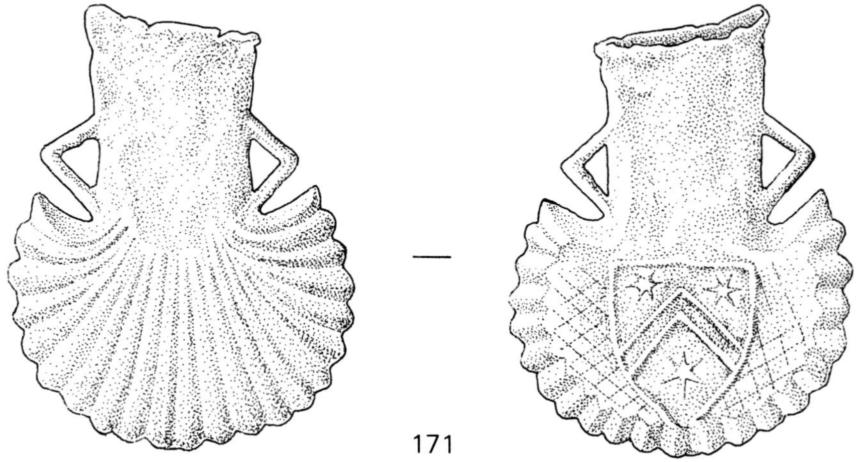

171

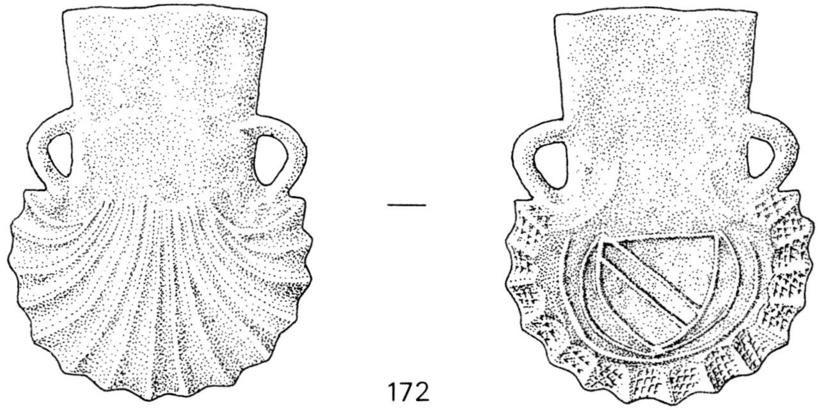

172

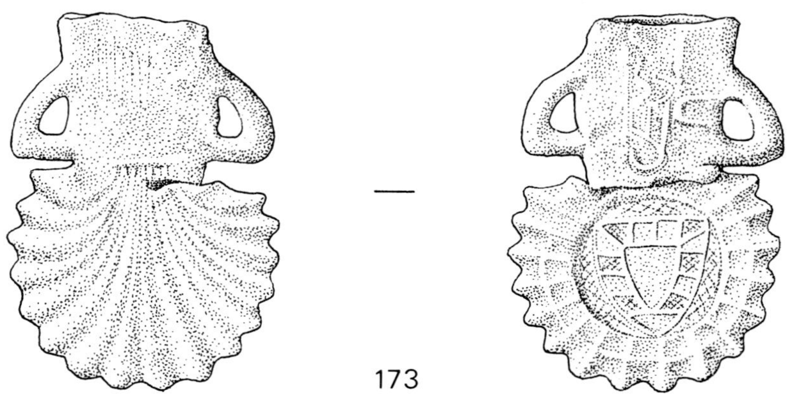

173

Pilgrim souvenirs. Figs 171-173. Scale 1 : 1

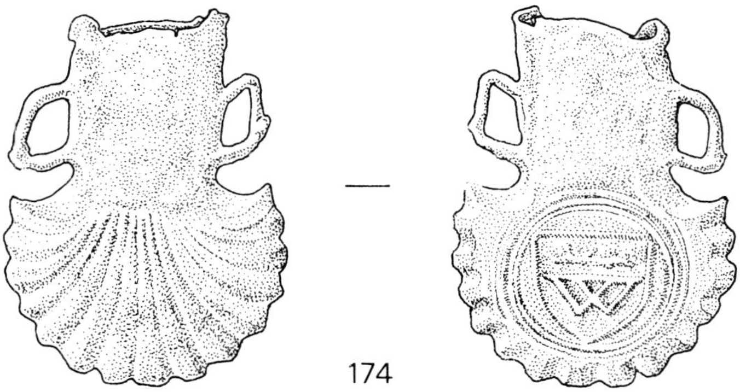

174

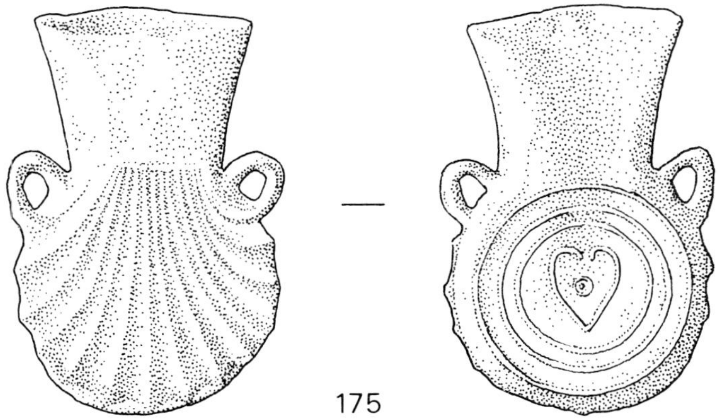

175

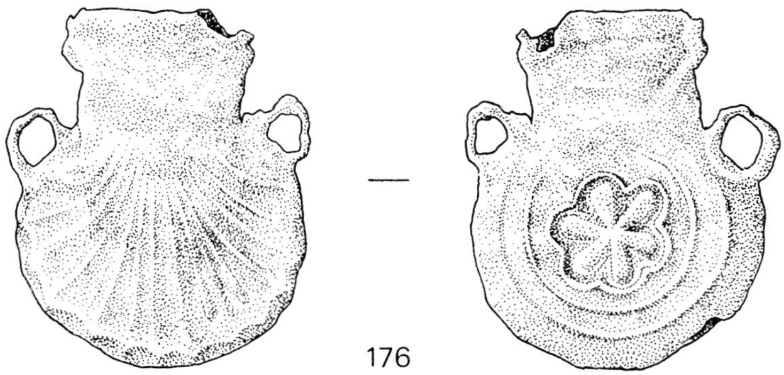

176

Pilgrim souvenirs. Figs 174-176. Scale 1 : 1

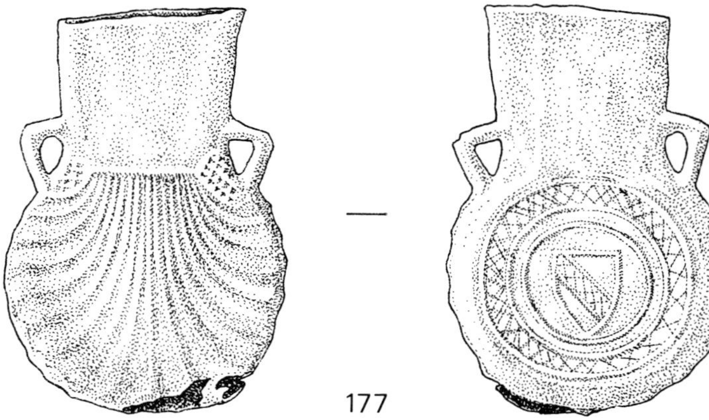

177

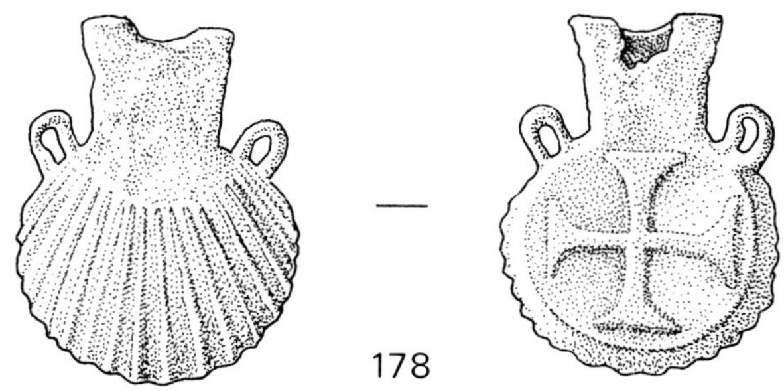

178

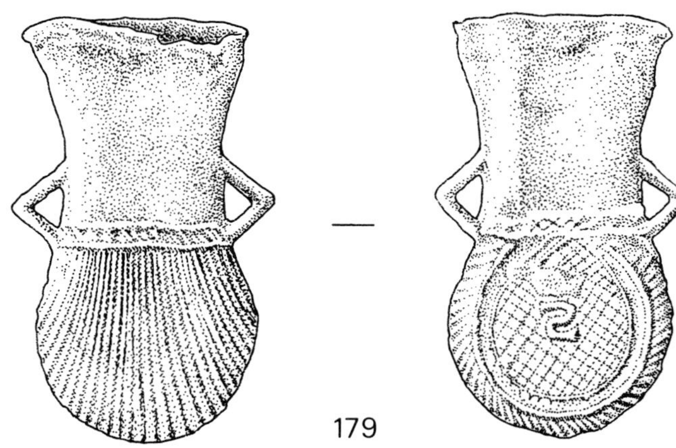

179

Pilgrim souvenirs. Figs 177-179. Scale 1 : 1

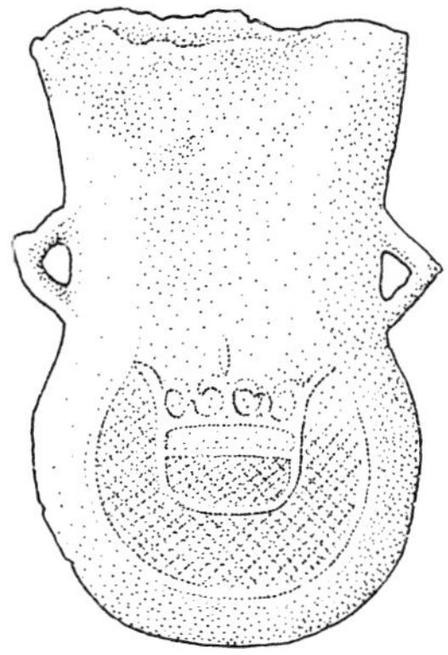
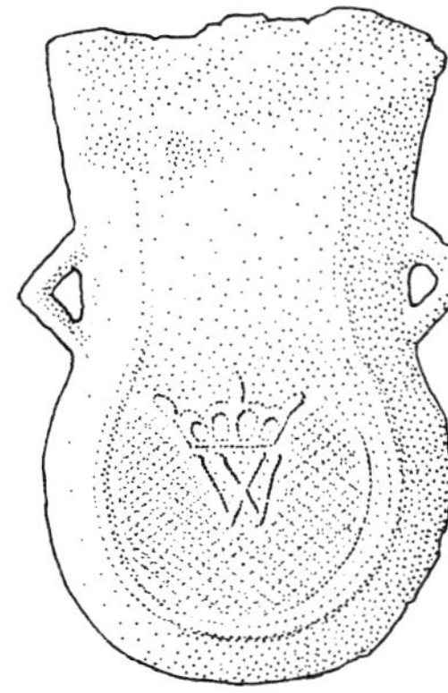

180

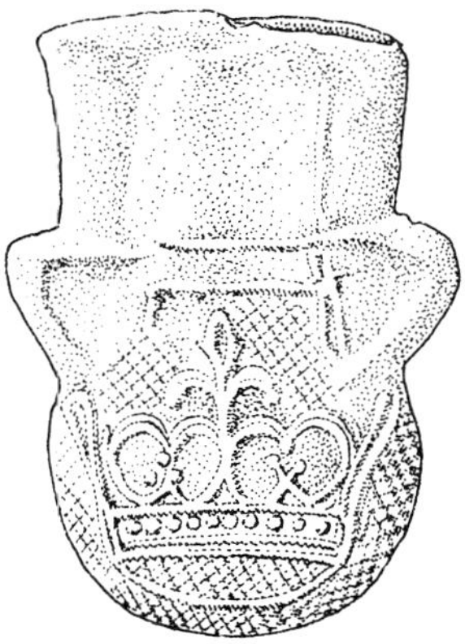
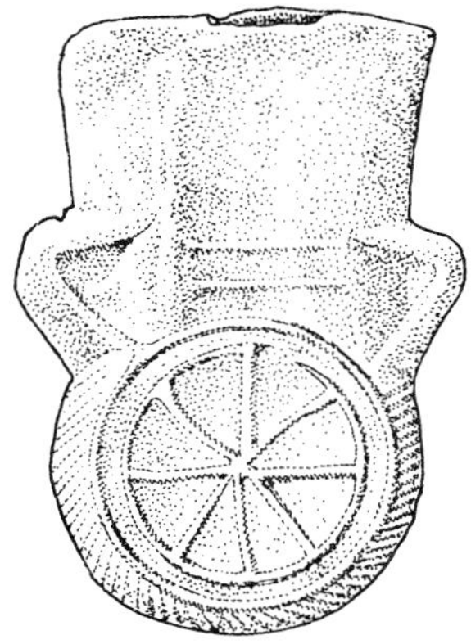

181

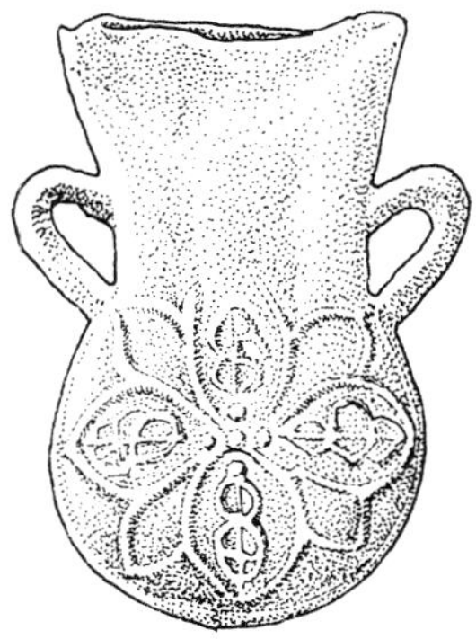
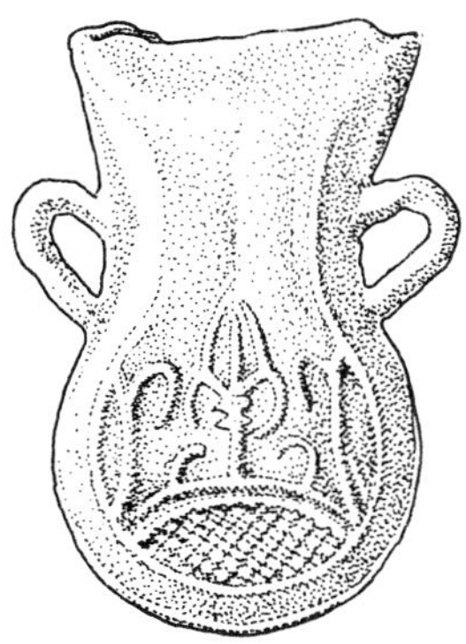

182

Pilgrim souvenirs. Figs 180-182. Scale 1 : 1

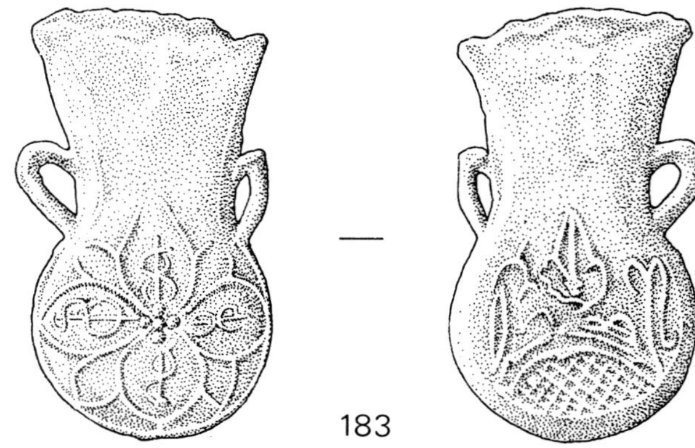

183

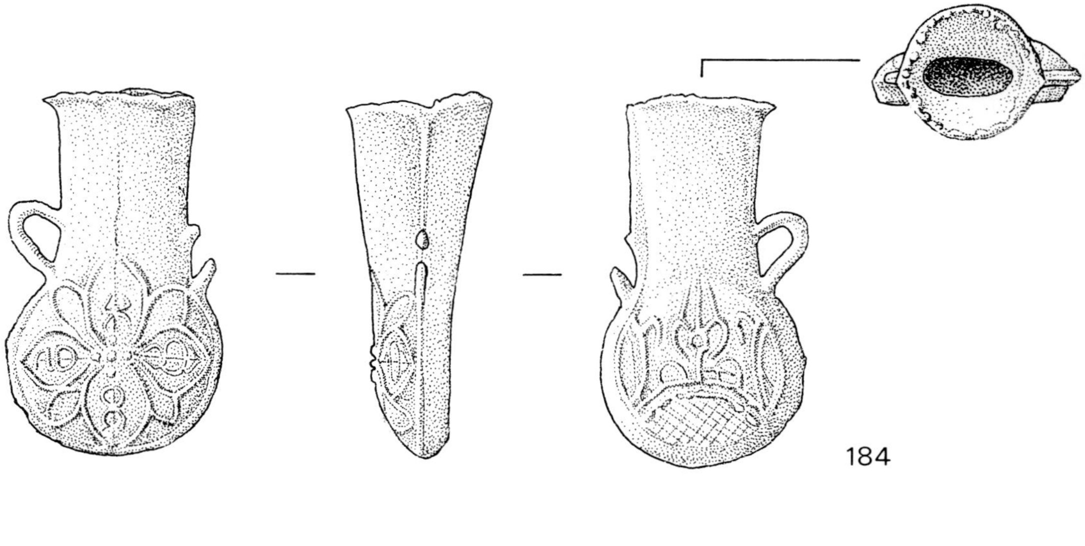

184

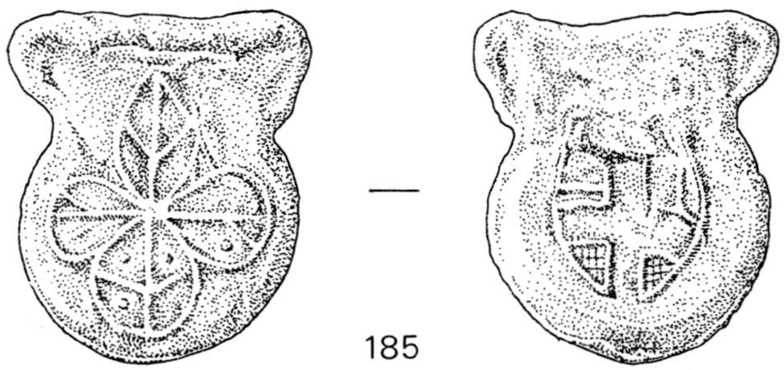

185

Pilgrim souvenirs. Figs 183-185. Scale 1 : 1

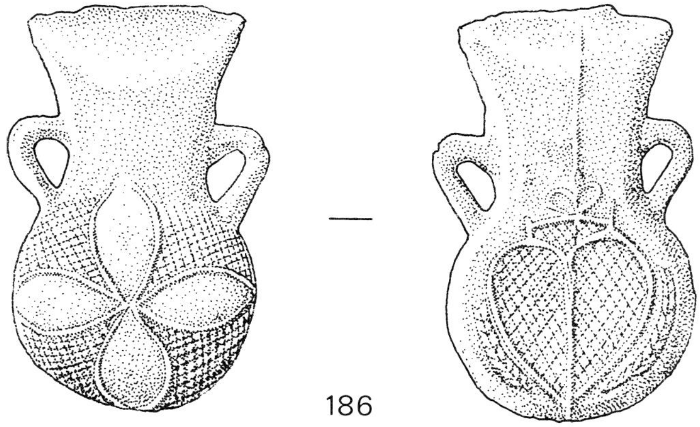

186

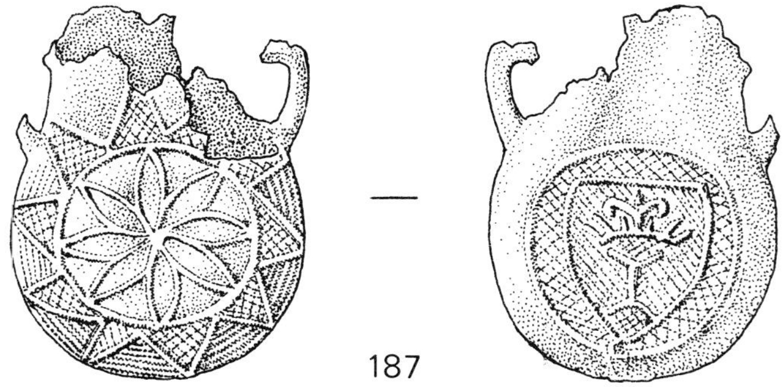

187

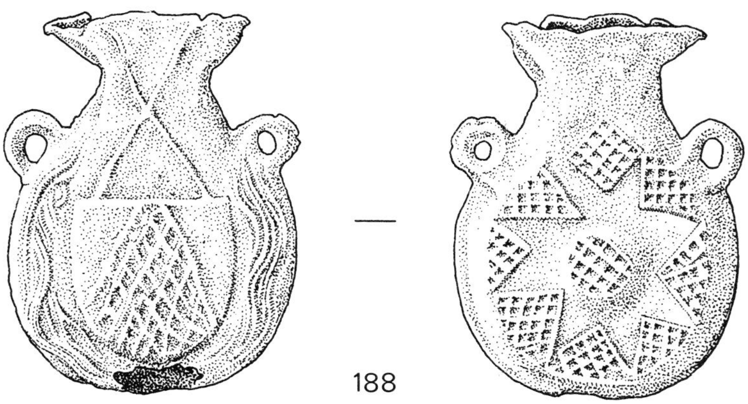

188

Pilgrim souvenirs. Figs 186-188. Scale 1 : 1

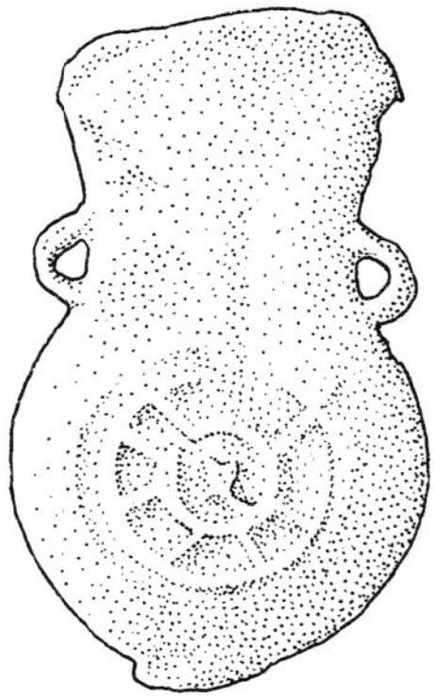
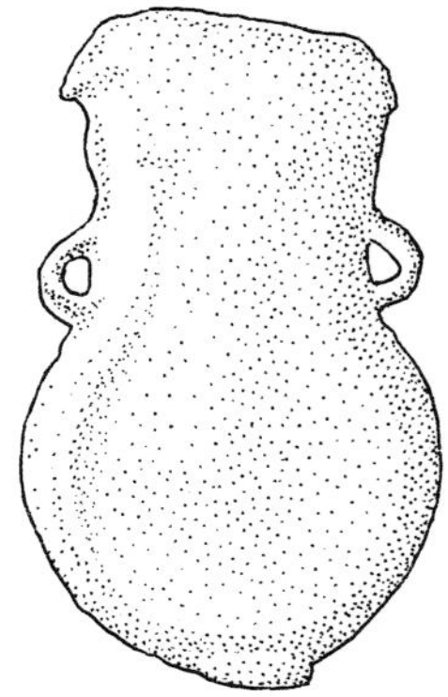

189

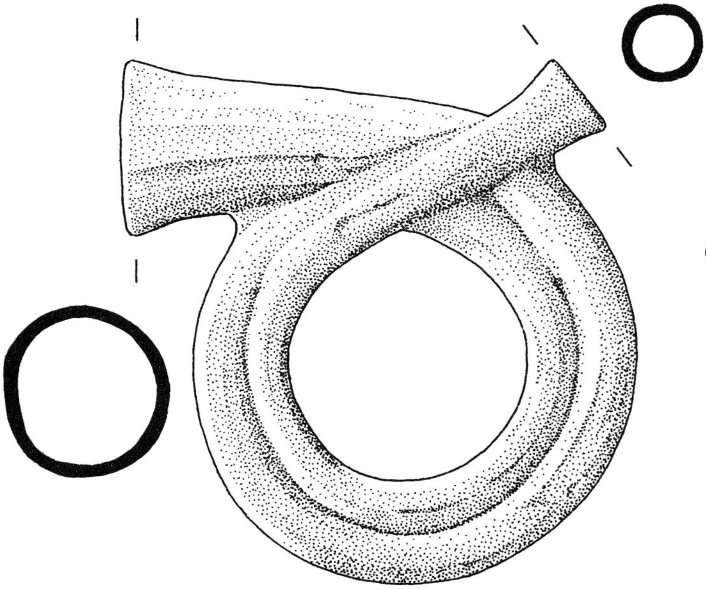

190
(×1:2)

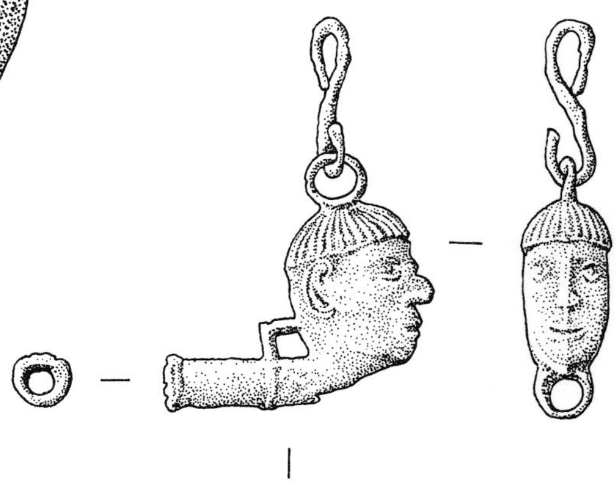
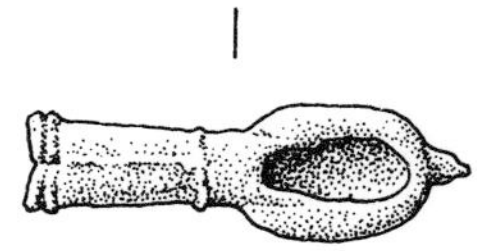

191

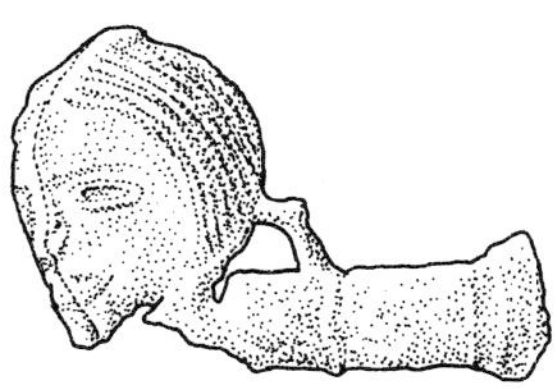

192

Pilgrim souvenirs. Figs 189-192. Scale 1 : 1, except 190 (1 : 2)

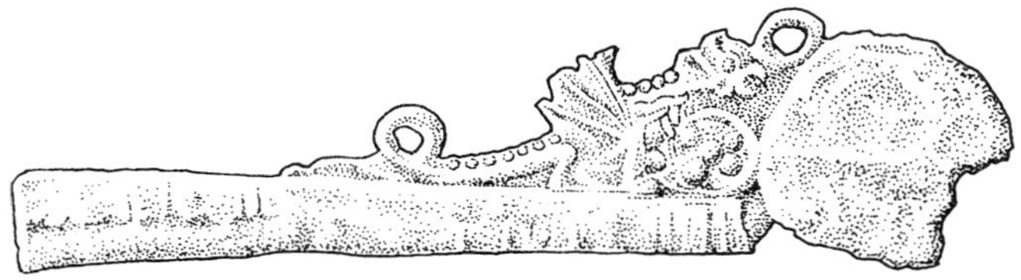

193

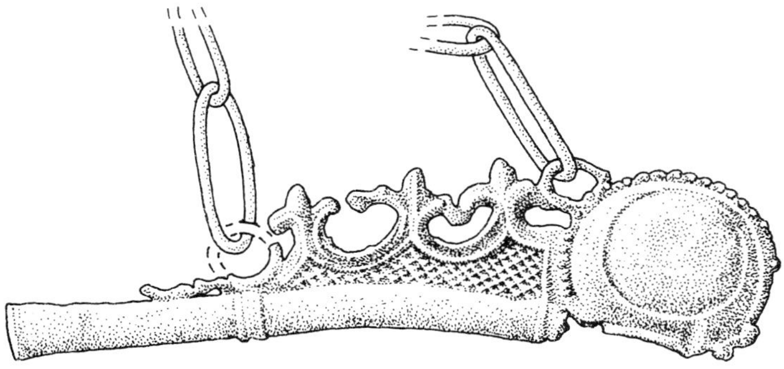

194

195

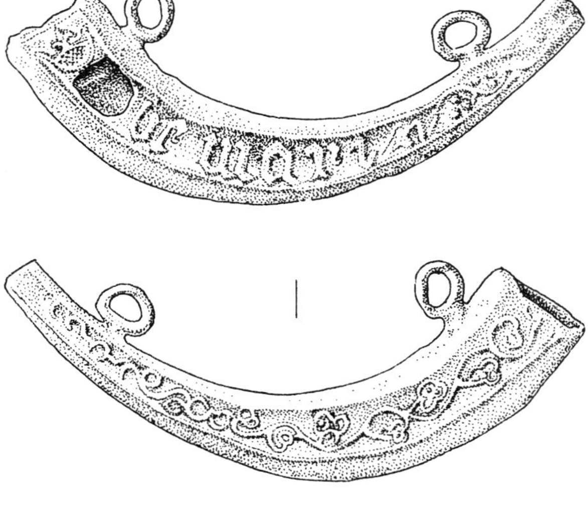

Pilgrim souvenirs. Figs 193-195. Scale 1 : 1

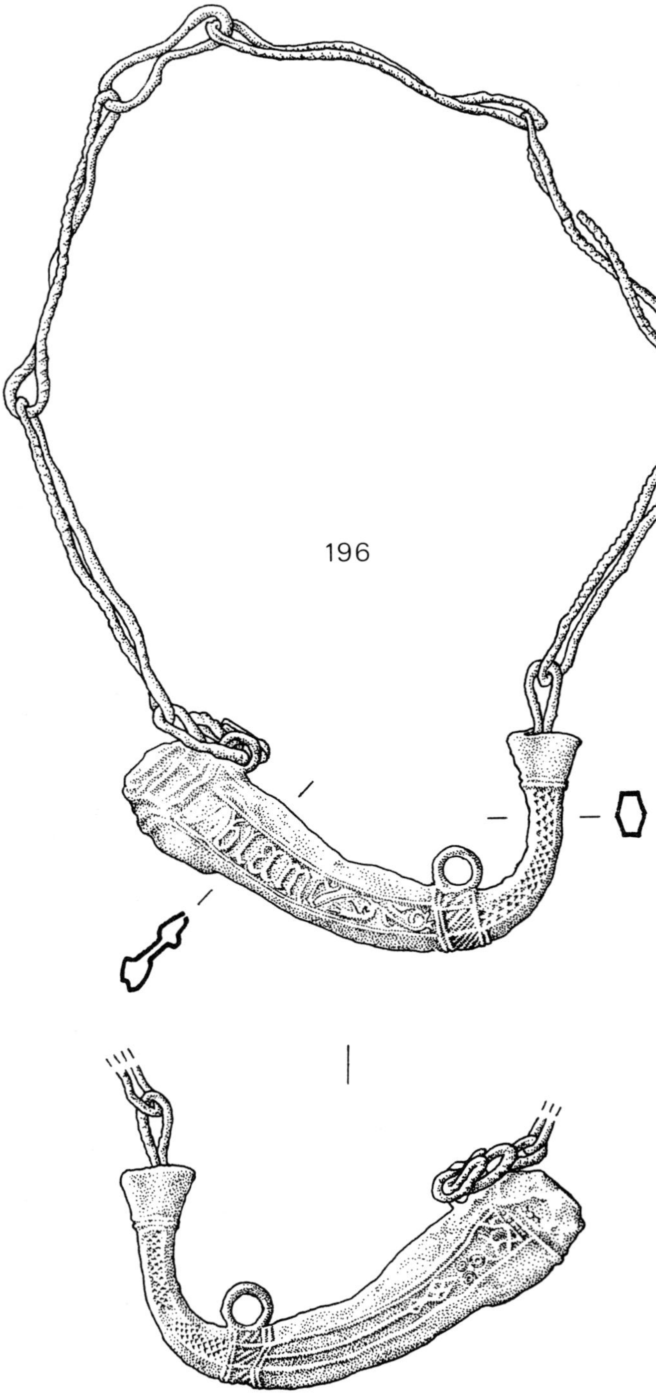

196

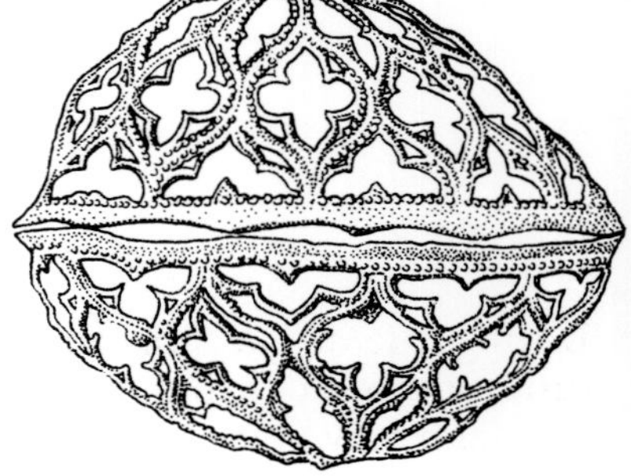

197

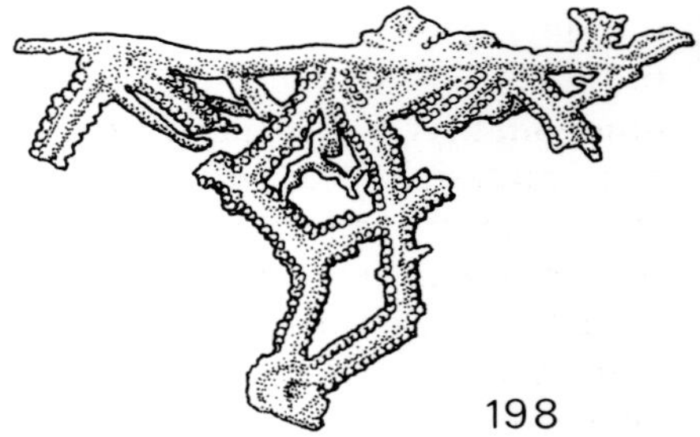

198

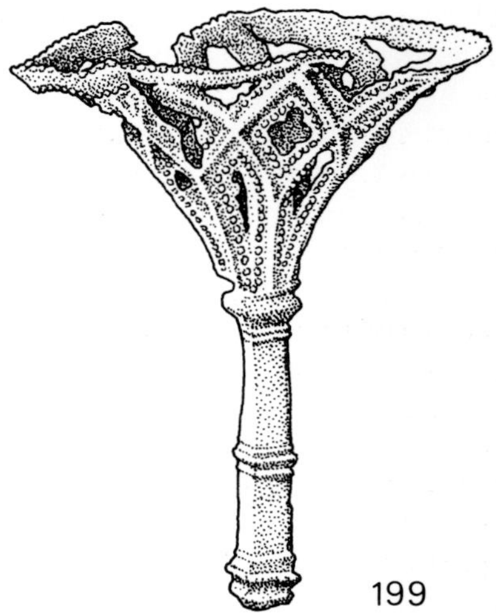

199

Pilgrim souvenirs. Figs 196-199. Scale 1 : 1

Livery and other secular badges

INTRODUCTION

During the fourteenth and fifteenth centuries, badges of a purely secular character were also very much in fashion and on many hats and hoods doubtless took their place alongside pilgrim souvenirs and devotional badges. A small proportion of these more worldly trinkets were intended to be primarily decorative or descriptive, with no ulterior significance – modest imitations in tin-lead alloy of the more picturesque, less functional type of fashionable brooch in precious materials (Cat 190-2). These ornamental brooch-badges of pewter were paralleled by base metal versions of other sorts of finery worn by the well-to-do as indicators of wealth and status, such as collars (Figs 295-8), pendants (Fig 251, 280), buckles (Figs 324-5) and other belt fittings. In addition to creating a decorative effect, however, a badge by definition generally had some statement or allusion to make on behalf of the wearer. Here it must be stressed again that a badge's cryptic message may now be too obscure to be clearly understood or may be capable of more than one interpretation. A few of the badges categorised below as secular, therefore, may, in fact, have had a religious connotation originally.

However, the message of some badges is seen to be unequivocally satirical (Cat 215-8) or even ribald (Cat 213-4). Other badges were manifestly designed to convey affection to a loved one (Cat 222-8) or to indicate to fellow men and women an enthusiasm for a particular accomplishment or for a certain sport or pastime (Cat 193-9). Just as pilgrim badges were widely used as health-preservers and disease-curers, some secular badges appear to have been specifically devised as wealth-providers, aimed at bringing their wearers material good fortune (Cat 219-21) and, through the use of well-tried magical symbols and formulae, at affording wide talismanic protection. Some badges were possibly designed for ceremonial wear on particular occasions (Cat 151, 158), while others appear to have been used to mark certain seasonal festivals, such as May Day (Cat 205) or Plough Monday (Cat 203-4).

By far the largest single category, however, was made up of livery badges (Cat 151-89). These identified the wearer as a person who was in some sense attached to a magnate (or to the king himself) and who in return enjoyed his lord's protection. They marked the wearer's secular allegiance in much the same way that pilgrim signs and devotional badges proclaimed his allegiance to a particular saint or cult. Livery badges came into fashion at the beginning of Edward III's reign and remained in general use until the latter part of Henry VIII's. The so-called livery of signs or badges was one of the three types of liveries distributed by magnates to their household servants and retainers; the other two were the livery of cloth, comprising doublet or doublet and hose, and the less important livery of hoods (Given-Wilson 1986, pp 236-7). Livery badges took the form of the device adopted by the lord as his mark or cognizance. Some lords used more than one badge. The device was normally a deliberately simple figure that would be easily recognised and quickly become a matter of common knowledge, at a time when the growing complexities of heraldry were making armorial bearings harder to identify. Unlike shields of arms and heraldic crests, however, these figures or cognizances were not subject to any hard-and-fast rules or to any official record. They were purely matters of personal fancy. This considerable informality adds to the difficulties of recognising and identifying some livery badges today.

Livery badges were often made of textile and embroidery or of silver and silver-gilt and were frequently worn on the chest or sleeve as well as on the headgear. In 1403 the supporters of Henry Percy, earl of Northumberland, were reported to be mustering with the Percy badge of the crescent moon on their sleeves (Halliwell 1846, I, p 206). Surviving livery badges, on the other hand, including all the Salisbury finds described below, are almost entirely of tin-lead alloy and, like pilgrim badges, they were provided with integral pins and clasps (e.g. Fig 216). These pewter badges were made by the same methods of serial production as were used for the manufacture of pilgrim souvenirs. It seems likely that livery badges in this cheap, relatively unpretentious form, would not have been grand enough for distribution inside a noble's household. More probably they were aimed at his 'affinity', the much wider body of well-wishers and adherents that was his essential power-base. In an increasingly competitive society, a magnate had to strive ceaselessly to maintain and enlarge his affinity and the distribution of badges played an obvious and significant part in this. It was the extended use of livery badges, beyond genuine household servants and officials such as stewards or councillors, that gave rise to considerable anxiety in parliament during the late fourteenth century and again a century later, associated, as the practice was, with the whole controversy over illegal maintenance and the building up of political factions and private armies.

In 1384 and again in 1388, for instance, the commons complained bitterly that the distribution of badges by lords was leading to the establishment of local tyrannies, since those who wore the badges were emboldened to perpetrate acts of oppression. 'It is certainly the boldness inspired by their badges that makes them unafraid to do these things and more beside . . . If the lords wanted to have peace and quiet in the kingdom they must drop the use of badges altogether' (Hector & Harvey 1982, pp 82-3, 355-6). Even the king was criticised for condoning a wider tyranny by keeping an unprecedentedly large retinue of 'sundry people' and by giving them 'sundry badges'. The indiscriminate distribution of livery badges – to tailors, tanners, drapers, butchers and other artisans – was also widely deplored and in the 1390s legislation was introduced forbidding the use of badges by anyone below the estate of esquire, except those 'continually dwelling in the house' of a lord. At intervals complaints were brought against those who violated the regulations. Thus in 1496 Sir Thomas Darcy of Temple Newsam, Yorks., was indicted for having given his badge, a silver buck's head, to a number of lowly yeomen and labourers who had for some considerable time been wearing the badges in their caps (Dunham 1955, p 55). The discovery of so many base metal livery badges at Salisbury, however, suggests that for the greater part of the fifteenth century the various restrictions and prohibitions on the use of livery badges were very largely ignored or at any rate were not considered by parliament to be an important political issue during this period.

Reference has already been made to circumstantial evidence that points to the manufacture of small pewter dress accessories (Figs 324-5) in fifteenth-century Salisbury and to a strong presumption that pilgrim souvenirs relating to Salisbury's role as a cult centre were also local products. There is also a hint that at least one livery badge was made at Salisbury (Cat 176). One or two moulds for casting certain livery badges have been found, not surprisingly, at London, the main industrial centre, where the special skills of the goldsmith or seal-engraver were probably commissioned for making some of the better-class moulds (e.g. Cat 151). The discovery of a livery-badge mould at the shrine of Our

Lady of Walsingham (Cat 156-7), however, suggests that a lord seeking a supply of pewter badges for his adherents might well turn for the appropriate expertise to the souvenir trade established at a major pilgrim centre. The detailed records relating to one such resort show that in the fifteenth century the shops around the church at Le Puy were stocked not only with religious souvenirs but with a wide variety of trinkets of a purely secular nature. These included figurines of men and women and of animals and non-religious badges, including royal badges designed to appeal to the national loyalties of French pilgrims (Cohen 1976, pp 194,208-9). There is, then, a strong probability that some of the secular badges included in the final section of this catalogue were also by-products of English pilgrim centres.

CATALOGUE

The remarks preceding the catalogue of pilgrim souvenirs on donors, lenders and provenance and the abbreviations used apply equally to the catalogue of livery and secular badges (see above, p 12).

The catalogue resumes with the most famous of all livery badges, the Black Prince's ostrich feather:

151 Livery or funerary badge: an ostrich feather, the badge of Edward the Black Prince (1330-76), *c.*1376. H.77 mm. Found during excavations at Old Sarum, 1909-15, 'from bottom of No.2 small pit' (i.e. garderobe pit 4, south of Kitchen Tower of the Courtyard House); *OS Diary* 1910, p.23. Burlington Fine Arts Club, 1916, pl xxiv. *1/1923. OS.C63* **Fig 200**

Other examples cast from the same and similar moulds show that beneath the knop at the base of the feather there was originally a quill surmounted by a scroll bearing the Black Prince's 'word' or motto *ich dene* (i.e. *ich dien*, Flemish for 'I serve'). The Prince's will makes it clear that this was his badge 'for peace', used, like the ostrich plumes he imported at vast expense, in the chivalric exercise of arms. The badge from Old Sarum seems likely to have been commemorative, perhaps commissioned for use at the Prince's state funeral in October 1376 (for fuller discussion see Spencer 1982, pp 316-20). An identical and entirely complete example of this badge was found in excavations near the site of Baynard's Castle, London; it belonged to a vast assemblage of material deposited, according to the evidence of coins and jettons, in the last quarter of the fourteenth century (Spencer 1987, p 223).

152 Livery badge: two ostrich feathers, the tops canted over left and right. Across the quills is a scroll inscribed *eadwrd* in black letter. 15th century. H. 35 mm. *Sal.Mus.Rep.* 1987-88, pl 3g. *219/1987* **Fig 201**

153 Livery badge: the scroll and quills from a badge identical to Cat 152. 15th century. W. 28 mm. Given by Mr R. Davis. *202d/1987*. Not illustrated.

Another complete example from London is in the Canterbury Museum. The badge could relate to either the son of Henry VI, Edward prince of Wales (1453-71), who certainly adopted the ostrich feathers as his badge, or to Edward IV's eldest son, Edward prince of Wales, later Edward V. It should be distinguished from another form of badge with double plume of ostrich feathers but with the scroll at the base of the quills (BM M & LA 56,7-1,2149; MOL 82.681). On the latter type the word *edward* (misread as P.GWAILS in Smith 1854, p 144) must refer to Henry VIII's son, Prince Edward, later Edward VI, since a pair of barbed stems between the feathers are united by a single (presumably Tudor) rose.

154 Livery badge: a hart lodged (i.e. lying down), its neck encircled by a crown for a collar, with a chain attached. The animal rests on a circular patch of grass, on the right of which stands a small tree or shrub. 1390-99. H. 36 mm. *195l/1987* **Fig 202**

A similar badge has been found at London (BM M & LA 56, 6-27, 17). Unlike the Salisbury find, this still retains the animal's head. Both badges are base metal versions of Richard II's personal cognizance of the white hart, which he first distributed at a tournament held in Smithfield, London, in October 1390. In much grander, jewelled form, the same badges are depicted in the Wilton Diptych (*c*.1395; National Gallery, London), where they are worn by King Richard himself and by his attendant angels. During the 1390s white harts of silver with gold crown-collars are known to have been bestowed on many of those whom the king wished to honour. The white hart motif was also applied to buildings and other royal possessions acting both as ornament and as a mark of royal ownership or status. By 1397 the white hart had become the greatest livery in England and its bearers, who may well have included the owner of this humble pewter version of the badge, then formed the nucleus of the king's army. According to one contemporary observer, the king's retainers took courage from their white hart badges and wore them with conspicuous pride (Harvey 1961, pp 6-10).

In *c*.1395 Richard II, following the example of the French royal house, adopted another personal badge, the broom plant, which in practice often simply took the form of the pea-like seed-pods of broom. In the Wilton Diptych the badge of the white hart worn by the king is encircled by broompods and both the king and the angels wear broompod collars. Broompods are also depicted alongside white harts and sunbursts on Richard II's effigy, which was commissioned in 1395. Many pewter pendants in the shape of broompods, modelled in the round, have been excavated, some from datable, 15th-century contexts. One has been found as far afield as Bruges (1985).

The specimen from Salisbury illustrated in Fig 203 (given by Mr B. N. Lee in 1990, *61/1990*) is typical of the many other surviving examples of this badge, which, though they may vary in size, invariably represent the pod as if it were tight with seed and sometimes show a calyx beneath the suspension loop. The pods are hollow and were evidently moulded by slush-casting (a technique probably facilitated in these instances by the use of pure tin instead of a tin-lead alloy); after the pod had been removed from the mould, its open, lower end was pinched together to form the pointed tip. Another example from Salisbury is illustrated in Mitchiner 1986, p 38, where it is wrongly said to be thirteenth century. These badges belong to the end of the fourteenth century at the earliest. It was not until *c*.1448 that Richard duke of York conceived the idea of using Plantagenet (derived from *planta genista*, Latin for broom) as a family surname; and the broompod was still in use at the end of the fifteenth century, for example, as a badge of William, Viscount Beaumont.

155 Livery badge: a hart lodged and held captive, not by a chain and crown-collar as in Cat 154, but by a circular, fenced enclosure. Probably end of 14th century. 29 x 38 mm. *205c/1987*
Fig 204

Badges from the same mould have been found at London (e.g. BM M & LA 36,6-10,52); in the case of the British Museum's badge the enclosure, with rails nailed to the top and bottom of the posts, has survived virtually complete, providing an unusual illusion of perspective, cast in openwork. Part of the tree that originally stood over the hart also survives and the animal retains one of its antlers. Also from London, at Bankside, comes a likely prototype for this kind of badge (Fig 205: MOL 86.202/42). Here again the hart, which has lost all but the stumps of its antlers, is shown beneath a tree. The tree's lower branches are couped and the encircling fence, fringed with grass, is fitted with a gate. Immediately in front of the hart, which is shown lying on grass, is a low-growing bush. A similar feature in front of the white hart painted on the back of the Wilton Diptych has been interpreted as rosemary, which is known to have been a badge of Anne of Bohemia, Richard II's queen (Harvey 1961,p 10). The best parallel for Cat 155, however, is provided by the stone effigy of Sir Thomas Markenfield in Ripon cathedral. He is shown wearing a livery collar of park palings behind which is a hart lodged. The hart has neither chain nor crown (Hope 1929, fig 184). A more exalted parallel is provided by an illumination of *c.*1440 showing members of the Neville family wearing a similar livery collar (Virgoe 1989, p 28). In this case, however, the front half of the hart emerges through the fence.

156 Livery badge: a hart lodged beneath a tree, the two lower branches of which are couped. The foliage at the top of the tree and the hart's antlers are missing. End of 14th or 15th century. H. 24 mm. *225k/1987* **Fig 206**

157 Livery badge: a hart lodged beneath a tree. Similar to Cat 156 except that the hart retains its prominent ears. H. 20 mm. *209c/1987* **Fig 207**

Aside from finds at Salisbury, other examples of this badge have also been found at Chester and King's Lynn (Spencer 1980, p 29). Many more have been recovered from fifteenth-century levels of the Thames foreshore at London, no fewer than six having been found at intervals near the north end of Southwark Bridge. Part of a stone mould for casting this same type of badge has been found when clearing a well near the shrine of Our Lady of Walsingham, Norfolk (Alexander & Binksi, 1987, pp 394-5). In all but two or three instances, the hart is shown, as in Cat 156-7, facing left. The tree is invariably depicted as if it were behind the hart and with the two lower branches couped. The lower branches are left uncut on another badge of the hart lodged found at Salisbury (Fig 208; pc); in this instance the hart's back has been pierced by a huntsman's arrow. Also from Salisbury comes the antlered head of a hart, which, if it originally took the same form as the others described here, would be about twice their size (Mitchiner 1986, p 121).

Richard II himself appears to have owned a jewel in the form of a hart beneath a tree (Palgrave 1836, III, p 356), but instead of matching Cat 156-7 this is more likely to have resembled the hart-and-tree motif adopted as a badge by the king's half-brother Thomas Holland, earl of Kent. This royal version of the badge is as yet known only from Holland's seal, where the hart has a crown collar and a shield with the royal arms hanging round its neck (Hope 1929, p 214 and pl XXIIIB). It was, incidentally, the alleged misuse of the livery of badges by Holland and others like him that led to the enactment of stricter legislation on livery badges by parliament in October 1399.

158 Badge: right-hand portion of a shield charged with the royal arms, *Quarterly France ancient and England*, the style of arms in use between 1340 and *c.*1406. The surrounding border carries part of a legend in Lombardic lettering, . . . :[*TH*]*AT : SET : IN : TRENNIT* . . . Though partly obscured by a secondary stitching-hole or nail-hole, the first letter appears to have been a letter D with a cross-bar, for 'th'. H. 38 mm. *204b/1987* **Fig 210**

A left-hand portion of a very similar badge (Fig 209) has been found on the Thames foreshore at Bankside, London, (MOL 86.106/5), providing another possible snippet of inscription – . . . : *KING. AND : HIS MAI* . . . Assuming that the phrases on both fragments are indeed complementary and that one might be taken to run on from the other, the gap that would still exist between them would allow the incomplete word 'mai' to be extended by only two letters, perhaps to 'mainy', meaning household, retinue or affinity. Though still lacking its beginning and ending, the inscription might then be taken to read '. . . King and his mainy that sit (or sat) in Trinity . . .,' possibly alluding to a gathering of the royal household or followers on a particular Trinity Sunday. A reference to Trinity term, as a session of one of the royal courts of justice, seems unlikely in this context. For instances of fourteenth-century badges that commemorate royal devotion to the Trinity, see Spencer 1982, pp 316-20.

Reflecting the period of greatest civil disorder, discoveries at Salisbury and elsewhere indicate that the second half of the fifteenth century was the time when the wearing of cheaply-produced livery badges was at its peak. From 1455 onwards factions, backed by private bands of soldiers, battled and blustered for political power and then, more than ever before, the retainers and, very probably, the wider affinity of the various magnates locked in strife chose to signify their respective allegiances by wearing badges of the appropriate livery. It was probably Sir Walter Scott who gave this bitter power struggle the misleading name of the Wars of the Roses. Those engaged in the conflict, even at the level of passive support, did not see themselves as protagonists for rival rose badges, and when they appeared as two armies on the battlefield, the participants wore the many different badges of their respective lords (Dunham 1955, p 25). Indeed, the red rose of Lancaster was not used at all by Henry VI (1421-71), though it had certainly been one of the many badges belonging to his forebears. For Edward IV (1442-83), on the other hand, the white rose of York, inherited from his Mortimer ancestors, was probably his most important badge, and it was to his supporters or loyal subjects that the following roseate badges most likely belonged. When new and bright they would have resembled the correct heraldic metal (*argent*) of the Yorkist rose.

159 Livery badge: a hollow pendant, the front moulded in the form of a Yorkist rose (i.e. with four petals, barbed of the calyx points), the back decorated with a compass-drawn flower. The suspension loop has been lost. Second half of 15th century. H. 26 mm. *203a/1987* **Fig 211**

Another, similar pendant from Salisbury retains the loop (Mitchiner 1986, p 248). In the base of these and other examples there is an opening which appears to have had no practical function and to have been an unavoidable consequence of the processes of slush-casting. Among the more conventional pin-badges found at Salisbury are a few depicting the Yorkist rose, sometimes with a crown (e.g. Figs 212-213; pc), sometimes combined with a sun:

160 Livery badge: a crowned Yorkist rose and, at its centre, a mirror-image of a shield bearing *Quarterly France modern and England*. Second half of 15th century. H. 37 mm. *195s/1987* **Fig 214**

161 Livery badge: a rose *en soleil*, with a circular aperture at the centre, rebated behind. Second half of 15th century. H. 27 mm. Given by Mr D.Morgan. *198e/1987* **Fig 215**

162 Livery badge: a rose and sun dimidiated. Examples from the same mould have been found at London. A smaller version of this badge, identical to MOL 79.403/2, has also been found at Salisbury. Second half of 15th century. H. 40 mm. *1909/1987* **Fig 216**

Late fifteenth-century deposits at London have yielded well over fifty badges of the crowned rose of York and several more depicting the rose in a fetterlock. The various combinations of rose and sun were alternatives popular with supporters of the house of York as well as with Edward IV himself. The rose *en soleil*, for example, appeared on the reverse of the gold ryal of 1465-6. Edward's favourite badge, however, was the sun in splendour, which he invented for himself after his defeat of the Lancastrian army at Mortimer's Cross in 1461 or, more particularly, after unusual weather conditions had created the illusion of three suns shining in the sky before the battle, a spectacle that Edward took as a good omen. On pewter badges the sun is represented with an open, friendly face and with straight rays, which are longer and shorter by turns. One of two such badges found at Salisbury is illustrated in Fig 217 (pc); the other is in Mitchiner 1986, p 118, where it is dated fourteenth century and wrongly associated with the roots and runners of a badge depicting a strawberry plant (*cf.* Cat 175) which have been taken for another 'sun'.

163 Badge or casket-mount: the circular, central motif of pierced lattice-work has a border of 'rays' surrounded, first, by a wreath which incorporates four roses and then by an outer border of rays. No pin was provided. Late 15th or early 16th century. D. 60 mm. *193k/1987*
Fig 218

The Museum of London possesses one identical and one very similar piece. The latter (MOL 57.32/1), on which the roses are clearly barbed, has been advanced as a possible badge that combined the Yorkist rose and sunburst motifs (Tudor-Craig 1973, pp 59-60).

While it may be possible to link many roseate badges with the royal house of York, it is not practicable to assign badges of the lion to particular kings or magnates. The number of options is too great. Some badges, however, may simply have been regarded as the lion of England and worn, perhaps, as an expression of popular nationalistic feeling during active phases of the Hundred Years' War with France.

164 Livery badge: a lion passant guardant, crowned. Another copy of this badge was found in an early 15th century context at Swan Lane, London. W. 55 mm. *225j/1987* **Fig 219**

165 Livery badge: a lion passant guardant, crowned. 15th century. W.30 mm. *191k/1987*
Fig 220

166 Livery badge: a lion counter statant, crowned; one of two such badges found at Salisbury. A more complete specimen from the same mould, found (1987) at St Katherine's Wharf, Tower Hamlets, London, in a deposit dating from the first half of the 15th century, is illustrated in Fig 222. W. 32 mm. Given by Mr R. Davis. *202c/1987* **Fig 221**

167 Livery badge: a lion counter statant, crowned. The lion's posture is known from other examples of this badge. Early 15th century. W. 52 mm. *190u/1987* **Fig 223**

168 Livery badge: a lion's face within a circular frame, from which project a series of pearl-like knobs. The Museum of London possesses an identical badge (no 8884). Probably first half of 15th century. H. 26 mm. *225l/1987*
Fig 224

169 Livery badge: the scroll and other lower parts of a badge depicting a sprig of mulberry, the punning device of the Mowbray dukes of Norfolk. The scroll is inscribed *movberi*. End of 14th or 15th century. W. 32 mm. *222/1987* **Fig 225**

On this, the commonest form of mulberry badge, the upper parts are moulded in the round and, when complete, would have depicted a single, almost life-size berry on a stalk, within a cluster of four ovate leaves (e.g. BM M & LA 56,7-1,2111, MOL 80.81/17). The delineation of the leaves and fruit matches illustrations of mulberry in fifteenth-century herbals (Hind 1935, I, fig 159). A similar sized sprig was also produced as a single-sided badge (Spencer 1980, p 28), while other probable Mowbray badges depicted a whole twig or branch of mulberry, with many leaves and berries, sometimes arranged as a wreath emerging from a vase.

Thomas, the first Mowbray duke of Norfolk, had mulberry trees as well as silver lions (another of his badges) embroidered on the trappings of his horse in preparation for his intended trial by combat with Henry of Bolingbroke in 1398. The Salisbury find is likely to date before the death of John, the fourth and last Mowbray duke. At the very latest, Mowbray badges might have been worn at a lavish Westminster tournament in January 1478, held in honour of Anne Mowbray, the duke of Norfolk's young heiress, after her marriage to the infant second son of Edward IV, Richard duke of York.

Similarly, another kind of badge, depicting berry-like fruit heaped up inside a hood, has all the sententiousness of a rebus. Though its meaning has yet to be recognised, a combination of its visual elements was perhaps intended to suggest a family name. Alternatively it is the sort of badge which might signify a popular saying of the day as are contemporary badges depicting a hood with a phallus filling the face opening (Bergen op

Zoom 1987, p 54; Whiting 1968, B452; Jones forthcoming).

170 Badge: a hood full of fruit. The edges of the face-opening are turned back and a seam is represented across the top of the hood and along the length of the liripipe (or tail at the back), which is wound twice round the gorget. Early 15th century. W. 39 mm. Given by Mr M.Green. *142/1978* **Fig 226**

171 Badge: very similar to Cat 170 and intact. *190w/1987* **Fig 227**

Yet another example found at Salisbury is illustrated in Mitchiner 1986, p 96, where the badge is attributed to St Dorothy. A fashionable hood, however, seems far removed from her story. Among versions of the badge found at London is one where much more exaggerated, applied dagging replaces the integral dagging of the liripipe (BM M & LA 56, 7-1, 2114). *Cf.* Cat 182 below.

172 Livery badge: a fragment depicting the goat-like head of a fabulous animal with long tusks and ringed or corrugated horns, two of the characteristics of the heraldic yale. Probably first half of 15th century. W. 23 mm. Given by Mr I. Smith. *200k/1987* **Fig 228**

That the fragment belonged to a particularly large badge is shown by a more or less complete example found at London in 1978 and illustrated in Fig 229. Here the yale is gorged with a crown and fettered. Though, once again, only the stumps of the horns survive, there is enough of them to show that one horn would have curved forwards, the other backwards. This peculiarity, the long mane and the cloven feet are further distinctive features of the yale, and it was the nature of the horns in particular that distinguished the yale from the heraldic antelope, the badge associated especially with Henry V and Henry VI (*cf.* Cat 115) (Druce 1911).

The yale seems to have made its first appearance heraldically as a badge of John Beaufort, duke of Somerset (*c.*1404-44), grandson of John of Gaunt. In view of their large size, the badges illustrated here would fit in best with fashions of the earlier fifteenth century. Yales might also have been worn, however, later in the fifteenth century and at the beginning of the sixteenth by adherents of John Beaufort's daughter and heiress, Margaret (1443-1509), the mother of Henry VII (Hope 1911).

173 Livery badge: a talbot-hound *sejant*, or squatting on its haunches, wearing a collar with two bells. 15th century. H. 31 mm. *190s/1987* **Fig 230**

174 Livery badge: a talbot very similar to that in Cat 173. H. 33 mm. *11d/1988* **Fig 231**

Three similar badges are known to have been found at Salisbury; for one of them, see Seaby 1987, pl V361. The talbot, a breed of large hunting dog, was used as a badge by the Talbot family during the fifteenth and early sixteenth century. The badge was made especially famous by the military prowess of successive generations of the family. John Talbot, the first earl of Shrewsbury (d.1453), who was referred to in *c.*1449 as 'Talbott our good dogge' (Bentley 1831, p 161), was for thirty years the envy and 'the terror of the French' until he was killed near Castillon, attempting the reconquest of Gascony. Later, two of his sons are alluded to by reference to the talbot badge, while of their nephew, Sir Gilbert Talbot, who was one of Henry Tudor's captains at Bosworth, it was said 'the Talbott he bitt wonderous sore' (Barnard 1925, p 82). In the late fifteenth and early sixteenth century the badge was described as a running hound or *a talbot passant argent* and both then and earlier was often so depicted (Barnard 1925, f 3r; Howard de Walden 1904, p 66; Ellis 1981, p 103; *cf.* a stone mould for casting a series of talbot badges, MOL 8909). Most of the numerous surviving pewter badges show the animal seated, however, facing right as well as left and in the main varying only in details of the collar. On a badge of this type found at Bristol, however, the damaged collar still retains the beginning of the name, Talbot, which tends to confirm that badges depicting the seated hound were, indeed, intended for the Talbot family (Marks & Payne 1978, p 36).

175 Livery badge: part of a strawberry plant, comprising the roots, a single strawberry and some of the stalks and runners. 15th century. W. 37 mm. *10b/1988* **Fig 232**

Consisting of seven roots, two strawberries, two leaves, a flower and four runners, the complete appearance of this relatively common badge is disclosed in Fig 233, from an example found on the site of Swan Lane car park, Lower Thames Street, London. A badge that may be closely related to it is among the eighteen badges exemplified in 1720 as belonging to 'the most ancient and illustrious family of Stafford'. Here again two strawberries hang on twin stalks but in this instance the stalks cross one another and rise from a single stem (Fox-Davies 1907, fig 11, no xvi and pp 28-41, 144-5). The same badge, with the ascription to Stafford, is given in two Tudor collections, College of Arms MS L.14, ff 107-8 and Vincent 172, p 515 (info. Mr J. A. Goodall, FSA). No documentary record has yet been found, however, of the use of strawberries as a badge by the Stafford dukes of Buckingham in the fifteenth century. Livery badges were rarely a matter of official record, however.

176 Livery badge: the sails of a windmill, designed to be part of a large composite badge. The sails appear to be unfinished and unused; intended openwork has failed to come out, runners from the mould are still attached to three of the sails and the central pivot-hole has not been perforated. This badge may therefore have been a waste product from a Salisbury workshop. Mid 15th century. 52 x 48 mm. *191n/1987* **Fig 234**

Other examples of the badge recovered at London (such as BM M & LA 1904, 7-20, 30 which has, in fact, lost practically all but the hub of its sails,) show that the sails were intended to revolve on a short spindle protruding from the upper part of a post-mill (Fig 235), which in turn carried the pin and clasp at the back. The mill, set on a grassy mound, has a gabled roof, a short ladder leading to the open door, which in some versions stands to the left instead of the right, and a steering-post, most of which is missing from the example illustrated. Sometimes the mill is shown to be made of boards of random lengths nailed end to end. A mill sail was the badge of Robert Willoughby, lord of Eresby, who is identified by reference to this badge in a political poem of *c.*1449: 'our Myllesaylle will not a bowte', (Bentley 1831, p 161). Lord Willoughby was an active supporter of the Lancastrian dynasty and was one of the many leaders killed at the battle of Towton in 1461, when the Lancastrian army was defeated by the new king, Edward IV.

177 Livery badge: the elephant and castle. The elephant has a dappled body, scalloped ears and cloven feet, and it walks stiff-legged over a patch of meadow. Only a fragment of its short trunk survives. The howdah or castle rests on a housing trimmed with bells and secured by a girth-band and takes the form of a highly stylised triple tower. 15th century. H. 42 mm. *190t/1987* **Fig 236**

Other examples found at London include badges from the same mould (BM M & LA 56, 7-1, 2152; MOL 8730). The elephant of the medieval bestiary was far removed from reality. It was said to have no joints in its legs, for example. The bestiary also explained that Indian and Persian warriors fought from wooden towers on the backs of elephants, and this fortified structure was always depicted. The elephant and castle was a badge of William, Viscount Beaumont (1438-1507) (Fox-Davies 1907, p 77). An active supporter of Henry VI, he was on the losing side at the battle of Towton (1461) and the battle of Barnet (1471) and spent the remaining years of Yorkist rule in exile or in prison.

178 Livery badge: the sun in the horns of a crescent moon. The sun has a face on the central disc surrounded by 16 rays which are straight and wavy by turns. Late 14th or 15th century. H. 43 mm. Drainage coll. (Brodie). Akerman 1855, p 72 and 1857, pl facing p 94; *Sal.Mus.Cat.* 1864, p 55 no 220 and 1870, p 11; Smith 1880, p 151. *iiE501* **Fig 237**

The sun and moon were emblems of Christ and the Virgin Mary respectively, and both were used as attributes of the Virgin after she had become identified with the 'great wonder in heaven; a woman clothed with the sun, and the moon under her feet' (Revelation XII, 1). The sun and moon were also widely used heraldically, the sun as a badge of Richard II and Edward IV (Fig 217), for example, and the crescent-moon as a badge of the Percy earls of Northumberland. As far away as the palace of the dukes of Mantua, Mantegna depicted (*c*.1474) a sun-and-moon almost identical to Cat 178 as a horse pendant. The connections of this Salisbury find, however, are likely to be much nearer at hand. A heraldic visitation of Wiltshire undertaken in 1623 and now preserved in the Salisbury Museum gives the arms of the Daunger family as a crescent moon with a sun between the horns. The sun has a face and sixteen rays alternately straight and wavy as in Cat 178. The herald who compiled the visitation also noted evidence for the use of this device in the fourteenth century.

179 Livery badge: a star of eight wavy rays clasped by a crescent moon. The star's radiance is depicted on the surface of the moon. Late 14th or 15th century. H. 23 mm. *191l/1987* **Fig 238**

180 Livery badge: a wavy star clasped by a crescent moon, the outer rim of which is strewn with trefoils. Late 14th or 15th century. H. 18 mm. *191m/1987* **Fig 239**

181 Livery badge: a wavy star clasped by a crescent moon, the surface of which is decorated with a line of large pellets. Late 14th or 15th century. H. 15 mm. Given by Mr I. Smith. *2000/1987*. Not illustrated.

Similar badges have been found at Tupholme, Lincs., Chester and London (e.g. MOL 80.447/1). A similar motif occurs on another Salisbury find (Mitchiner 1986, p 196) described by Mitchiner as a 'two layered pendant badge'; it is, in fact, a strap-end. The star and crescent was a lesser livery briefly instituted by Henry IV at the beginning of his reign (Given-Wilson 1986, pp 241-2). The occasional difficulty of distinguishing heraldically between the sun (*cf.* Fig 217) and the star is illustrated in Shakespeare's *Henry V*, III, vii : '*Rambures.* My lord constable, the armour that I saw in your tent tonight, are those stars, or suns, upon it? *Constable.* Stars, my lord.' A similar mistake in wrongly identifying the De Vere star-badge played a significant part in the outcome of the battle of Barnet in 1471 (Ross 1974, p 168).

182 Livery badge: a pendant, modelled on both sides, in the form of a tailed hood of chequered cloth, hollow-cast but now laid flat. The liripipe is drawn forward, as if to sweep round and bind the collar, which is dagged at the edge. A suspension-ring is attached to the liripipe. Second half of 15th century. 28 x 35 mm. *192a/1987* **Fig 240**

Virtually identical badges have been found at London; e.g. MOL 87.168/4, which differs only in showing the gorget to be more tightly bound by the encircling liripipe. Another variant, with a slightly different woven pattern, is illustrated in Mitchiner 1986, p 188, and is there classified as an emblem of St Dorothy. It seems more likely that this kind of hood was one of the badges adopted by Sir Walter Devereux, Lord Ferrers (*c*.1432-85). In 1475, when it was worn by the contingent of men-at-arms and 200 archers taken by Ferrers on Edward IV's military expedition to France, the badge was described as a 'ffrench wyfis hood boundyn' (Barnard 1925, p 28). In view of the animosity between France and England in these closing phases of the Hundred Years War, 'French wife's hood' was presumably a mockingly derogatory description of the badge, implying a hood of such unfashionable cut and plainness that only a peasant woman would have worn it. A life-size hood of the same proportions as Cat 182 with its deep front and padded face-opening, would have shaded the face of its owner, who, if female, might have been considered unfashionable, modest or both. After a lifetime of active support for the Yorkist cause and dynasty, Lord Ferrers was killed at the Battle of Bosworth. His descendants continued to use the hood as a badge until at least the middle of the sixteenth century.

183 Livery badge: a rectangular padlock, the sides slightly waisted and with trefoils at the corners; the key-hole is a little off-centre, though aligned with the middle of the shackle. 15th century. H. 29 mm. *190r/1987* **Fig 241**

A 'square-cornered padlock' was the badge of Francis, Viscount Lovel (1454-1487), chamberlain to Richard III and one of the few members of his household to escape death at the battle of Bosworth. The badge is depicted on his stall-plate in St George's Chapel, Windsor. At least two other versions of this badge have been found at Salisbury, and others have turned up at London. One of the London finds, almost identical to Cat 183 is illustrated in Mitchiner 1986, p 187, as a pilgrim souvenir from the Lock, a lazar-house in Kent Street, Southwark. One of the hospitals maintained by the city authorities on the outskirts of London specifically to ensure the isolation of lepers seems an improbable attraction to pilgrims, however. On other London finds the body of the lock is depicted perfectly square, conforming even more closely to the description of the Lovel lock as square-cornered. The lock was so designated to distinguish it from the commoner badges of the fetterlock, associated with the Yorkist royal house. On pewter badges the fetterlock is represented as a barrel-padlock, cylindrical in form.

184 Livery badge: a bridled horse in full career, its long, flowing tail adding to the sense of movement. Perhaps early 15th century. W. 35 mm. Mitchiner 1986, p 213. *193m/1987* **Fig 242**

The absence of collar and traces seems to rule out the draught-horse badge used in the later fifteenth century by William Herbert, Earl of Pembroke. This Salisbury badge may go back, therefore, to the turn of the century when a running white horse was a badge of the Fitzalan earls of Arundel, who were leading members of the factions supporting Henry of Bolingbroke both before and after his accession as king (Fox-Davies 1907, p 75). Thomas Fitzalan (1381-1415) died during Henry V's Agincourt campaign.

185 Livery badge: the stump of a tree eradicated proper. Probably first half of 15th century. H. 43 mm. *10d/1988* **Fig 243**

An almost identical badge comes from the Thames at Bankside (MOL 83.629). This rebus (a pun on the name Woodstock) was one of the badges of Edward III to be adopted by his grandson Henry of Bolingbroke (Henry IV). From Henry the badge passed to his third son John, duke of Bedford (1389-1435) and it was by reference to this badge that Bedford was identified in a mid-fifteenth-century poem: 'The Rote is ded' (Bentley 1831, p 161). Uncle to the baby king Henry VI, John duke of Bedford was heir presumptive until his death. During the king's infancy he was made Protector but deemed it more important to concentrate on his other role as Regent of France, hoping thereby to fulfil Henry V's ambitions.

186 Livery badge: a swan in an aggressive attitude, its wings raised high and its arched neck and body forming a reversed-S shape. The swan stands on a circle of ground dotted with flowers. 15th century. H. 37 mm. *190v/1987* **Fig 244**

In the fifteenth century the swan was a Lancastrian badge and was used in particular by both Lancastrian heirs to the throne, Henry of Monmouth and Edward, son of Henry VI and Margaret of Anjou. An almost identical badge (Fig 245) was found with a large quillon dagger, *c.*1430, at the Anchor Pier, Bankside, London and several other examples of this badge have been recovered (e.g. MOL 8740; Liverpool Museum 8185). From Salisbury comes another badge which is also similar to Cat 186, except that the swan faces the other way (Seaby 1987, pl V361B). In a few other instances the swan faces right and on one of these badges the swan's neck is encircled by a coronet (Cherry 1969, pl xxv, 4). The consistency of this considerable group of badges suggests that they were issued at one particular period. Perhaps they were among those which Margaret of Anjou caused her son to distribute as a livery in 1459, when seeking to identify his supporters and to bolster his position as heir to the throne (*ibid.*, 50).

187 Livery badge: a swan standing, with its wings upraised and its beak slightly open. The body is hollow with a narrowing open end at the tail. The wings were cast at right angles to the body and were then bent upwards. A pin was cast beneath the wing at the back and was aligned behind the swan's legs, now missing. The badge required the use of a complicated six-piece mould. The opening in the tail is a feature of other contemporary hollow-cast pewter birds, usually designed as pendants, and it is tempting to suppose that these apertures sometimes held a tuft of real feathers (but see Cat 159). Late 14th-early 15th century. H. 35 mm. *191j/1987* **Fig 246**

Another swan of this type was recovered from a deposit at Bull Wharf, London, dated by coins and pilgrim signs to the late fourteenth century. From the same deposit came another swan badge, in this case two-dimensional, with the wing only slightly raised and its general configuration reminiscent of the Dunstable swan jewel in the British Museum. The swan badge was worn in the fourteenth century by the Bohuns and some other noble families as a mark of their descent from the Swan Knight of medieval romance (Cherry 1969, pp 45-48).

188 Livery badge: a wheatear crowned. Second or third quarter of 15th century. H. 43 mm. *225z/1987* **Fig 247**

For a similar badge also found at Salisbury see Seaby 1987, pl V359A. Other versions of the badge depict the wheatear without a crown or with its stalk uppermost. The wheatear was a badge of Henry Holland, duke of Exeter (d.1475) and a great-grandson of John of Gaunt. In 1449 he was alluded to by reference to his badge: 'The Whete yer woll theym susteyn' (Bentley 1831, p 162). Henry Holland was destined to sustain the cause of the Lancastrian dynasty and thereby found himself on the losing side at the battle of Towton in 1461. After a period in exile, he returned to become part of the Lancastrian army that was defeated by Edward IV at Barnet in 1471. There he was wounded and left for dead, but he eventually recovered and spent the rest of his life imprisoned at the Tower of London. The wheatear was also used as a badge by Henry Holland's father, John, also duke of Exeter (d.1447). It appears on John Holland's seal matrix as Admiral of England, Ireland and Aquitaine, dating from 1445-6 (Tonnochy 1952, no 24).

189 Livery badge: fragmentary badge of a bundle of five arrows held at the middle by a belt. Late 15th century. H. 54 mm. *190z/1987* **Fig 248**

An intact example of a very similar badge, still with its casting flashes (Fig 249; MOL 82.8/16), shows that the bundle comprised what is, heraldically, a sheaf of arrows (i.e. one erect and two in saltire) and two additional, blunt-ended, target-practice arrows. The belt-buckle is also seen to be a standard late fifteenth-century type. These badges call to mind two of the lines describing the yeoman forester in the Prologue to Chaucer's *Canterbury Tales*:

> 'A sheef of pecok arwes, bright and kene,
> Under his belt he bar ful thriftily.'

English archers normally carried their arrows in a bundle, point upwards, through a loop on their belts. Several other surviving versions of this badge differ only in size or in being held by a looped cord instead of a belt. They are to be distinguished from the 'garbs' of arrows noted in Cat 102. Five arrows tied at the middle were a badge of Arthur, prince of Wales (1486-1502), son of Henry VII (Fox-Davies 1907, p 153).

190 Badge: a pair of spurs suspended from their lower leathers so that the shanks and rowels point downwards. Originally they appear to have been surmounted by a crown, of which only the base now survives. Late 14th century. H. 45 mm. *191r/1987* **Fig 250**

Here the mould-maker has taken pains to preserve not only the general form of the spur but also the decorative detail, such as the scalloped flanges and the curling bell-flower crests that appear, as it were, behind the wearer's heels. The resulting miniatures invite comparison with an actual spur catalogued as no 29 in the first part of the Salisbury Museum's *Medieval Catalogue*. In the opinion of Mrs Blanche Ellis, the shape and proportion of the spurs on this badge are a little earlier than those depicted on the brass of Sir William Bagot (d.1407) at Bagington, Warwicks. (London Museum 1940, fig 32, no 5). The large rowels, curved sides, single ring terminals, curled decorative crests and the circular studs depicted on the upper leathers are all features consistent with a date near the end of the fourteenth century. These spurs have not yet been recognised as a livery badge and may simply belong to a more general class of decorative badge which feature military equipment and weapons, such as daggers:

191 Pendant: a miniature dagger-sheath with loop for suspension. The top is cupped to house the lower guard of a rondel-dagger like the one described below (Cat 192). The rest of the sheath is of diamond-section. Probably early 15th century. H. 39 mm. *191u/1987* **Fig 251**

192 Pendant: a miniature rondel-dagger with blade of diamond-section. The upper guard is missing. The dagger would have been worn in a sheath like that described above (Cat 191). Probably early 15th century. H. 46 mm. *191u/1987* **Fig 252**

Several other examples of sheaths of the same form, though of varying sizes and sometimes decorated with scroll-work, have been found elsewhere. Corresponding daggers have also turned up. A complete dagger (from Butler's Wharf, Bermondsey) comparable to Cat 192 is depicted in Fig 253; what appears to be another found on the site of Nieuwlande (Netherlands) has been catalogued as a pilgrim-staff badge from Compostela (Bergen op Zoom 1987, p 63; van Heeringen, Koldeweij and Gaalman 1987, p 62; see also comment following Cat 87 above). The hilt of another rondel-dagger found at Salisbury (Fig 254; pc) takes a somewhat different form, with its spherical pommel and grip swelling at the centre. In only one instance has a miniature, pendent dagger-sheath been found (at Trig Lane, London) with its dagger still inside (Spencer 1982, p 315).

Some badges are in the form of a long-bow with arrow drawn or of a loaded cross-bow. An example of the former, found at Salisbury (pc), is illustrated in Fig 255. Though included here among badges of a military character, its true purpose may have been to advertise the prowess of its wearer as a lover, rather than as an archer. It seems to be a badge or brooch of this type, described as a 'baw bond (? bow band) and the arow therein', that is included among the rings and other love-tokens in a late medieval love poem (Silverstein 1971, no 143, line 21). Consistent with this view of the bow-and-arrow as a symbol of male virility is a cross-bow badge in which the stock terminates at the butt-end in a young man's head (Bergen op Zoom 1987, p 56, no 305). The proverb, 'the bolt finds the notch', perhaps also belongs to this context.

Another badge found at Salisbury (and now in the Blackburn Museum) depicts a pole-axe (Fig 256), virtually identical to others found at London (e.g. BM M & LA 1904, 7-20, 27; Spencer 1968, pl III,11). It is, however, possible that such axe-badges were pilgrim souvenirs, perhaps commemorating the cult of St Alphege, archbishop of Canterbury, who was killed at Greenwich by a blow on the head from an axe and was alluded to as Canterbury's first martyr in Thomas Becket's last sermon. Knightly equipment more akin to the Salisbury spurs-badge appears on badges representing a pair of laminated, plate gauntlets. A fragment of one of these badges has turned up at Salisbury (Fig 257, pc); two others, more or less complete, have been excavated from an early fifteenth-century deposit at Swan Lane, London.

193 Badge: a knight advancing towards an imaginary opponent. The horse sets off at a gallop over grassy hummocks. The knight wears a surcoat and helm and carries a shield charged with a chevron. There now survives only a fragment of his lance, which pointed obliquely upwards above the horse's ears and towards his opponent's helm. 14th century. H. 43 mm. *1910/1987* **Fig 258**

This and many similar badges found elsewhere celebrate the glamour and excitement of the tournament, the most picturesque and splendid form of entertainment available for onlookers who crowded into the tilting grounds in the later fourteenth and fifteenth centuries. Some badges appear to give expression to the chivalric aspirations of the spectator, for the jouster is sometimes represented as a sprightly youth with no helm and, sometimes, no rerebrace, and with a lance that has a blunted end or a coronal (Spencer 1980, p 30). Badges celebrating other manly sports, like archery or wrestling, were also made for those who wished to make their interests known.

194 Badge: a hare and hound. The greyhound wears a collar with a hook for its leash. Late 14th or 15th century. H. 48 mm. *195m/1987* **Fig 259**

195 Badge: the hound from a badge very similar to Cat 194. W. 41 mm. Given by Mr W. Wareham. *43/1988* **Fig 260**

Connected, as it was, with one of the chief sports of the gentry, the greyhound eventually served as a heraldic badge. It was used by Margaret Beaufort, for example, and was also adopted by her son, Henry VII, as the dexter supporter of the arms of England. In France a bizarre cult associated a sanctified greyhound with the protection of children (Schmitt 1979) and it may have been with children in mind that badges of the greyhound were labelled unequivocally as bringing good luck to those who wore them (Gay 1928; p 153; Haedeke 1976, p 73; Koenigsmarková 1987, no 172). But the presence of the hare in Cat 194 suggests that this type of badge simply stood for the love of the chase, a passion shared by the mass of people, if only at the level of poaching. Indeed, anyone could savour the dramatic irony of the situation, with the hare taking cover in the one place where the greyhound could not see it. The other sorts of hounds, those that hunted by scent rather than by sight, were also represented on fifteenth-century badges, though most of these seem likely to have been livery badges (Cat 173-4).

196 Badge: a man goes riding with his falcon. He wears a garland round his head, a padded doublet with a thigh-length skirt and a knightly girdle round his hips. The falcon, perched on his left hand, is damaged by corrosion. Late 14th century. W. 40 mm. *1950/1987* **Fig 261**

Alongside the Salisbury find is illustrated (Fig 262) an unblemished prototype found at London (MOL 82.8/15). Here the man is seen to have a two-pointed beard, his doublet is of patterned cloth and his shoes or soled hose have extremely long points. He wears a glove on his left hand and his horse's harness is covered with bells. The same subject, a man going hawking, is depicted as an occupation of the month of May in medieval calendars. The badge was doubtless worn, not simply as a celebration of spring, but in honour of hawking itself – a favourite sport of royalty and the well-to-do, to whom it was largely confined by law and sheer cost. The quarry was waterfowl. Falcons were so highly prized that pilgrimages were undertaken for sick or injured birds. Sometimes the birds themselves, or their images in wax, were taken to the shrines, principally to St Thomas of Canterbury and to St Thomas Cantilupe at Hereford. The survival of many kinds of cheaply-produced badges relating to falcons and falconry (though some may well have been livery badges) suggests that the sport was highly regarded by people at large. Among those found at Salisbury are the following:

197 Badge: probably a livery badge, depicting a hawk's lure, comprising a pair of bird's wings joined by a pad of leather or fabric. When complete, this would have been fitted with a looped leash at the top, the loop serving also as the means of suspending or attaching the badge. Second half of 15th century. H. 25 mm. *191v/1987* **Fig 263**

This is one of two badges of this sort found at Salisbury. A few others have turned up in fifteenth-century deposits at London (one of them, described as a cloak lined with ermine, is illustrated in Mitchiner 1986, p 243). They depict the kind of lure used by falconers for the training of young hawks. In heraldry such a lure is blazoned 'a hawk's lure, leashed' or 'two wings conjoined in lure, leashed, and inverted.' In 1531-2, lures of this type were depicted on the banner of 'Mayster Ichingham' (Howard de Walden 1904, p 112).

198 Badge: a falcon with a scroll above its back inscribed in black letter *: spege . tollys . may.* The missing head, with hooked beak, and neck, with collar and ring, are known from fragments of identical or similar badges (e.g. MOL 75.1/27). 15th century. W. 55 mm. Mitchiner 1986, p 214. *193r/1987* **Fig 264**

199 Badge: falcon's claw and part of a scroll inscribed *[dis] may tollis* from a badge identical to that in Fig 266 (found at London, 1979) and similar in style to Cat 198; here, however, the falcon faces right and stands above the label. 15th century. Width of fragment, 30mm. Given by Mr I. Smith. *200m/1987* **Fig 265**

The significance of the mottoes on these badges is uncertain, though they may allude to falconry, since the Middle English word *toll* was used as a verb and noun to mean lure or decoy. Thus one of the poor scholars in Chaucer's *Reeve's Tale* says 'With empty hand men may na haukes tulle.' Another, perhaps garbled, inscription, reading *ihc mai . . . adi* appears at the foot of a comparable, though inferior, Salisbury find (Fig 267, pc). A falcon of a different type is depicted on yet another badge found at Salisbury; here the bird, wearing a bell and with wings upraised, stands, not upon its prey as stated in Mitchiner 1986, p 215, but on a wreath-like circle of ground (as in Cat 186).

Two other badges depicting birds remain to be considered:

200 Badge: bird with curved beak and extremely long tail and wearing (the remains of) a crown and a collar with a ring. Late 14th or early 15th century. W. 75 mm. *225i/1987* **Fig 268**

Several other copies and variants of this large badge have been found at London. Whether it faces left or right (as here), the bird is invariably given an extremely long tail, curved beak and, when they survive at all, short talons. In these respects the badges come closest to resembling medieval popinjays (parrots). Indeed a badge found in Amsterdam (1988) depicting a bird virtually identical to, though somewhat smaller than, Cat 200 carries the (reversed) inscription *papagaei* (info. Mr H.J.E. van Beuningen). Another badge, from Bull Wharf, Upper Thames Street, London (1979), depicts a very similar bird in a more familiar parrot-like attitude, perched upright and looking backwards. This badge was found near the site of the mansion belonging to the fourteenth-century tycoon, Sir John Pulteney, who had the curtains and coverlets of his beds patterned with violet popinjays. Aside from badges, there are many other illustrations of the bird's popularity as a decorative and heraldic motif, such as the 'papejayes' and blue cockerels on worsted hangings left by Elizabeth de Burgh to her daughter in 1355 (Evans 1949, p 43) or the 'papiayez' and periwinkles depicted on the silk covering the aventail of Gawain's helmet in 'Gawain and the Green Knight'. The *Oxford English Dictionary* (s.v. *popinjay*) cites several other medieval examples of the decorative use of the popinjay and of the application of the word 'to a person in an eulogistic sense, in allusion to the beauty and rarity of the bird'. Of all the many birds kept captive as pets in the Middle Ages, the popinjay was also the most coveted, not least because of its ability to mimic human speech.

201 Badge: an owl, the face of which has been given, probably inadvertently, a humanoid expression. 15th century. H. 33 mm. *225y/1987* **Fig 269**

At least two other copies of this badge have been found at Salisbury and several more have turned up at London (e.g. London Museum 1940, pl LXXIV, no 58). According to the bestiaries the owl was symbolical of the Jews, who preferred the night of their ignorance to the fair day of Christian belief. If that were the intended meaning of these badges, then their purpose was presumably apotropaic. That there are many other possible explanations of the owl motif is evident from the most recent study of the symbolism of the owl in medieval art (Vandenbroeck 1985).

Some pewter badges appear to have been made to celebrate the seasons and seasonal festivals. Decorative badges in the form of holly twigs doubtless became magical talismans when worn for the feast of Christmas, combining, as they did, peasant lore and fable with symbols of Christ's Passion.

202 Badge: a sprig of holly. 15th century. W. 40 mm. *190x/1987* **Fig 270**

There can be much less doubt about the seasonal significance of badges depicting a plough. Celebrating what has been described as 'the most important single piece of machinery in the feudal economy, . . . an absolute essential in the life and prosperity of all levels of society' (Camille 1987, p 426), these badges, it may be suggested, were made for wear during Plough Monday, the first Monday after Twelfth Night (6 January), when pseudo-pagan fertility rites marked the resumption of work on the land after the Christmas festival. With its phallic associations, the plough was central to these revelries, the main feature of which was the procession of disguised ploughmen and boys who dragged a plough from door to door, extracting gifts from householders. Before the Reformation some of this money was allocated for the support of the plough light, maintained by the ploughmen's guild, before their altar in the parish church (Chambers 1866, pp 94-6; Hole 1976, pp 157-8).

203 Badge: in the form of a plough. Through its long, curving plough-beam is fitted, near the front, the plough-foot, which helped with the steering, and, near the middle, the coulter, which cut the ground ahead of the plough-share. Immediately behind the pointed plough-share is a mould-board, deep enough here to conceal not only the share beam but part of the two upright members of the frame. The badge is decorated with a crown, which sits on top of the plough-beam, between the plough-tail or upper handle and the top end of the coulter. 15th century. W. 40 mm. *191q/1987* **Fig 271**

204 Badge: depicting a plough with a lower, furrow-handle as well as the plough-tail. The latter is fitted with a semi-circular loop similar to the rope hand-hold represented on the furrow-handle in the famous depiction of a ploughman in the Luttrell Psalter. Only the base and one fleuron of the crown survive. 15th century. W. 38 mm. Given by Mr A. G. Pilson. *107/1987* **Fig 272**

Part of a badge very similar to Cat 204 has been recovered, with late fifteenth-century material, at Butler's Wharf, Bermondsey (1987). Another badge from St Katherine's Wharf, Tower Hamlets (1987) shows the plough facing left (Fig 273), in a sense wrongly, since the mould-board, which turned the soil over to the right to make a furrow, was, strictly speaking, only visible on the right-hand side of the plough; but the coulter is correctly shown immediately in front of the share. Interesting variants have been discovered at Canterbury. One Canterbury plough is more stylised, its beam terminating in a grotesque animal head and the whole structure, apart from the share, is decorated with dot-and-circle ornament on a hatched ground. The other Canterbury find, also facing left, is a wheel plough, which was steered by a wheel instead of the plough-foot at the front (Fig 274). Another badge found (1984) at Trig Lane, London, combines some of the features of both Cat 203 and

204. The whole subject is again topped by a highly decorative crown. The hand-hold on the curving furrow-handle is represented as rope and the share, mould-board and plough-foot stand on a scroll inscribed in black letter *God sped [th]e ploue* – God speed (prosper) the plough (Fig 275: the third 'd' in the inscription differs slightly from the other two and was probably intended to represent the old crossed d, standing for th; *cf.* Cat 158). The words of this traditional Plough Monday prayer also appear above a drawing of a plough team on a late fourteenth century manuscript of William Langland's poem *Piers Plowman*: 'God spede ye plow and sende us korne ynoug' (Camille 1987, p 431).

The next badge is believed to have been made for the celebration of another festival whose pagan rites persisted into the Middle Ages and beyond, namely the spring festival connected with the May King, or Jack-in-the-Green, and his associates:

205 Badge: in the form of a milkmaid dressed for Mayday celebrations. The ankles and feet are missing. Her low-waisted gown is buttoned down the front, and down the lower part of the sleeves. The cape of her hood is dagged and, characteristically for a woman, is open at the front below the chin. She holds a jug in her left hand, while on her head are perched three flagons or conical measures, supported by a wreath of twisted cloth. Last quarter of 14th century. H. 55 mm. *1909/1987* **Fig 276**

At first sight the figure in the badge might seem to belong to the popular medieval tradition of the dishonest ale wife, who is often represented with an ale-measure as a symbol of her fraudulence. This is how she is depicted, for example, in the doom painting, on the side of the damned, in the church of St Thomas, Salisbury. But it is the peculiarly cumbersome headdress and the slightly raised skirt that indicates the more likely identity of the Salisbury badge. Part of a similar badge, comprising the milkmaid's garland or headpiece of three flagons has been found at London (Mitchiner 1986, p 193, catalogued as three pillars). These medieval badges appear to antedate by some 300 years the main pictorial records of traditional Mayday rituals (Judge 1979, pp 3-7) and, in particular, of milkmaids going from door to door, dancing before the houses of their customers and taking as their equipage a wreath of flowers in one hand and a flagon in the other and a pyramidal garland of pewter vessels for carrying on the head.

Other fourteenth-century badges found at London represent the milkmaid as swaying in stately dance and holding a milking-pail instead of a jug (e.g. MOL 88.446) and in some instances two pails supported from a yoke. Another milkmaid-badge (Fig 277) found (1987) at St Katherine's Wharf, Tower Hamlets, London, shows her holding the same kind of conical vessel as those appearing on the head of the Salisbury find. The chaplet of flowers she is also holding brings a touch of gaiety to the rustic character of her clothes, a heavy hood with deep shoulder cape, her gown drawn up over the belt, revealing a bit of leg and a pair of hefty half-boots and enabling her to cavort more freely. It is interesting to note that pewter badges of the dancing Mayday milkmaid were still being made as late as the end of the seventeenth century: BM M & LA 1921 2-16 71. The conical flagons of the late fourteenth-century badge from Salisbury (as well as flagons of different shapes) are, incidentally, echoed by hollow-cast pewter pendants, several examples of which have been found at Salisbury (Fig 278, pc).

The workaday vessels depicted on the medieval badges had by the eighteenth century been replaced in the Mayday dances in London by much grander assemblages of silver utensils, hired out for the purpose by pawnbrokers at so much an hour. At that time, too, if not earlier, milkmaids might also take a cow with them and dance round it during the Mayday procession (Chambers 1866, I, p 573).

The care of horses, on the other hand,

appears to have been associated with another fragmentary pewter badge found at Salisbury (Fig 279; pc). This can be identified as part of a miniature replica of a curry-comb, which would have had a handle as well as two rows of teeth when complete (as in Fig 280; MOL 86.59/1) and would have had a loop at the end of the handle making it available for use as a pendant. Curry-combs, either as implements or badges, had no connection whatever with the currying of leather or the curriers' guild, as stated by Mitchiner 1986, p 243. They were, and still are, used in the grooming of horses. The pendants described here, like others depicting curry-combs of a somewhat different form, are inscribed with the word *fauel*, i.e. favel, which in Middle English was the name given to a fallow or chestnut horse. This sort of horse became, in turn, a symbol of dishonesty and fraud and by the first half of the fourteenth century gave rise to the expression 'to curry favel' (which we know today as 'to curry favour'), meaning to use insincere flattery or unworthy compliance to gain personal advantage. Presumably such uncomplimentary punning badges could only have been worn by owners who wished to indicate that they were worldly-wise and alive to the danger of flatterers and hypocrites (Jones 1989, pp 207-8).

206 Badge: depicting a cat with a mouse in its mouth and standing on a scroll bearing the inscription *VISI MUS* in mixed lettering. The forequarters of the mouse and the cat's ears are missing. 15th century. W. 40 mm. *Sal.Mus.Rep.* 1987-88, pl 3g. *221/1987* **Fig 281**

207 Badge: the scroll from a badge similar to Cat 206, bearing the inscription *VISIS MIN*. 15th century. W. 37mm. Given by Mr D. Morgan. *198f/1987* **Fig 282**

Another variant of Cat 206 has also been found at Salisbury; this came from the same mould as several other badges found at London, the best preserved of which is British Museum M & LA 96, 5-1, 76 (Fig 283). Here the wide-eyed cat has long, pricked ears and the legend reads *VISIS MU*. Finally, other versions of the badge, found in Canterbury and on several fifteenth-century sites at London, show the cat, still with captive mouse, wearing a saddle, trimmed with bells, strapped round its girth. The scroll on these badges reads *vesiu .ipab* in Gothic black letter. This garbled inscription and the alternative *VISI MUS* and its variants perhaps all derive from the words 'voici mus' (here is the mouse), since 'mus' could be regarded as an acceptable French (as well as English or Latin) word for 'mouse' at this period. On all versions of this badge the cat is depicted with a pair of tails. Whatever their meaning, the two tails seem to be peculiar to the badges, which are otherwise consistent with other medieval art-forms, such as bestiaries and misericords, in representing, as they so frequently do, the cat as a mouser, even though the weasel or ferret were then regarded as more effective and tenacious in that role. The cat and mouse were sometimes intended to symbolise the Devil and the sinner (Whiting 1968, C80), but here the allusions seem more likely to be political.

208 Brooch or pilgrim sign: a fleur-de-lys in a circular, beaded frame from the right-hand side of which protrudes a loop. The brooch is provided with the usual pin and clasp at the back. The loop is therefore intended for the suspension of a trinket from the badge itself. First half of 15th century. *Cf.* Cat 54-7. W. 23 mm. *225x/1987* **Fig 284**

Other examples with side-loops (including one from the same mould) have been found at London (MOL 80.65/17). The vast majority of brooches of this type, however, have the loop at the base of the frame (*cf.* Spencer 1980, p 19). A few fleur-de-lys brooches with basal loops have also been found at Salisbury (Figs 285-92, private collections). One example is slightly larger than the general run and is decorated with zig-zag ornament (Fig 285). Another (Fig 286) has a bracket formed from convergent scrolls between the frame and the loop, now missing. Another, still retaining its S-link, is illustrated in Fig 292, while yet another is figured in Seaby 1987, pl V356A.

If brooches of this kind were indeed designed as pilgrim souvenirs, there are grounds for suggesting that they originated from Canterbury (Spencer 1982, p 316). Their primary purpose, however, was evidently to support and provide the attachment for an amulet of medallic form or for a pendant trinket,of the type represented by the flagon in Fig 278 or the whistle in Cat 147. A few pendants have remained secured to their brooches. To a brooch almost identical to that in Fig 292 and found (1985) on the Thames foreshore at Queenhithe, London, a miniature bagpipe is still attached. From another recovered (1982) from the Thames at Brooks Wharf, London, is still suspended, from a pair of long, spindly links, a purse like that in Fig 309, while to a brooch very similar to that in Fig 285 and also found at London, is attached by one elongated link a purse of the single loop type (Cat 220). Like the Salisbury example in Fig 292, several fleur-de-lys brooches retain the flimsy, pewter S-links from which pendants were often suspended (MOL 82.221/20), raising the possibility that the purchaser was left to make his own choice from a variety of pendants. The brooches themselves varied also, a four-leaf flower or four circles (Fig 293; pc) and occasionally other motifs being substituted for the fleur-de-lys, as in the following example:

209 Brooch or pilgrim sign: a (now damaged) cross patée in a circular, beaded frame, from the base of which projects a loop. 15th century. H. 19 mm. Given by Mr I. Smith. *200h/1987* **Fig 294**

A negative version of this brooch, depicting the cross patée in openwork, was used for suspending a small purse with a frame of late fifteenth-century type (David Miller, St Albans: *List 18* (1988), fig 123). Another Salisbury find, a pendant in the form of a conventional vine-leaf (Fig 295; pc), is just the kind of ornamental knick-knack that could have been worn on one of these brooches. This type of pendent leaf has also turned up in quantity outside Salisbury in fifteenth-century contexts. What is quite certain, however, is that the leaves and small pewter bells (sometimes wrongly identified as hawk's bells) were used to adorn necklaces and other items of cheap jewellery formed from slender strands of pewter, cast to resemble twisted wire (Fig 297, MOL 86.362 & 86.408/1). What is also certain is that there are no cogent grounds for connecting the pendent leaves with the pilgrimage to Westminster as argued by Mitchiner 1986, p 181. Sometimes the pewter 'wire' was formed into elongated links in such a way that the side-loops, with their pendent leaves, came together in pairs at the centre of each loop. Neckchains of this latter kind have been found at London (Fig 298; found at St Katherine's Wharf, 1988) and Canterbury, while the following fragment found at Salisbury is further evidence of the widespread popularity of such fragile trinkets.

210 Necklace: fragment of pewter 'wire' with two side-loops for pendent ornaments. *Cf.* Fig 297. 15th century. L.66 mm approx. Given by Mr I. Smith. *200p/1987* **Fig 296**

211 Badge: a harp. 14th or 15th century. H. 49 mm. *195n/1987* **Fig 299**

Similar badges have been found at London. Other badges depict bagpipes and pipers or musicians playing the portable organ and other instruments. Such a badge might well have been worn by an itinerant minstrel to advertise his craft to pilgrims and other travellers or worn by members of one of the fraternities of minstrels which had been formed by the late fifteenth century.

212 Badge: a strutting cockerel, one of two identical finds from Salisbury. 15th century. H. 22 mm. *191p/1987* **Fig 300**

Several more from the same mould affirm its wider popularity (e.g. MOL 8719); at least two come from fifteenth-century deposits and one found at Wapping, London, retains some of its original paint. These badges may have been intended to honour cock-fighting, a favourite street-corner pastime among medieval youths. But this cock has no spurs, which feature prominently on some other sorts of cockerel-badges (e.g. Luton Museum BL/9/122/55). He therefore perhaps stands more in the tradition of Sir Chantecler the Cock, king of the dunghill and parody of male conceit, best known today through Chaucer's *Nun's Priest's Tale.* In the same pert spirit are roughly contemporary, hollow-cast pendants in which the cock holds a scroll in its beak saying on one side *Lok on me* and on the other *Kocrel* (Smith 1854, p 145). By the end of the fourteenth century, if not before, the cockerel was universally recognised as a symbol for lust and adultery. Thus lechery might be depicted as a beautifully dressed woman with loose dishevelled hair, carrying a cockerel. At the same time, 'kokkynge' was accepted as meaning lechery. The word retained the same significance in the sixteenth century, when 'cocky' meant 'lecherous'. Similarly, the word 'haenken' was used in Flemish to mean woman-chaser and in France wise-women devised recipes to restore 'l'ardeur des coqs' to impotent husbands (info. Mr Malcolm Jones; see also Jones forthcoming).

213 Badge: a cockerel mating with a hen. Late 14th-early 15th century. W. 30 mm. *195p/1987*
Fig 301

214 Badge: cockerel from a badge similar to Cat 213. W. 32mm. Given by Mr R. Davis. *202e/1987*. Not illustrated.

Virility, already hinted at in Cat 212, becomes the obvious message of this type of badge, which is as unequivocally sexual as the early fifteenth-century poem beginning 'I have a gentle cock' and ending, 'every night he percheth him in mine ladye's chaumber' (Davies 1963, pp 153-4).

At least two other relatively complete examples of this badge are known to have been found at Salisbury and very many more have been recorded at London, including one from a late fourteenth-century dump at Swan Lane. An almost intact specimen from fifteenth-century deposits at London (MOL 89.122/1) is illustrated in Fig 302. Examples of these popular badges, which were most probably of English make, reached the villages of Reimerswaal and Nieuwlande, near Bergen op Zoom (Zealand) in the Schelde estuary (Bergen op Zoom 1987, p 57). Yet from the same sites a great quantity of bizarre pornographic badges, dating mainly from the second half of the fourteenth and first half of the fifteenth centuries, has been recovered (*ibid.*, pp 49-56). This high proportion of bawdy pewter badges is evidently characteristic of other medieval sites in the Netherlands (info. Mr H. J.E van Beuningen). In fact no badges appear to have been made in England to match the extraordinary bawdiness of contemporary pewter badges found in such numbers on the continent, in France and the Low Countries especially. Some of these badges seem to parody the pilgrim sign and to mock the pilgrim by depicting male or female genitals as pedestrians, sometimes equipped with the pilgrim's staff (itself a well-known medieval phallic symbol), hat and rosary (Koenigsmarková 1987, figs 174, 176), or as travellers on horseback or on board ship. Genitalia also take the place of both the human and sacred elements in a blasphemous burlesque of a procession celebrating the Assumption of the Virgin (*cf.* Cat 45-6). Badges of this sort may have been no more than gross vulgarity. But if they also aimed to revile image-worship and pilgrimage, they are probably to be regarded as the pictorial equivalent of some of the less restrained sacrilegious remarks attributed to fifteenth-century Lollard sympathisers.

215 Badge: a fox preaching to geese. The fox stands in a polygonal pulpit (modelled in relatively high relief) and leans on a staff. Geese stand around the pulpit, two looking up at the fox in rapt attention, while two others may even be falling over backwards, lulled to sleep by the sermon. Another goose to the fox's right has either been lured to perch on the top of the pulpit or, when the badge was complete, was perhaps shown to be forcibly held there by the fox, who already has a dead goose tucked under his belt and may have others concealed beneath the bulges of his pseudo-monk's habit. 14th or 15th century. H. 48 mm. *44/1981* **Fig 303**

Parts of identical badges have been found at London. (MOL 78.84/13, 87.131/3). The proverb 'When the fox preaches, beware your geese' was known throughout most of western Europe in the later Middle Ages, having been disseminated not only verbally but pictorially by way of illuminated manuscripts, sculpture, carvings, textiles and wall-paintings (Rodin 1983). This badge is a clear indication that the theme, having also entered the repertoire of popular art, had unusually broad appeal. A fox dressed as a monk preaching to a congregation of gullible geese implied a role-reversal in which the deceiver pretended to be the representative of the good. The scene was therefore used to put across a critical view of hypocrisy and sanctimoniousness in the religious establishment, the fox's hypocrisy being usually revealed by a glimpse of a captive goose tucked into his hood (e.g. Varty 1967, pl 72). On the Salisbury-type badge, however, perhaps because the fox appears not to have been shown in profile with a consequent sight of his cowl, an early victim is instead thrust under his belt, while another may have been enticed into a position beneath his right fore-paw. The subject was also construed as symbolising the way in which the Devil uses his cunning to trap unsuspecting souls.

216 Badge: an ape, wearing a hood and standing on a fish, pounds the contents of a mortar with an immensely-long pestle, and adds a stream of urine to the concoction from his own over-large penis. Early 15th century. H. 45mm. *196a/1987* **Fig 304**

217 Badge: another version of Cat 216. The mortar has handles and the fish a more predatory look. Early 15th century. H. 44 mm. *Sal. Mus. Rep.* 1987-88, pl 3d. *220/1987* **Fig 305**

218 Badge: fragment of another version of Cat 216-7, the face being more ape-like. H. 24 mm. Given by Mr I. Smith. *200l/1987* **Fig 306**

Fragments of three other versions of this badge have also been found at Salisbury (pc) and many more have turned up at London (e.g. London Museum 1940, pl lxxiv, 60; pl lxxii, 49, where the creature is wrongly described as a woodwose. Woodwoses depicted on badges are consistent with those in other media). One of them (Museum of London 8717) is almost identical to the first of the Salisbury finds catalogued here, while another comes from an archaeological context at Swan Lane dated shortly after 1422. Another entirely complete specimen, very closely related to Cat 216-8, has recently been found in the Oosterschelde at Reimerswaal in the Netherlands (Fig 307; pc) while another badge of the same subject, but from an entirely different design, has been recovered from the site of Nieuwlande (Bergen op Zoom 1987, p 52). The various components of this grotesque scene, the mortar and pestle, the hood and the fish, are all well-known medieval sexual symbols (Wagner 1937; Jones forthcoming) and, here too, might well be construed as having a sexual connotation. The constant association of urine with the diagnostic technique of medieval doctors and of the mortar and pestle with the work of the apothecary make it more likely, however, that the ape has taken on the role of a doctor. If his hood can be interpreted as a cowl, then he is very probably burlesquing a monk physician. In that case, the back of the slippery fish on which the physician is precariously standing may underline the insecure basis of his remedies.

The image is one that could well have escaped from the grotesques inhabiting the borders of Gothic manuscripts. Here apes are more conspicuous than any other animal, usually parodying reality and poking fun at human actions particularly among the upper levels of society. From the middle of the fourteenth century there are numerous examples of ape-physicians peering diagnostically at urinals, administering remedies and preparing them, by pounding with outsize pestles and mortars (Janson 1952, p 168; Randall 1966, figs 56-7). The badges' implied criticism of physicians is consistent with the propaganda put about at many shrines, where, in contrast to the miraculous cures afforded by a saint, ordinary doctors were held up as expensive failures. 'Thomas is the best doctor of the worthy sick' was the claim moulded on pewter ampullae sold to Canterbury pilgrims in the thirteenth century. In the fourteenth century William Langland railed against 'false fisiciens that helpen men to die' and in 1464 Margaret Paston wrote anxiously to her husband, 'For Goddys sake be war what medesyns ye take of any fysissyans of London; I schal never trust to hem be cause of your fadr and myn onkyl, whoys sowlys God assoyle' (Gairdner 1904, IV, p 104).

219 Badge: probably an amulet, of coin-like appearance, decorated with a long cross of three strands flory with crowns and fleurs-de-lys in alternate quarters and with the letter A above each fleur and M and E above the crowns. Second half of 15th century. D. 30 mm. Given by Mr W. Wareham. *143/1978* **Fig 308**

Although the badge is reminiscent of the reverse types of many French jettons, the design is probably not based on any single jetton but, like the jettons themselves, is derived ultimately from the gold coinage of Philip IV to Philip VI. The general design is closest to the *petit royal* or *demi-masse* of Philip IV (1295-1302), but the stylistic treatment of the crowns, the lys, the leaves on the cross-ends and even the lettering suggests that the badge dates from *c.*1450. On the wearing of coins and coin-like badges for magical purposes, *cf.* Spencer 1978, pp 249, 263 n 71 and Cat 220 below.

220 Badge or amulet in the form of a pendent purse containing a coin. The purse, covered with a lattice-pattern of pierced quatrefoils, is represented with tasseled draw-strings and with a further tassel at the base. When found, the purse contained a jetton-like, imitation coin, also of tin-lead alloy, with the arms of England on one side. Each side of the pendant was cast separately in the same, open mould. The pair were then soldered together continuously along the top edge (including the loop) and at two spots on the base, leaving a slender gap at the sides through which a coin, genuine as well as imitation, could be inserted. Early 15th century. H. 49 mm; diam. of coin, 17 mm. *218/1987* **Fig 309**

A similar coin was found inside a purse-badge recovered from fifteenth-century dumps on the site of the City of London Boys' School (1986); the purse has two loops (*cf.* Fig 310) to which a pair of elongated pewter links are still attached. A similar but narrower purse-pendant found in St Saviour's Dock, Bermondsey (1988), holds a slightly smaller pewter coin with degenerate markings.

The pendant was probably worn for magical reasons in the hope that it would attract wealth to its wearer. A badge in the Museum of London (no 85.428/1) depicting an open purse is inscribed *grommerci* (= *grant merci*, God give me great reward); another (no 80.248/1) shows a purse full to the brim with pennies. Although impoverished pilgrims might rely on charity, realists recognised that well-filled purses, like those celebrated in the badges, were the traveller's best friend. This is the repeated refrain of a fifteenth-century poem (Greene 1935, pp 260-1):

> In euery plas qwere I wende
> My purse is my owne frende;
> Therfor gladly may I syng,
> 'Gramercy my own purse'.

Broadly the same message is conveyed by the contemporary poem, London Lickpenny, which tells of the plight of an impecunious countryman on a visit to the capital; here the antithetical line 'But for lack of money I could not speed' reverberates like a litany throughout.

As suggested above (Cat 208), the Salisbury purse may have been worn in conjunction with a small brooch, like that in Fig 284. Another pendent purse found at Salisbury and illustrated in Fig 310 (pc) differs from Cat 220 in having two suspension loops. Examples of the badge found elsewhere sometimes have three tassels at the base (*cf.* Cat 222).

The arms on the imitation coin appear to be those of the period 1340-*c.*1406, a date consistent with the early 15th century archaeological context of another example of the badge discovered at Swan Lane, London. This date rules out an earlier suggestion (Spencer 1978, pp 246-7, 255-7) that this type of pendant might have been a souvenir of the pilgrimage to the tomb of Henry VI (*cf.* Figs 155-6). There nevertheless exist a number of smaller purse-badges with frames or bars of late fifteenth-century forms (*ibid.*, Fig 4, nos 73, 75). One from Salisbury with its purse-frame represented as hanging from a square brooch is illustrated in Seaby 1987, pl V354A. Such badges might still have been connected with the cult of Henry VI (*cf.* Cat 116).

221 Badge or amulet: part of an openwork purse decorated with beaded lattice-work. 15th century. H. 23 mm. Given by Mr M. Snell. *101/1987* **Fig 311**

The fragment comes from near the top of the type of pendant illustrated in Fig 312 (from the Thames foreshore at Southwark Bridge, south side). This, like Cat 220, is made up of a separate back and front, but here the suspension loops are at the sides and the purse is pear-shaped, with a circular aperture at the centre.

222 Badge or love-token: a pendant in the form of a purse of trapezoid shape, moulded in the round and depicted with tasseled drawstrings and three tassels at the base. On the front is shown a flowering heart. 15th century. H. 29 mm. *106/1987* **Fig 313**

A few pilgrim souvenirs, both ampullae and pilgrim signs, incorporate the flowering heart device as a symbol of heavenly love (Spencer 1980, p 24). But the motif was probably used much more often to suggest earthly love. It is a recurrent feature of fifteenth-century betrothal and wedding rings, for example, and was there intended both to express love and to invite reciprocal feelings. Nicholas Wyfold, grocer and alderman of London, who died in 1456, had a seal with a flowering heart and the motto 'a Luy Dere Hert'. Generally with three separate flowers though sometimes with many more, the flowering heart was frequently the subject of pewter badges (e.g. Smith 1857, pl XXVIII, fig 7; University Museum, Cambridge 22.781), which were manifestly lovers' tokens and include two examples found at Salisbury; for one of them see Mitchiner 1986, p 175, where it is classified as a pilgrim badge from Bromholm. The other heart (pc), which has lost all but the base of the flower stalks, has a scroll marked *amovrs* threaded through the middle. Another badge from Salisbury which belongs unmistakably to this class takes the form of a crowned heart with a scroll inscribed *herte be trewe* (Mitchiner 1986, p 126, where the legend is totally misread). The same inscription also occurs on the following Salisbury find:

223 Badge or lover's token: a hand holding a heart which is inscribed *hert be true.* 15th century. H. 33 mm. *225h/1987* **Fig 314**

More complete copies of this badge found elsewhere show that the hand is the hand of God, issuing from heraldic, nebuly clouds and beams of sunlight or radiance. The same conflation of religious and personal sentiment, that is also a regular feature of, say, some fifteenth-century posy rings, is to be found on several other base metal love tokens, such as the mid fourteenth-century brooch in Fig 315 (found at Billingsgate, London, 1984; *cf.* Bergen op Zoom 1987, pp 54-5 and Mitchiner 1986, p 103, where it is completely misconstrued). Here two arms, one representing the man, and one the woman, meet to support a heart wounded by love's arrow. At the same time they form a crowned letter M, emblem of the Virgin Mary (*cf.* Fig 72). A matrix for producing a similar badge in metal foil occurs on a multiple die-piece, *c.* 1340, found at London (Alexander & Binski, 1987, p 395). Two arms joined in friendly hand-clasp, in a manner reminiscent of the clasped hands of medieval love-rings known as *fede* rings, may have belonged to another form of trinket that passed on occasion between lovers at Salisbury:

224 Badge or love token: a fragment depicting two clasped hands emerging from close-buttoned sleeves. 14th or 15th century. W. 38 mm. *209e/1987* **Fig 316**

225 Badge or love token: head and shoulders of a woman with fashionable coiffure, surrounded by a circular frame decorated with dot-and-circle ornament and a pearled edge. Late 14th century. D. 22 mm. *225m/1987* **Fig 317**

There are many comparable badges with stereotyped portraits of women who are entirely lacking in saintly appearance and attributes (e.g. Smith 1848, pl XXXVII, 6; Smith 1852, pl XVI, 8; Spencer 1982, p 315). On three such badges from London, one recovered from the Thames at Queenhithe (1979), the others from spoil removed from the site of Billingsgate lorry-park (1984), the frames are inscribed *love love love.* A triangle of leather found in Karthhuizerwijk, Bruges (1984) is stamped with a similar medallion bearing the words *amor vincit omnia,* love conquers all (Goubitz 1988, pp 147-8). The same amatory motto appeared on the gold brooch worn by the Prioress in Chaucer's *Canterbury Tales,* and is inscribed on several surviving ring-brooches, some of which are of a size used in the fourteenth century for attaching the hose to the braygirdle or suspender-belt.

226 Badge or love token: a right hand, the thumb and a finger joined to make a loop, with cuff and part of buttoned sleeve. 15th or 16th century. W. 29 mm. Mitchiner 1986, p 205. *193n/1987* **Fig 318**

227 Badge or love token identical to Cat 226. *225bb/1987*. Not illustrated.

These badges appear to adopt the form and gesture characteristic of certain hand-shaped amulets that were directed against the evil eye (British Museum 1976, p 225). More complete copies of the badge, however, like that in Fig 319 (MOL 8741), show that a branching stem of at least three four-petalled flowers is being decorously proffered by the hand, which has a twin-hooped lover's ring (a gimmel ring) on the little finger. The flowers are not a new form of Yorkist rose as stated by Mitchiner (*loc.cit.*). Another Salisbury find, retaining one of the flowers, is illustrated in Seaby 1986, pl V196A.

228 Badge or lover's token: a daisy-plant with three large flowers, the two outer ones shown in profile. 15th century. 38 mm. *225aa/1987* **Fig 320**

The purpose of this badge was doubtless purely decorative and amatory. A similar half-opened daisy is wrongly described as a hollow mantle of the Merchant Tailors' Company in Mitchiner 1986, p 243. Any resemblance to the daisy-plant badge (marguerite) of Lady Margaret Beaufort, as depicted, for example, on the west gates of Henry VII's Chapel, Westminster Abbey, is probably fortuitous. Another suitable and somewhat prettier lovers' gift discovered at Salisbury depicts a conventional flowering plant (Fig 321, pc), as symmetrical in habit as the pear-tree depicted on another Salisbury badge (Mitchiner 1986, p 176, where the stiff branches, foliage and fruit are there mistaken for a 'spreading spray of arrows alternating with crossbow bolts' and because of this are wrongly attributed to St Edmund). Another badge or brooch found at Salisbury takes the form of a plant with globular buds or fruit on long stalks (Fig 322; pc). Variants of this badge have been found at King's Lynn and London (Spencer 1980, p 31).

The central portion of another widely-distributed badge, that can also be presumed to be a lover's token (Jones forthcoming), has also turned up at Salisbury (pc) and is here represented by means of an identical and virtually intact specimen from London (Fig 323; MOL, 80.70/6; see also Spencer

1980, p 32). The badge shows a violet growing on a grassy bank within an arbour of trees. Another version of the badge excavated at Swan Lane, London, is inscribed *veolit in maye, (?) lady*. This, in turn, invites comparison with a contemporary French badge in the Museum of Decorative Arts, Prague, showing a man and woman sitting beneath a tree, the man proffering his heart, the woman looking distractedly at the garland in her hand, all above the inscription *an : may* (in May) (Koenigsmarková 1987, pl 171). For the medieval poet May was pre-eminently the month of love and the violet was an emblem of true and faithful love. In a fourteenth-century quatrain (Wenzel 1978, pp 159-60), 'true love' is used to describe the flower of that name, Herb Paris (*paris quadrifolia)*, which like the violet in the badge is characteristically set in a Maytime arbour or bower. This is preceded, however, by another reference to true love which may surely be taken also as an allusion to the wearing in hats, hoods, and purses of the sorts of amatory badges considered above:

> 'Trewe loue among men that most is of lette [late]
> In hattes, in hodes, in porses is sette.
> Trewe loue in herbers (arbours) spryngeth in May,
> Bote trewe loue of herte went is away.'

List of Figures of Livery and Secular Badges

* An asterisk denotes an item deposited on loan to the Museum

Fig No	Cat No	Provenance	Accession No	Page
246	187	Salisbury	191j/1987*	106
247	188	Salisbury	225z/1987	106
248	189	Salisbury	190z/1987*	106
249	—	London	MOL	106
250	190	Salisbury	191r/1987*	106
251	191	Salisbury	191u/1987*	107
252	192	Salisbury	191u/1987*	107
253	—	London	pc	107
254	—	Salisbury	pc	107
255	—	Salisbury	pc	107
256	—	Salisbury	Blackburn Museum	107
257	—	Salisbury	pc	107
258	193	Salisbury	191o/1987*	108
259	194	Salisbury	195m/1987*	108
260	195	Salisbury	43/1988	108
261	196	Salisbury	195o/1987*	108
262	—	London	MOL	108
263	197	Salisbury	191v/1987*	109
264	198	Salisbury	193r/1987*	109
265	199	Salisbury	200m/1987	109
266	—	London	pc	109
267	—	Salisbury	pc	109
268	200	Salisbury	225i/1987	109
269	201	Salisbury	225y/1987	110
270	202	Salisbury	190x/1987*	110
271	203	Salisbury	191q/1987*	110
272	204	Salisbury	107/1987	110
273	—	London	pc	110
274	—	Canterbury	pc	110
275	—	London	pc	111
276	205	Salisbury	190y/1987*	111
277	—	London	pc	111
278	—	Salisbury	pc	111
279	—	Salisbury	pc	112
280	—	London	MOL	112
281	206	Salisbury	221/1987	112
282	207	Salisbury	198f/1987	112
283	—	London	BM M & LA	112
284	208	Salisbury	225x/1987	112
285	—	Salisbury	pc	112
286	—	Salisbury	pc	112
287	—	Salisbury	pc	112
288	—	Salisbury	pc	112
289	—	Salisbury	pc	112
290	—	Salisbury	pc	112
291	—	Salisbury	pc	112
292	—	Salisbury	pc	112
293	—	Salisbury	pc	113
294	209	Salisbury	200h/1987	113

Fig No	Cat No	Provenance	Accession No	Page
295	—	Salisbury	pc	113
296	210	Salisbury	200p/1987	113
297	—	London	MOL	113
298	—	London	pc	113
299	211	Salisbury	195n/1987*	113
300	212	Salisbury	191p/1987*	113
301	213	Salisbury	195p/1987*	114
302	—	London	MOL	114
303	215	Salisbury	44/1981	114
304	216	Salisbury	196a/1987*	115
305	217	Salisbury	220/1987	115
306	218	Salisbury	200l/1987	115
307	—	Netherlands	pc	115
308	219	Salisbury	143/1978	116
309	220	Salisbury	218/1987	116
310	—	Salisbury	pc	116
311	221	Salisbury	101/1987	117
312	—	London	pc	117
313	222	Salisbury	106/1987	117
314	223	Salisbury	225h/1987	117
315	—	London	pc	117
316	224	Salisbury	209e/1987	118
317	225	Salisbury	225m/1987	118
318	226	Salisbury	193n/1987*	118
319	—	London	MOL	118
320	228	Salisbury	225aa/1987	118
321	—	Salisbury	pc	118
322	—	Salisbury	pc	118
323	—	London	MOL	118
324	—	Salisbury	pc	9
325	—	Salisbury	pc	9

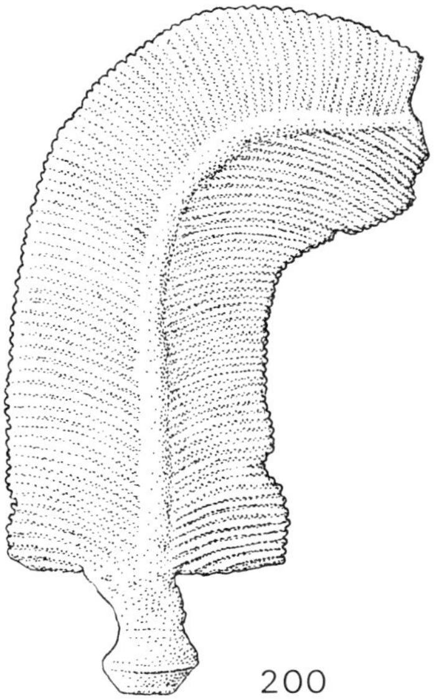

200

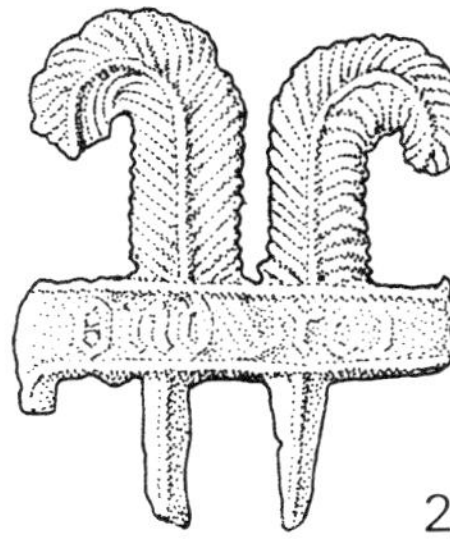

201

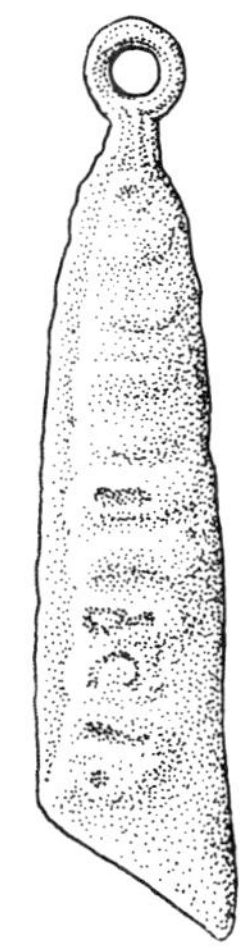

203

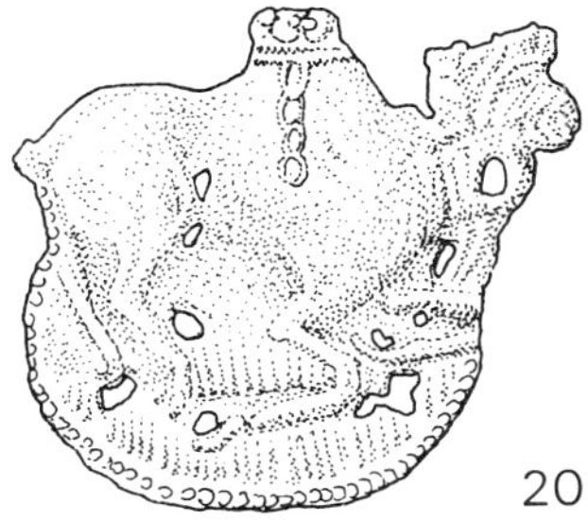

202

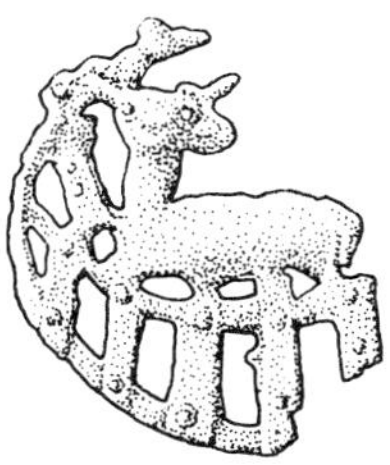

204

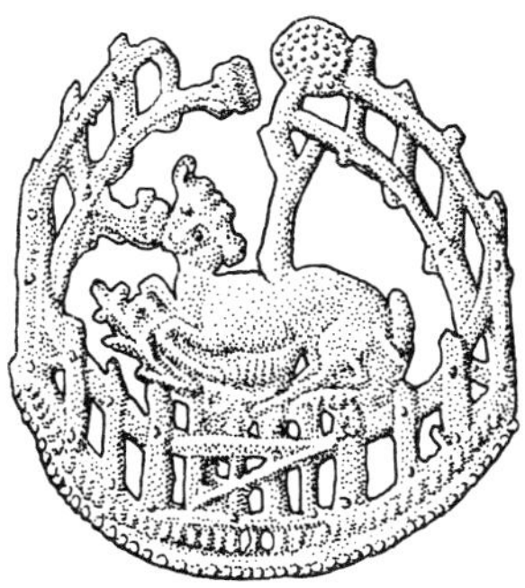

205

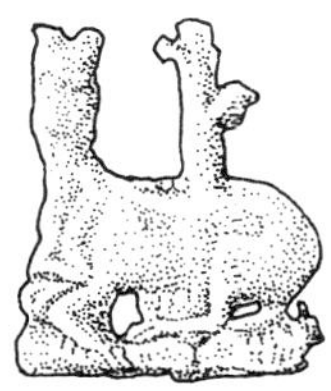

206

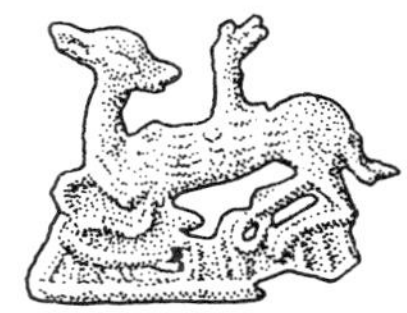

207

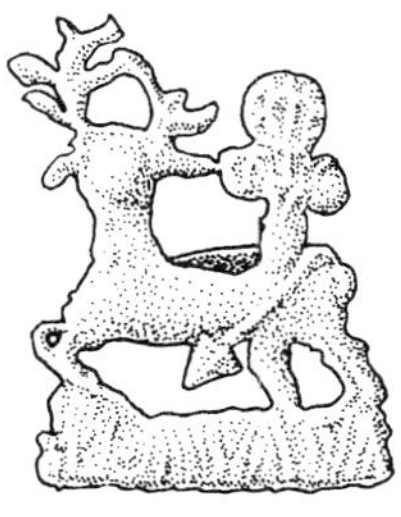

208

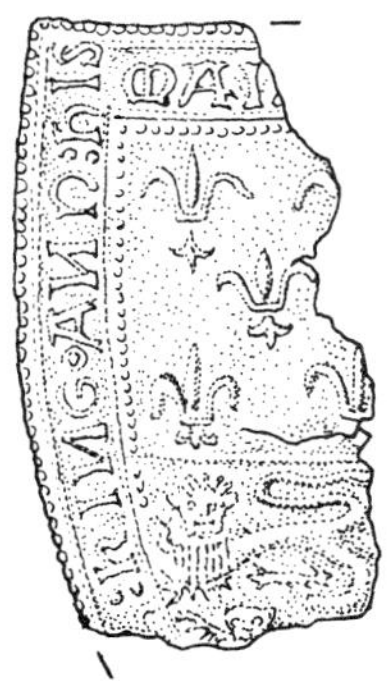

209

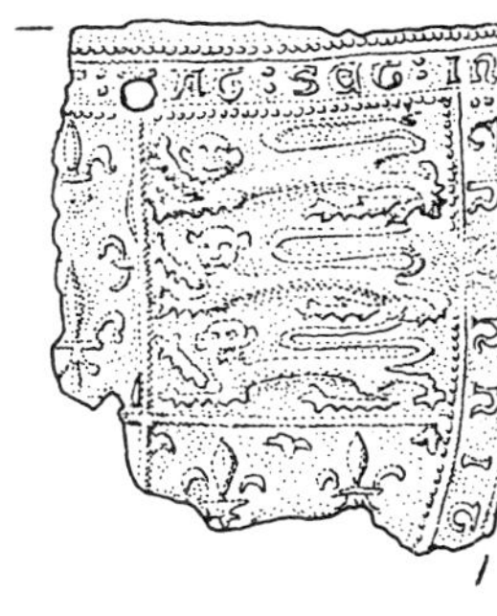

210

Secular badges. Figs 200-210. Scale 1 : 1

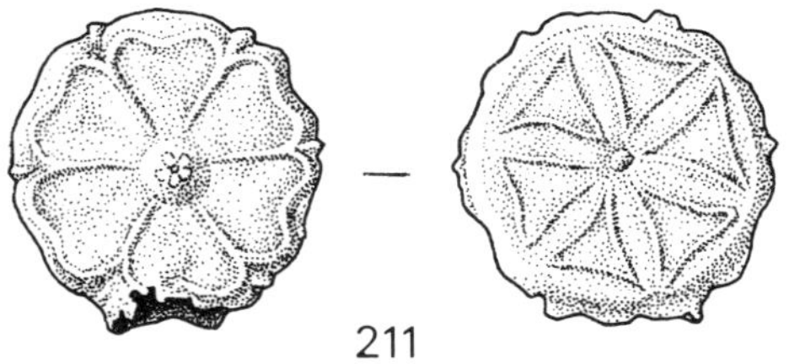
211

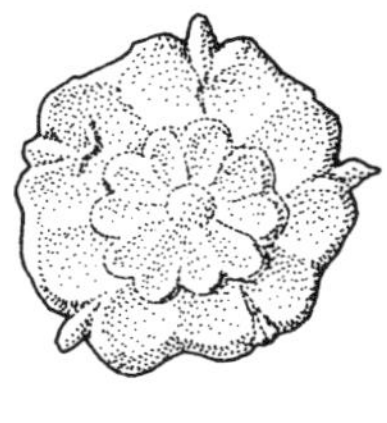
212

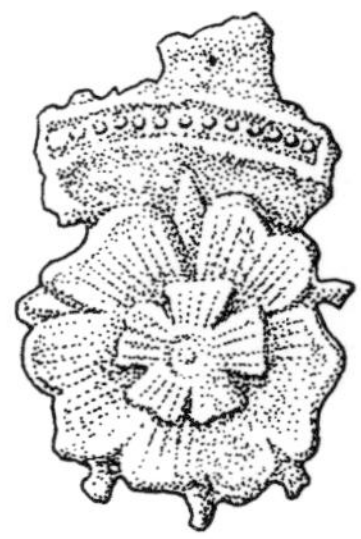
213

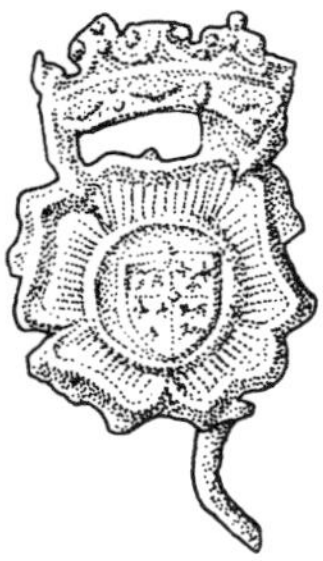
214

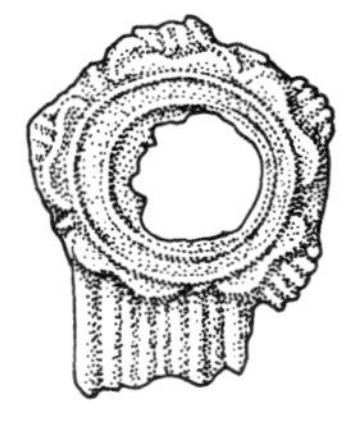
215

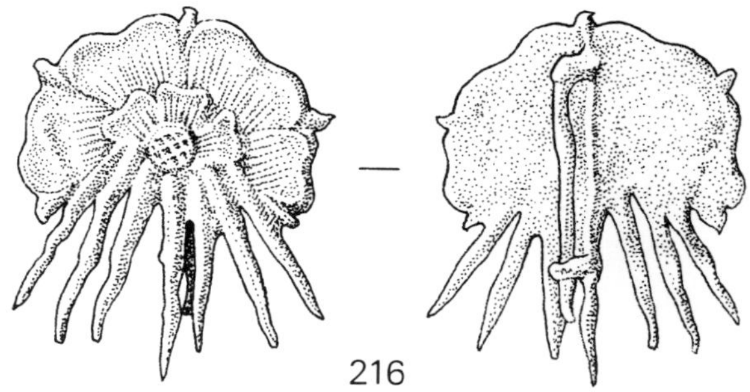
216

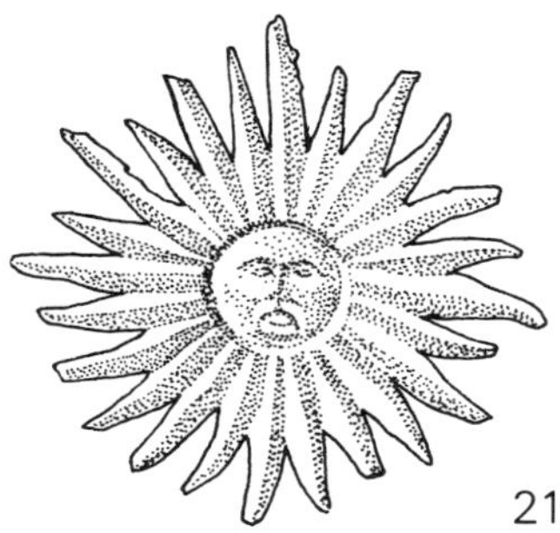
217

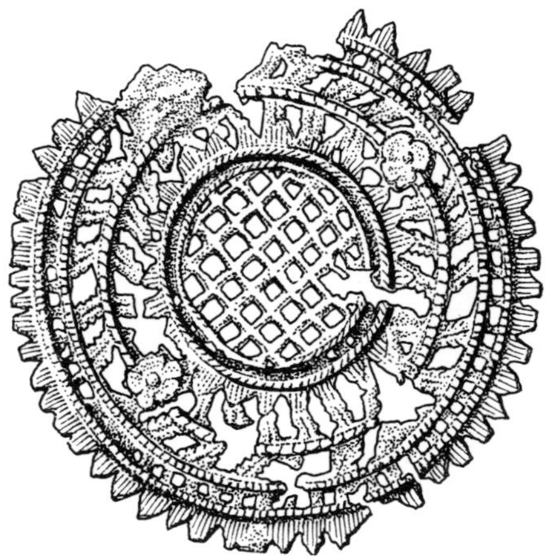
218

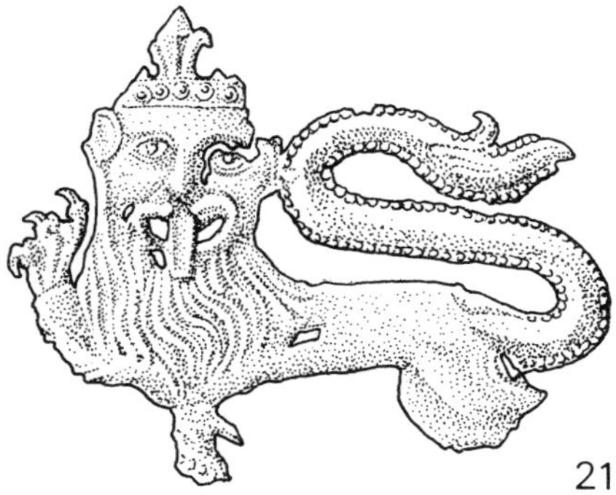
219

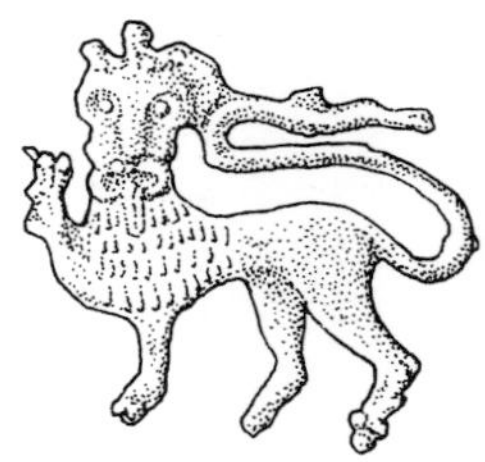
220

Secular badges. Figs 211-220. Scale 1 : 1

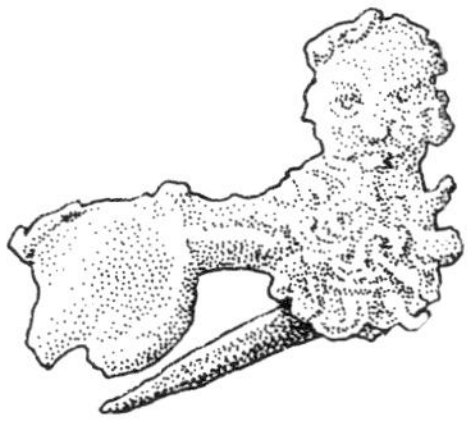

221

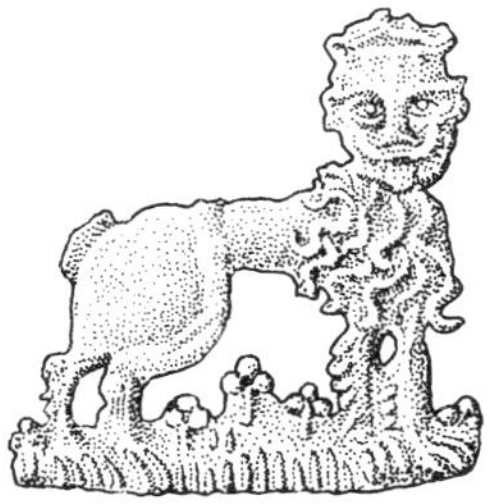

222

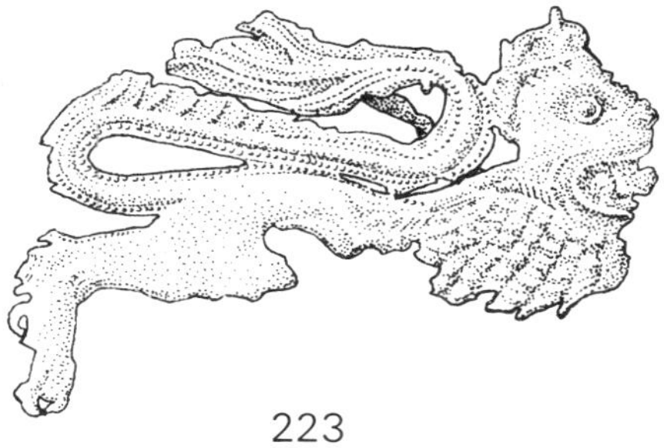

223

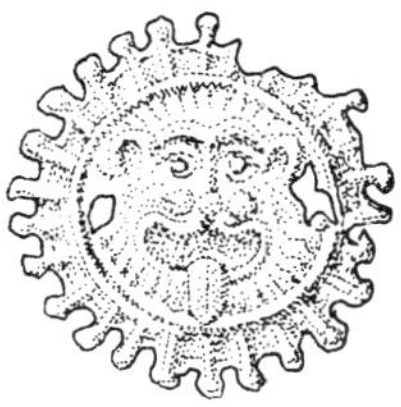

224

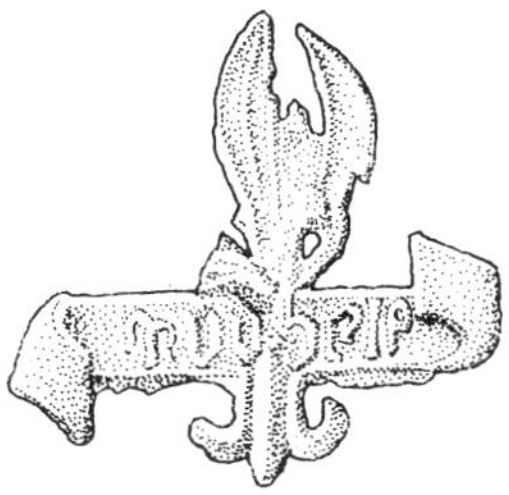

225

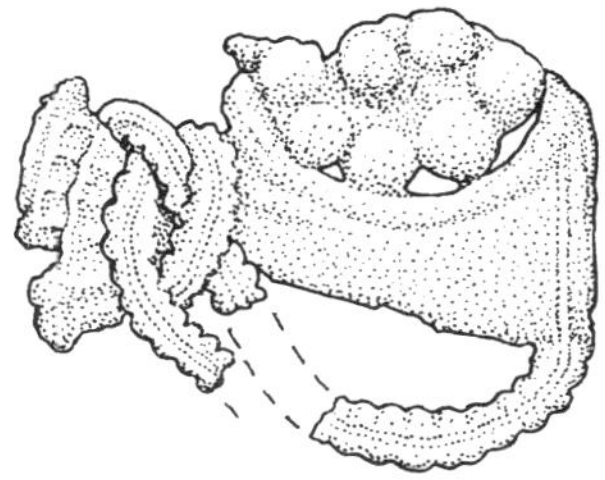

226

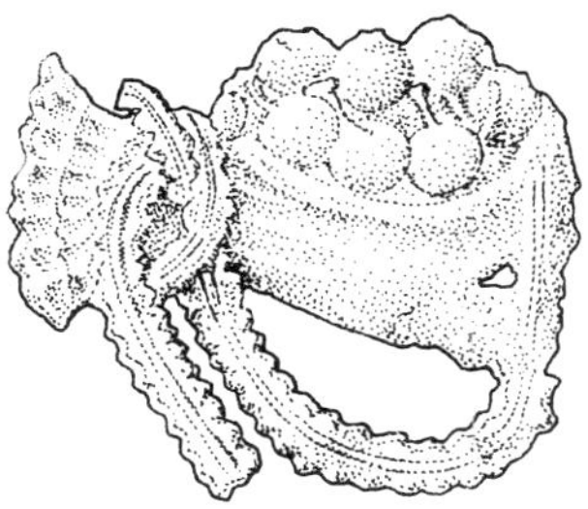

227

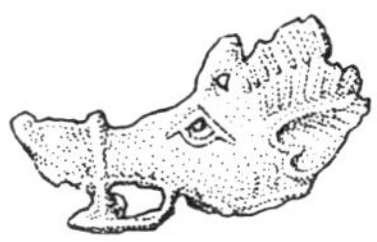

228

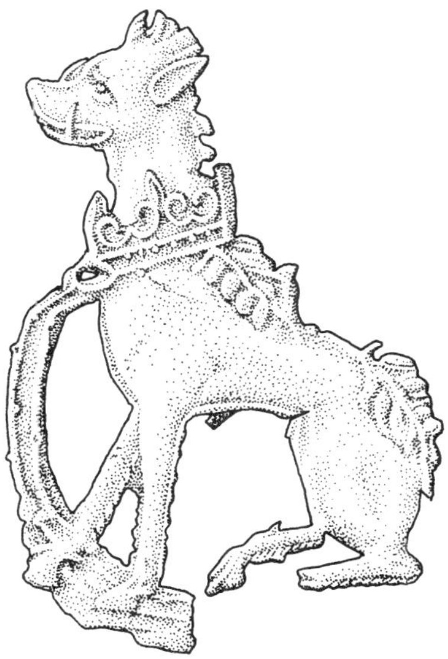

229

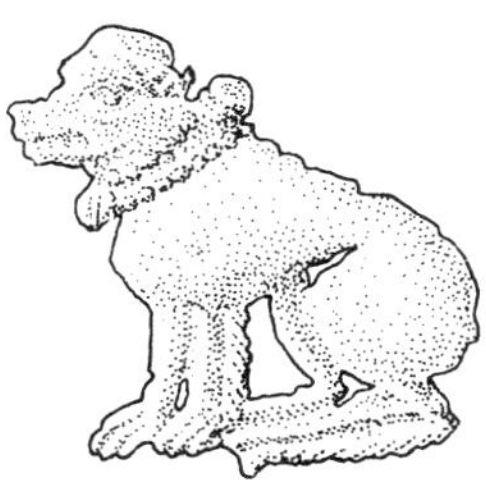

230

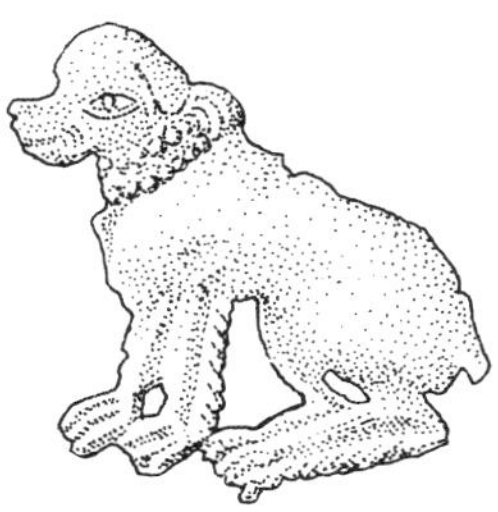

231

Secular badges. Figs 221-231. Scale 1 : 1

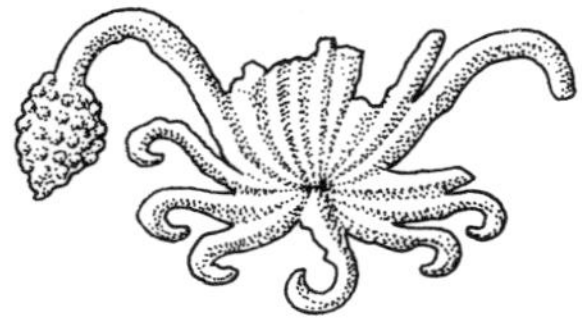
232

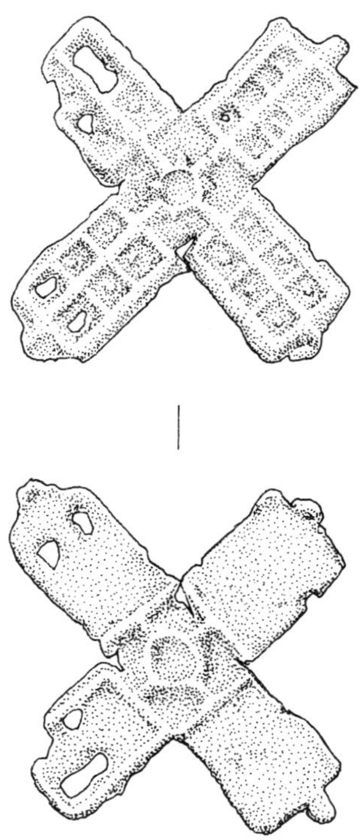

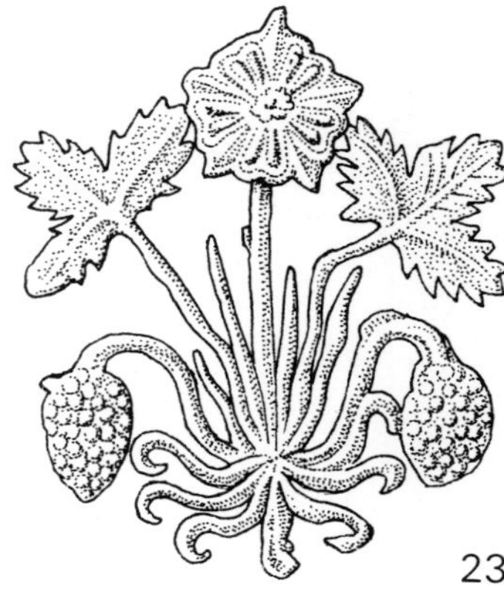
233

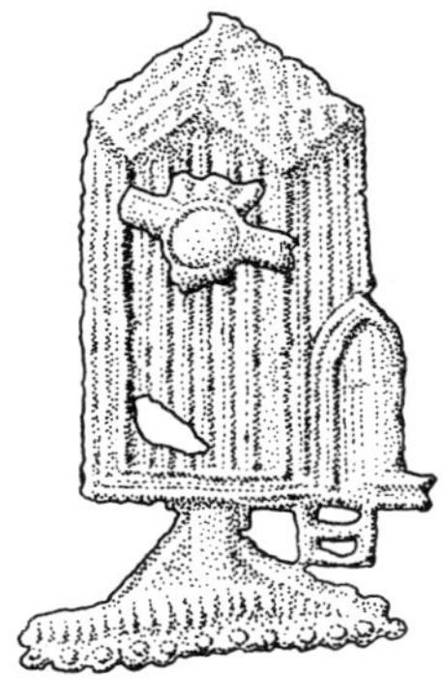
235

234

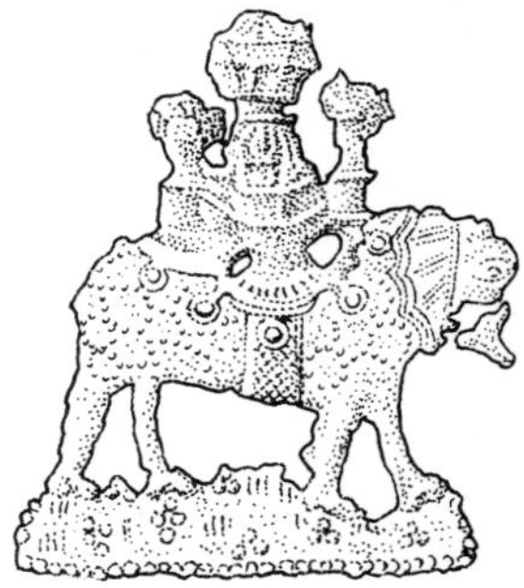
236

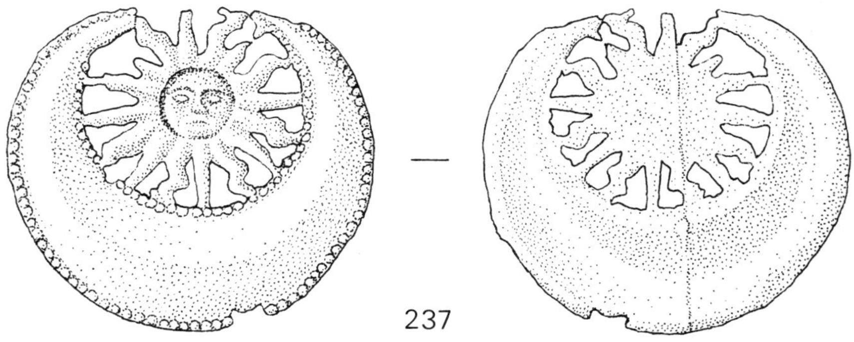
237

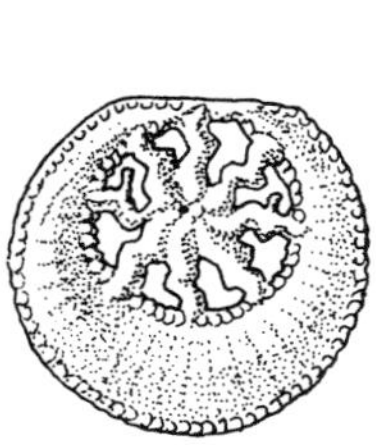
238

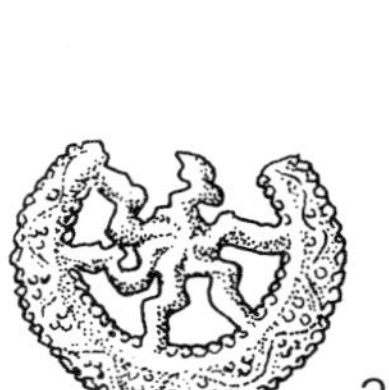
239

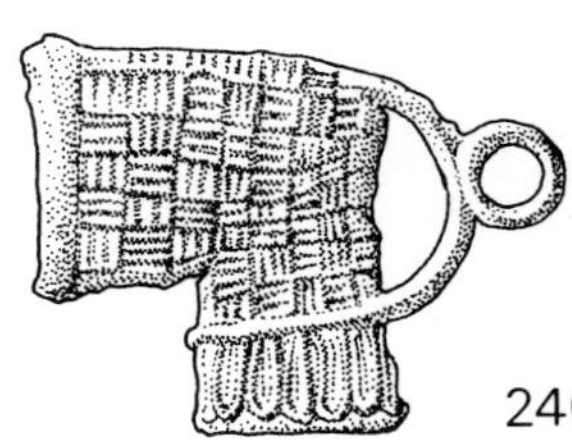
240

Secular badges. Figs 232-240. Scale 1 : 1

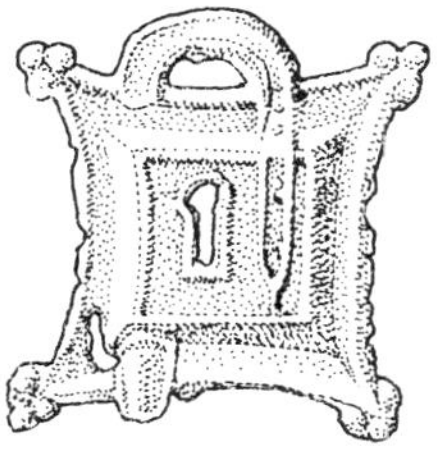

241

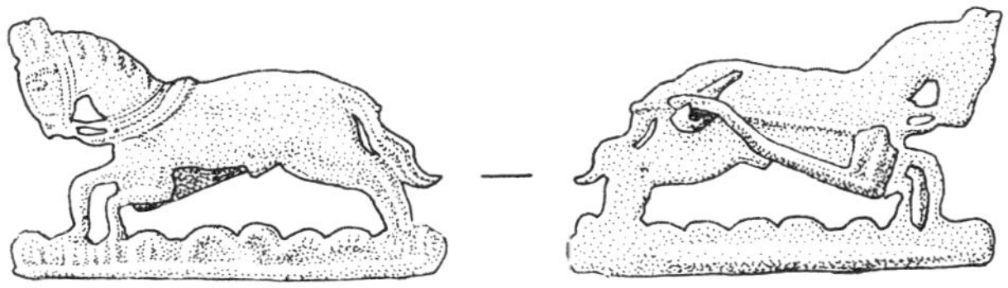

242

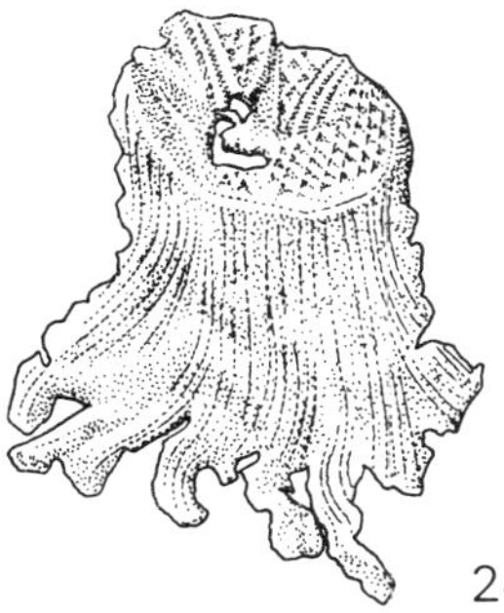

243

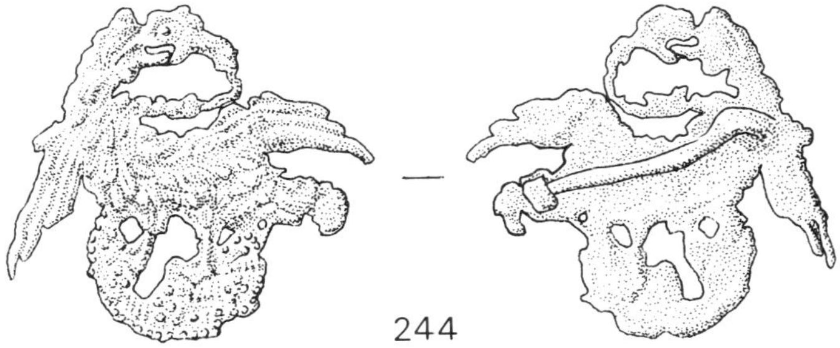

244

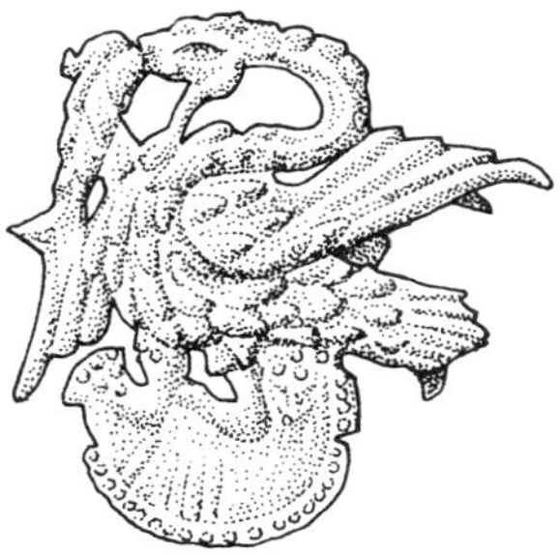

245

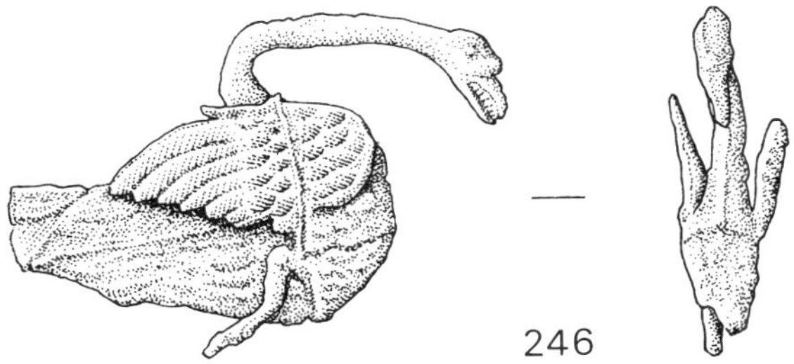

246

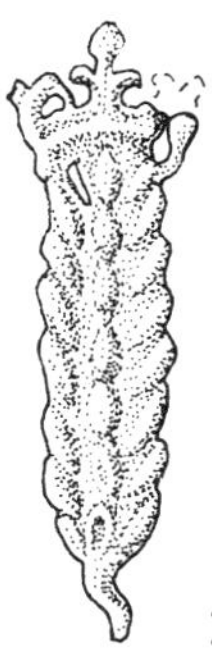

247

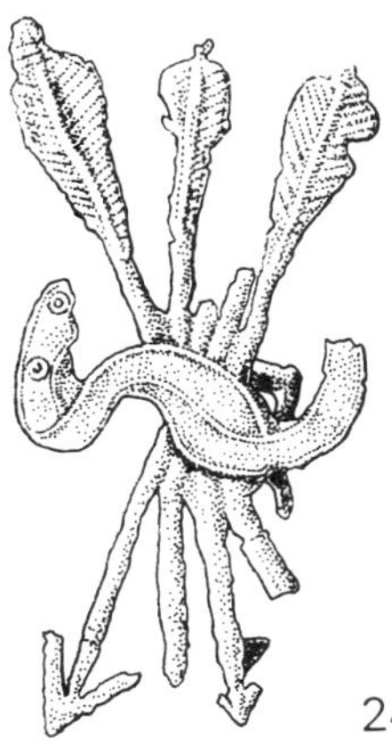

248

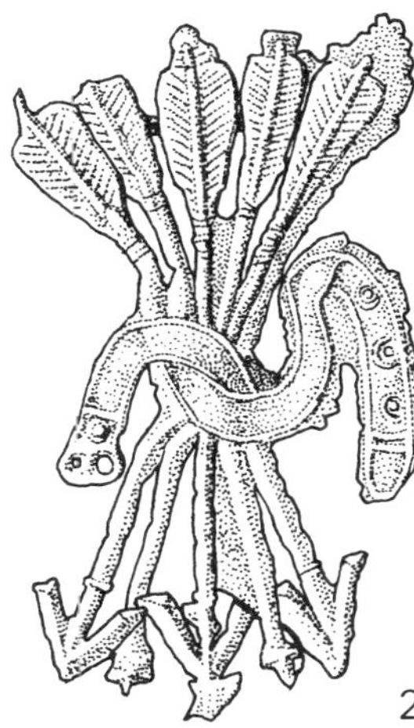

249

Secular badges. Figs 241-249. Scale 1:1

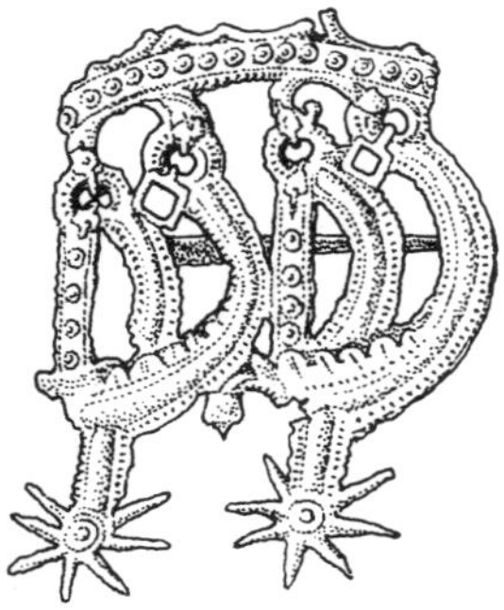
250

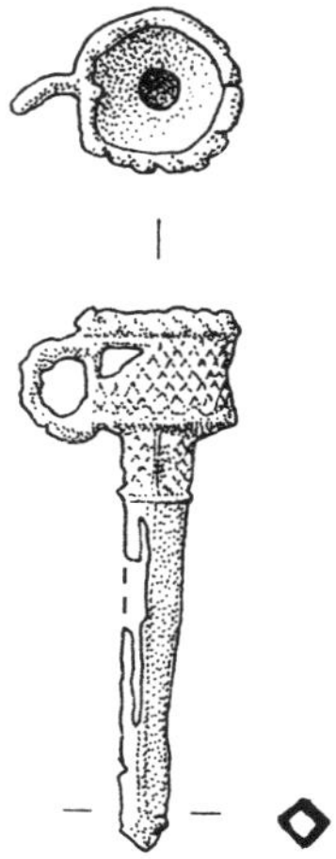
251

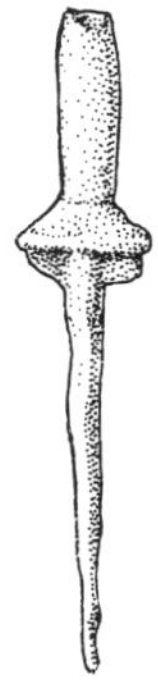
252

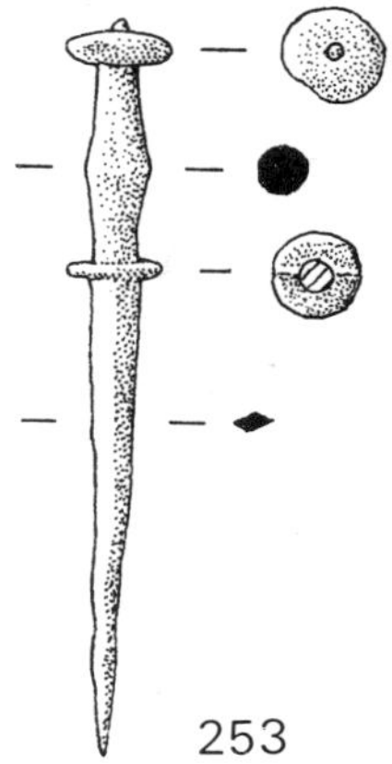
253

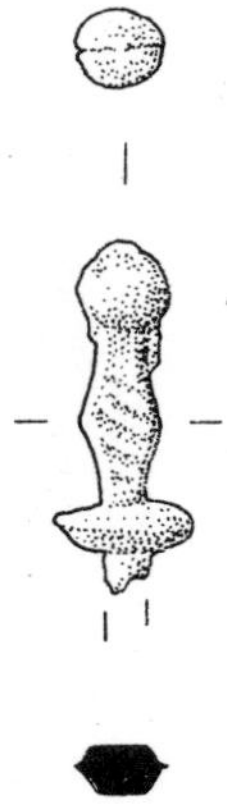
254

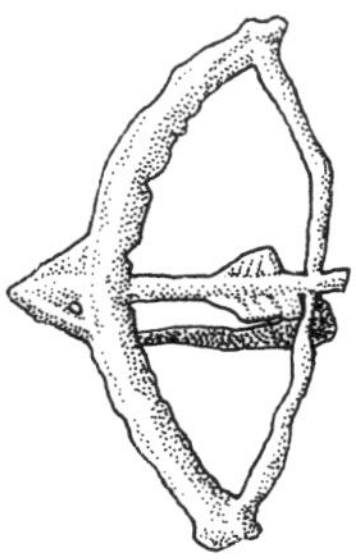
255

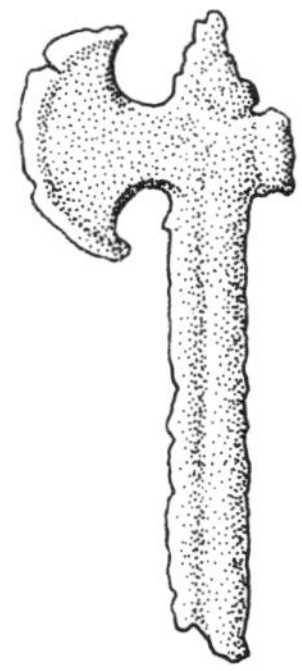
256

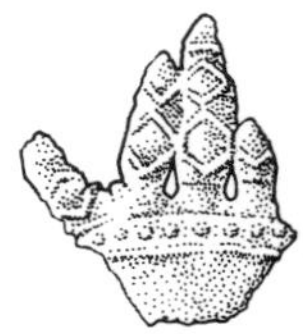
257

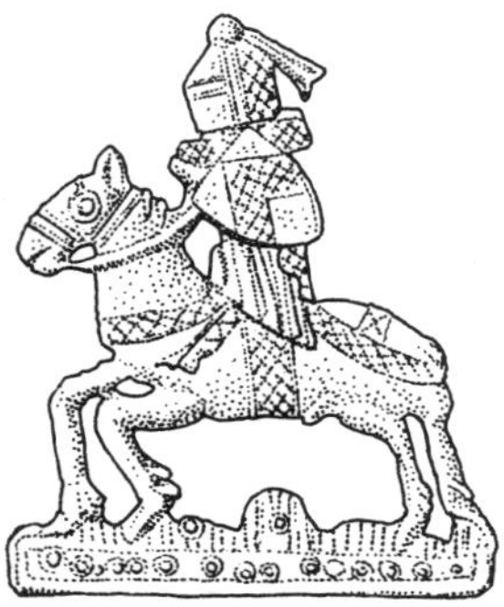
258

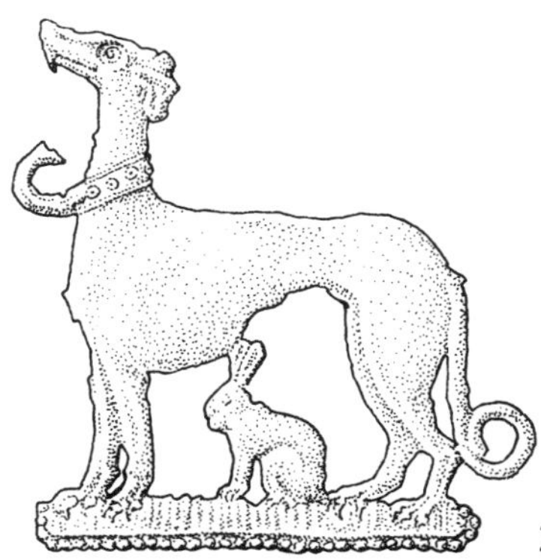
259

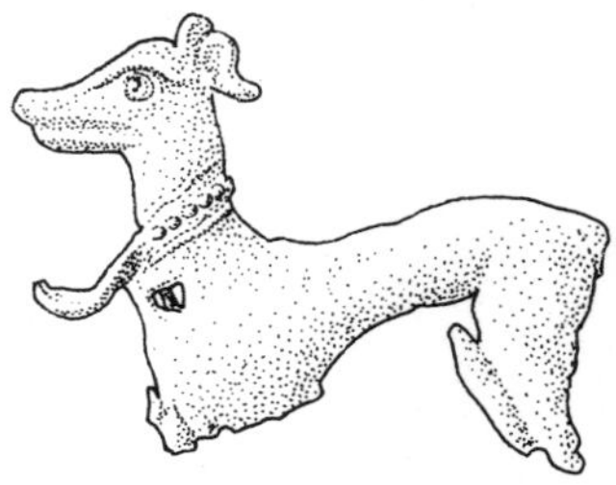
260

Secular badges. Figs 250-260. Scale 1 : 1

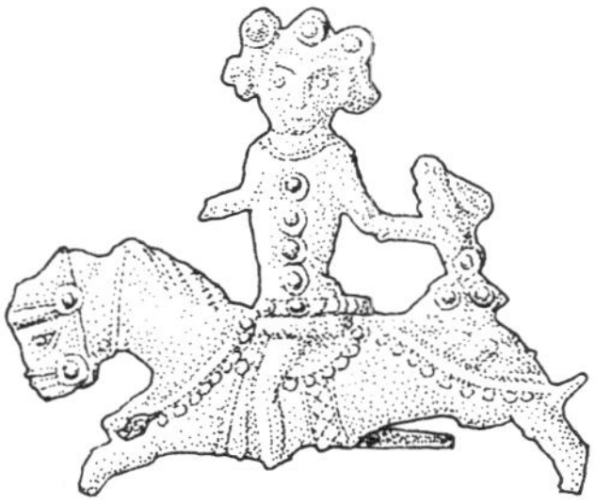

261

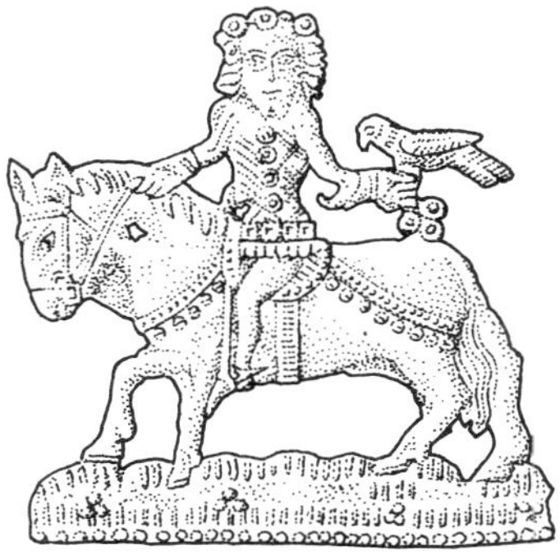

262

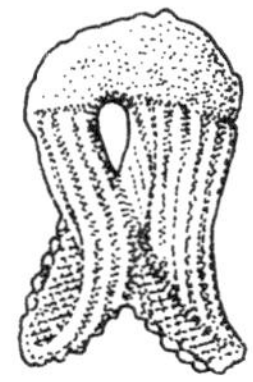

263

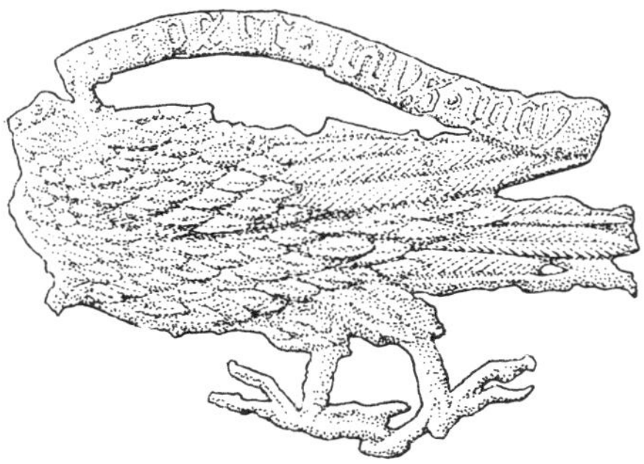

264

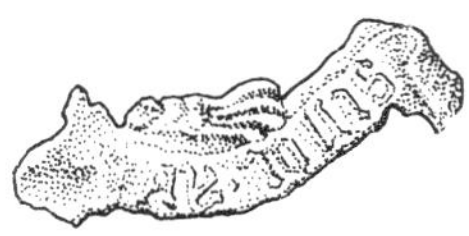

265

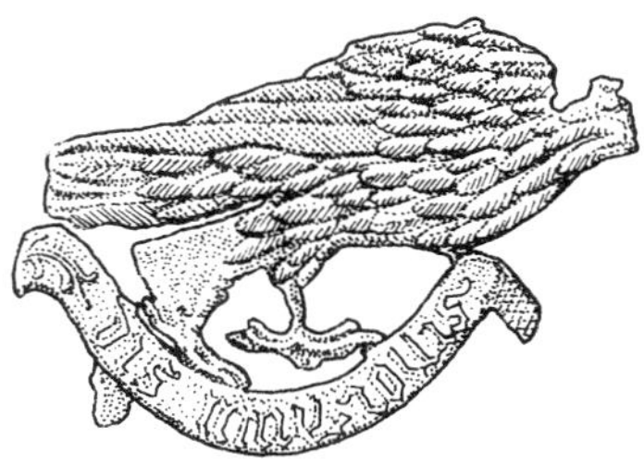

266

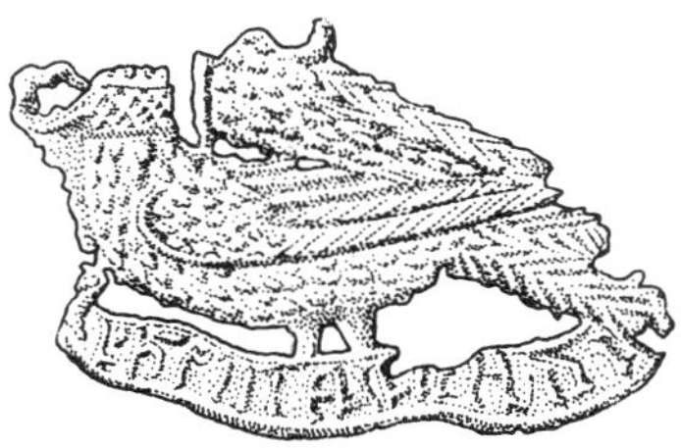

267

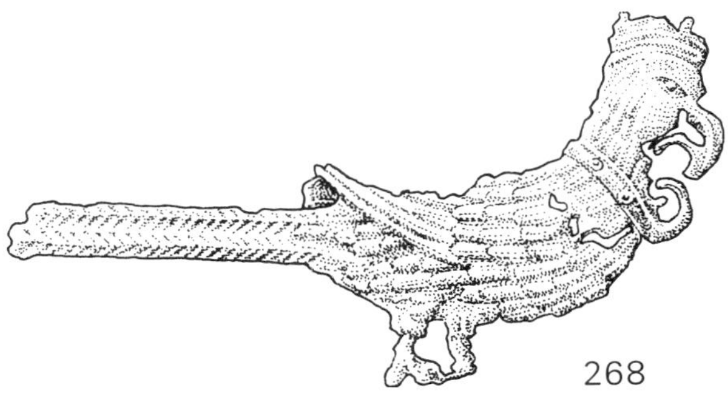

268

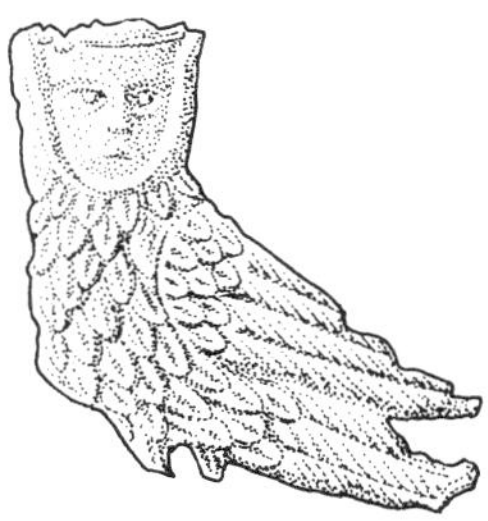

269

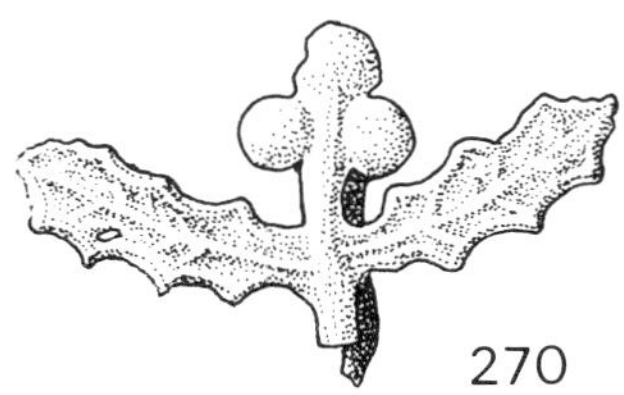

270

Secular badges. Figs 261-270. Scale 1 : 1

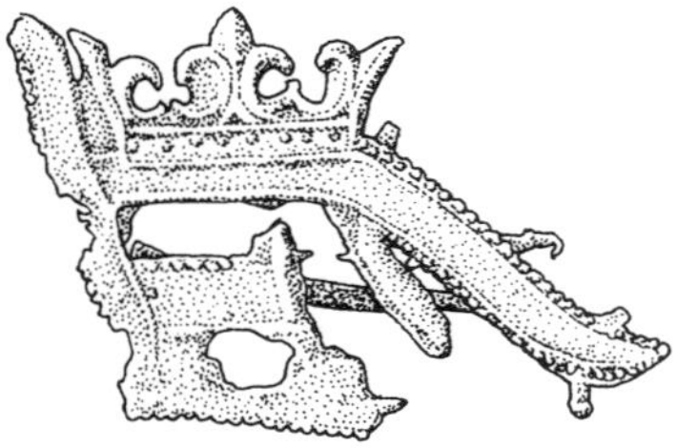
271

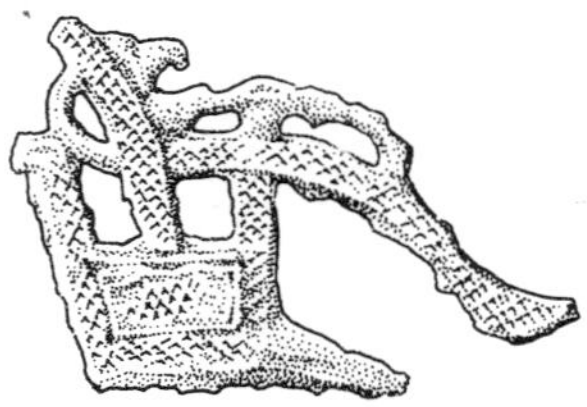
272

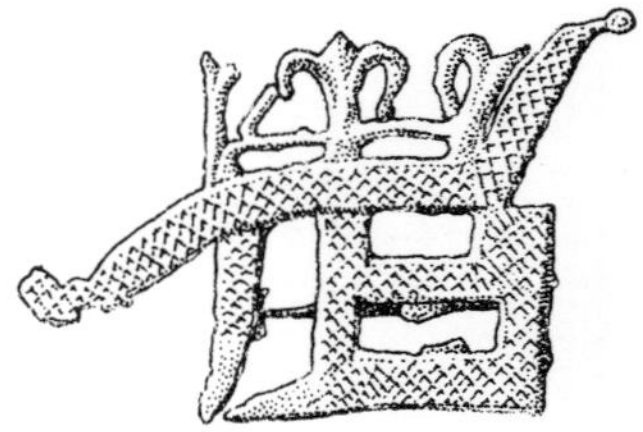
273

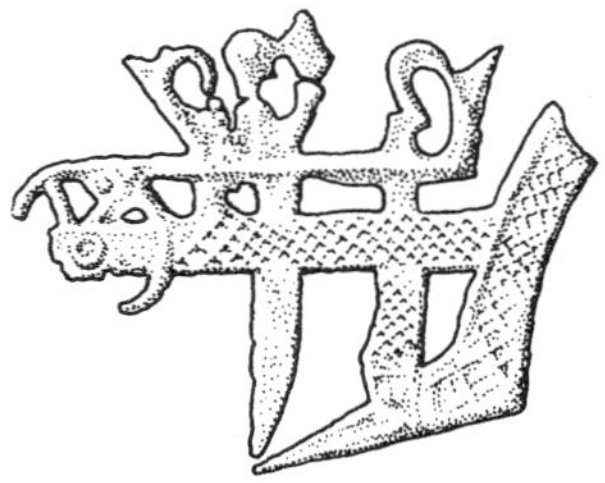
274

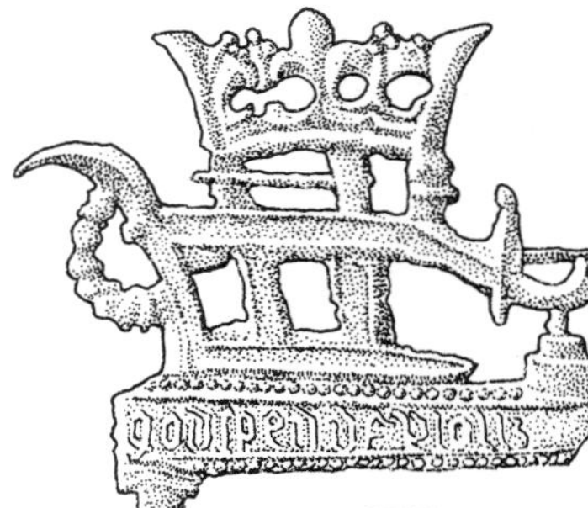
275

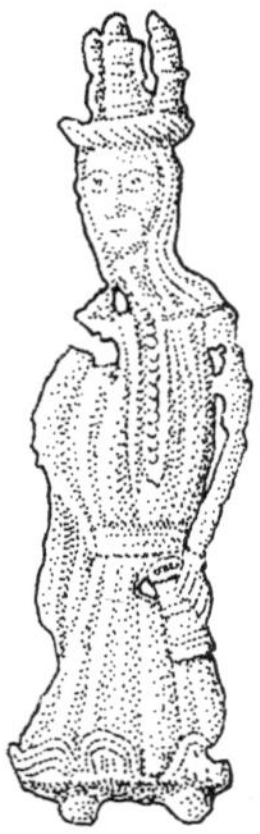
276

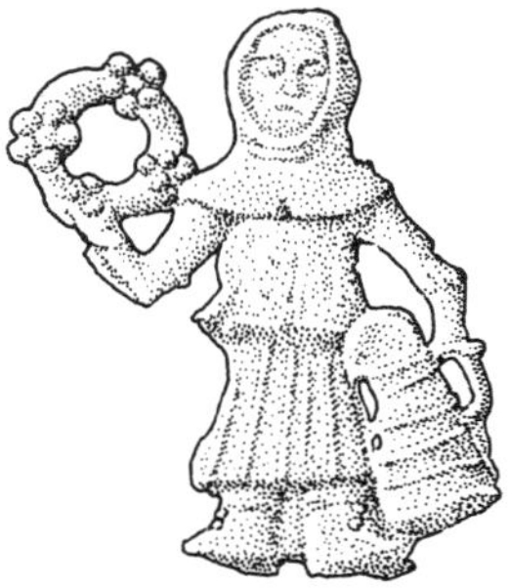
277

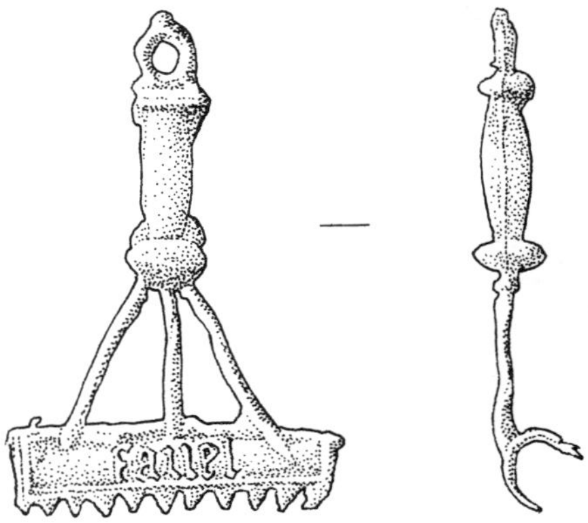
280

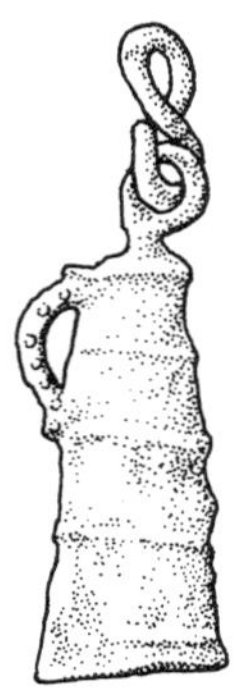
278

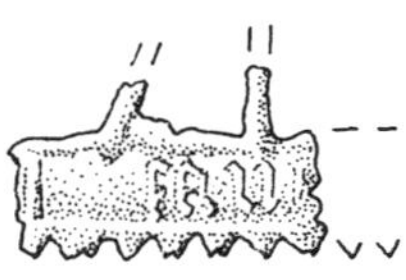
279

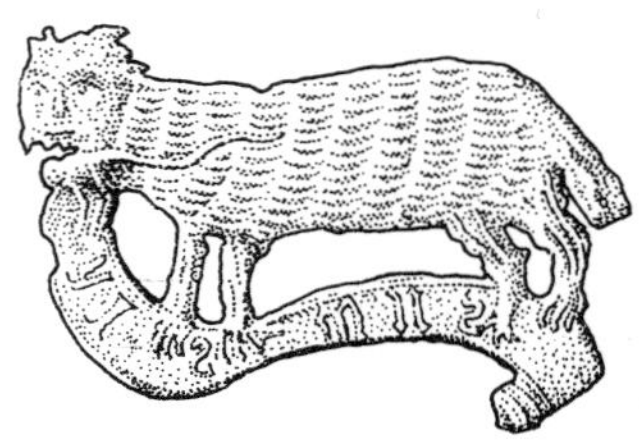
281

Secular badges. Figs 271-281. Scale 1:1

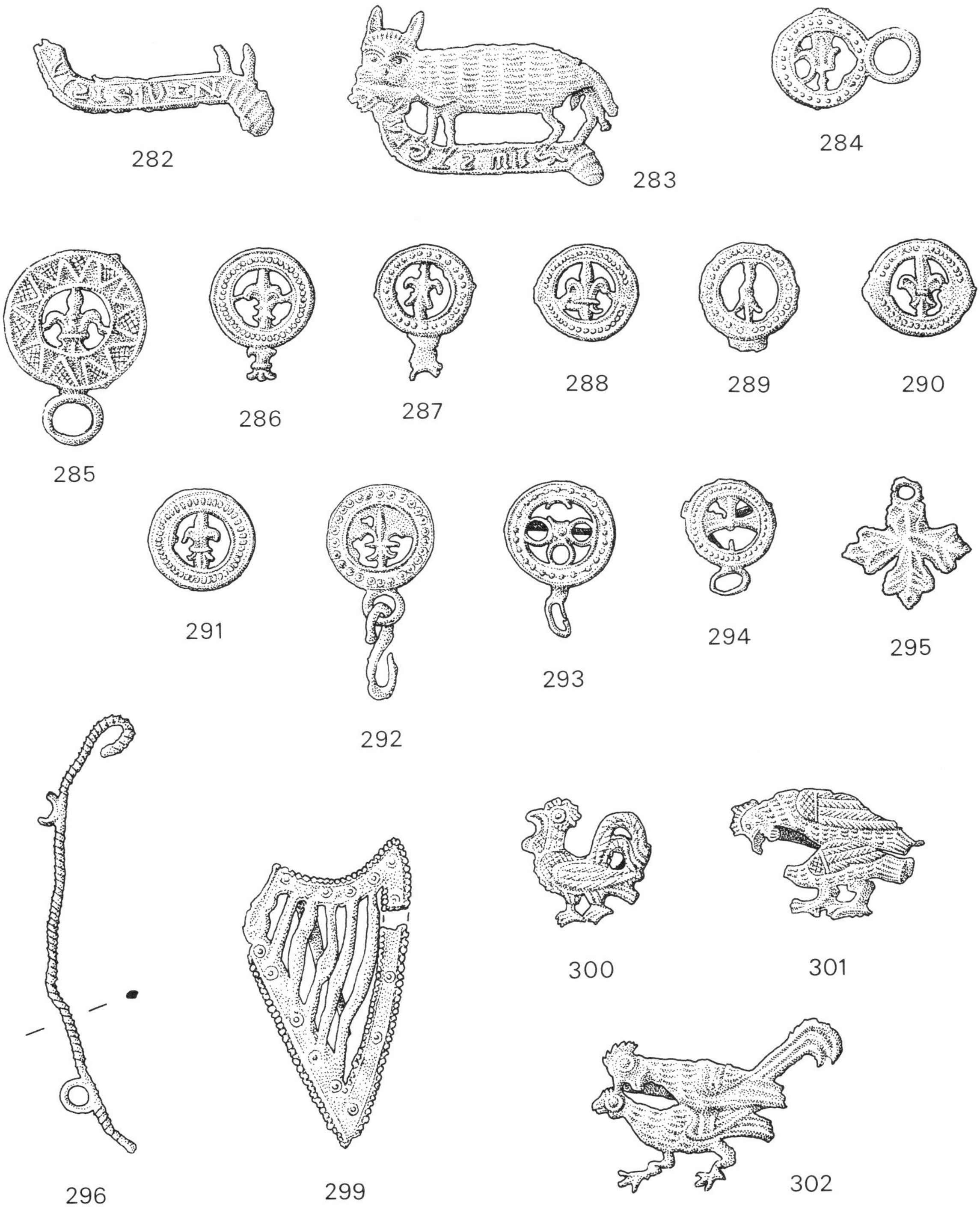

Secular badges. Figs 282-296, 299-302. Scale 1 : 1

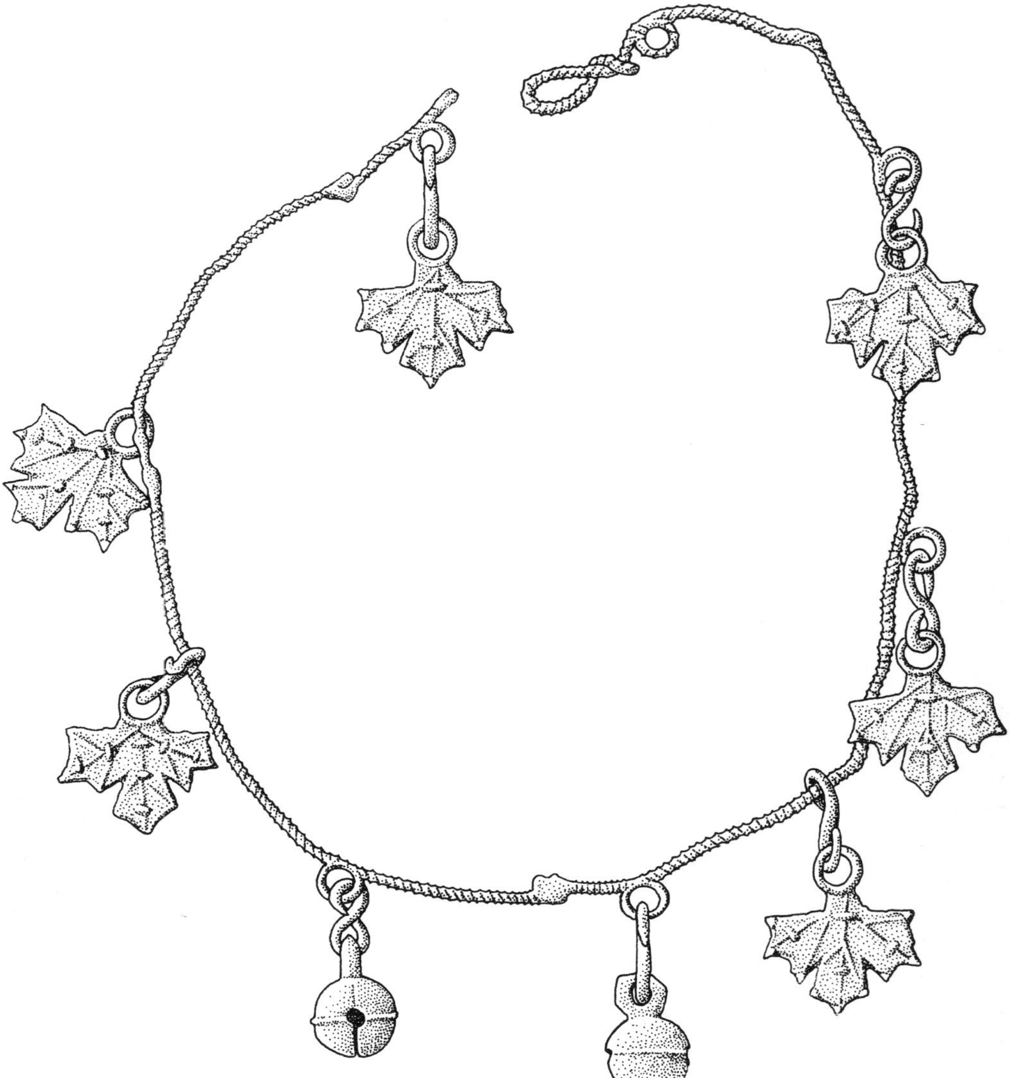

297

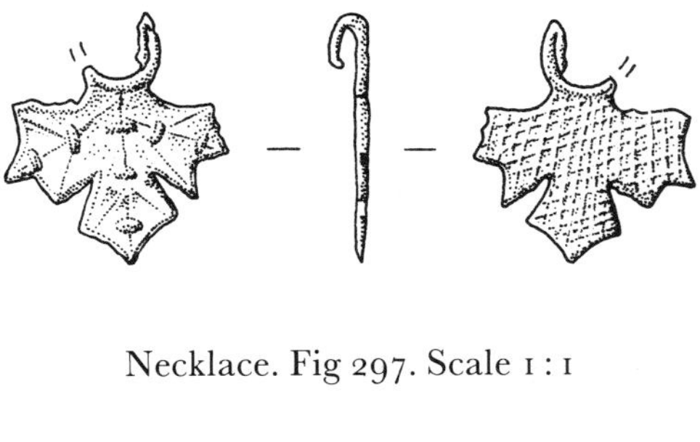

Necklace. Fig 297. Scale 1 : 1

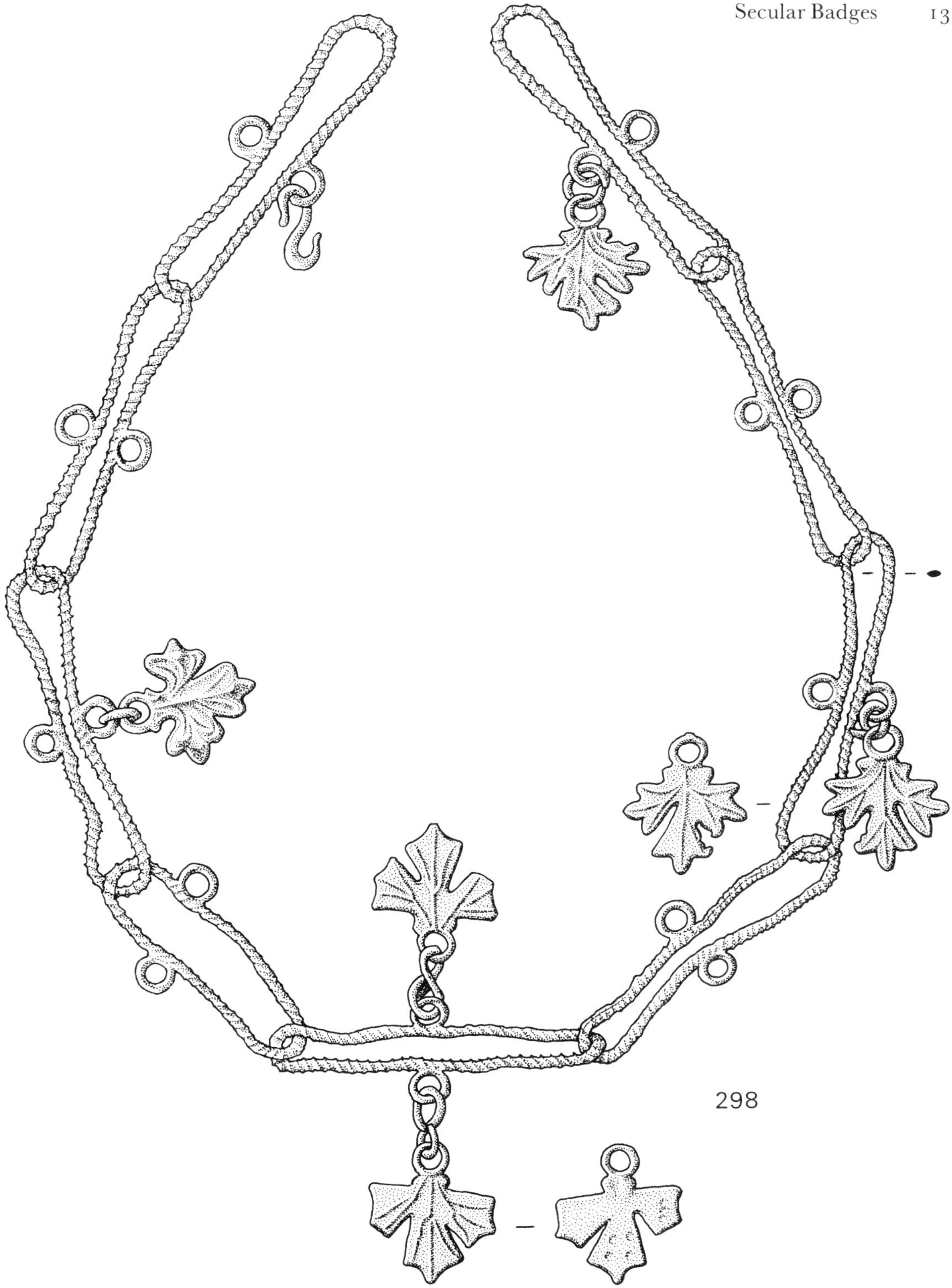

Necklace. Fig 298. Scale 1 : 1

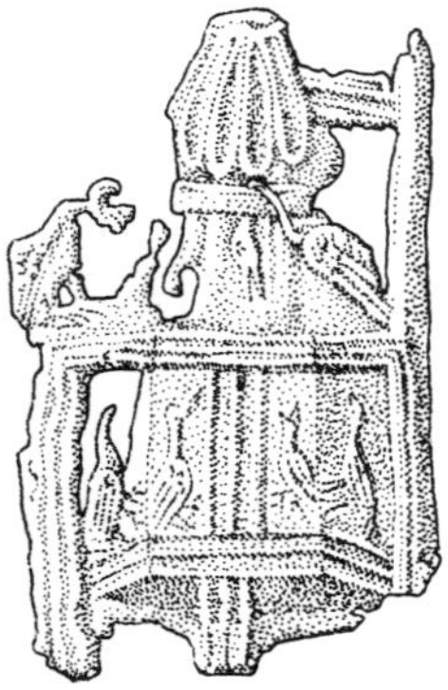

303

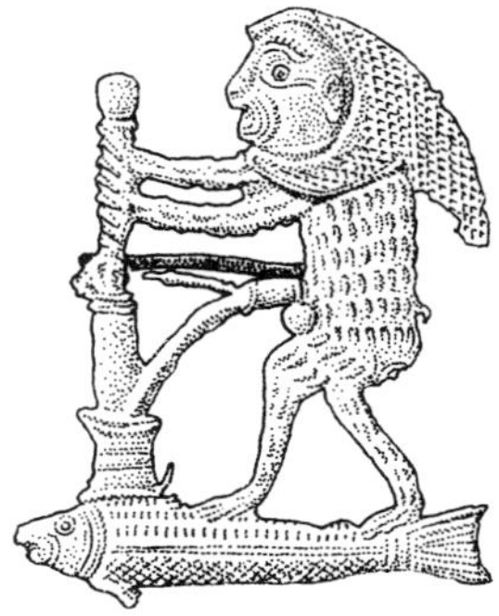

304

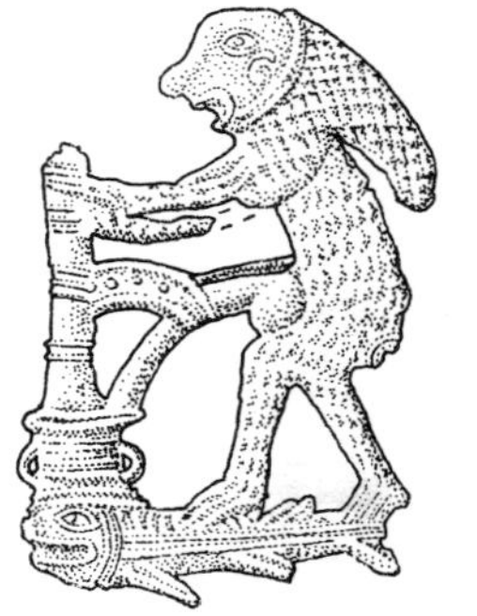

305

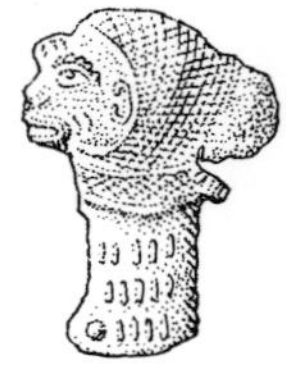

306

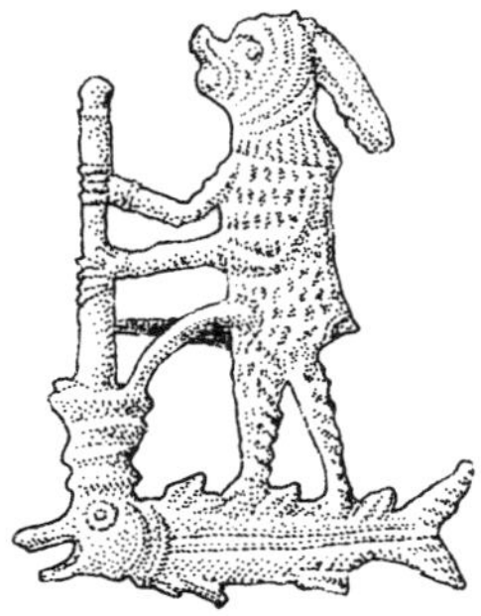

307

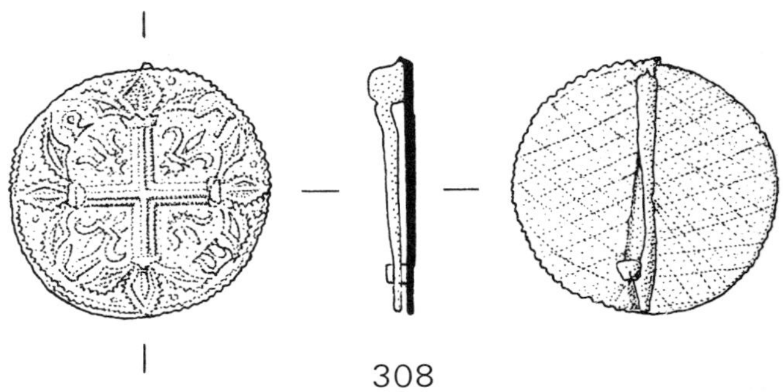

308

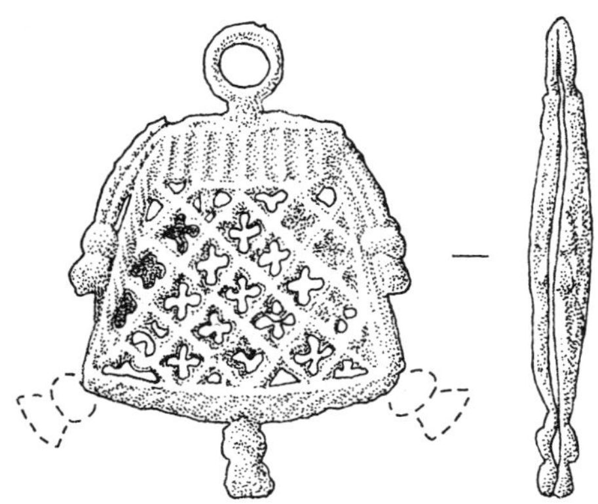

309

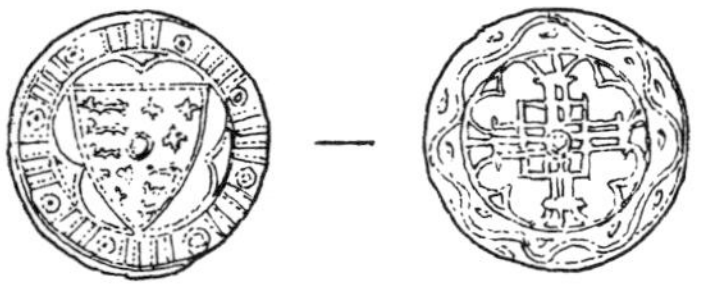

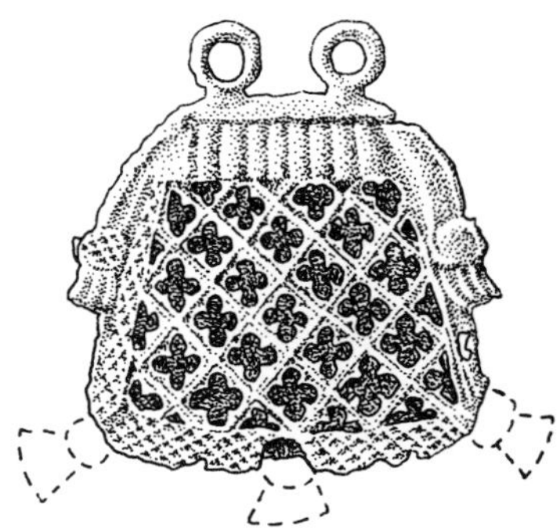

310

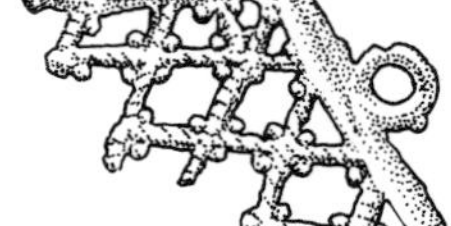

311

Secular badges. Figs 303-311. Scale 1:1

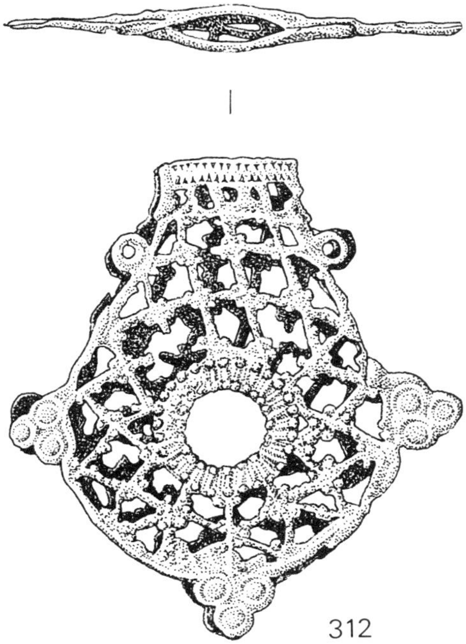

312

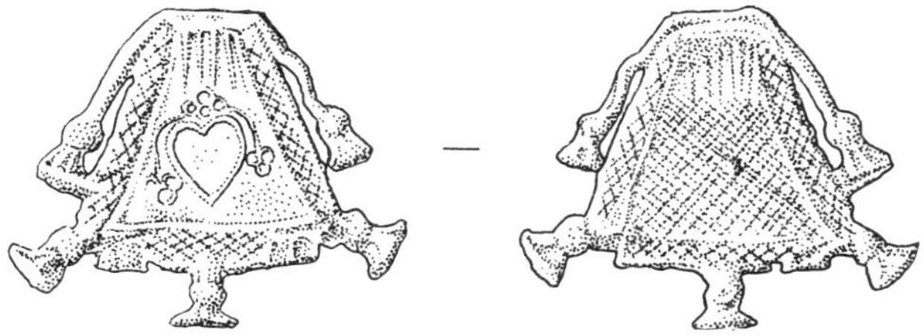

313

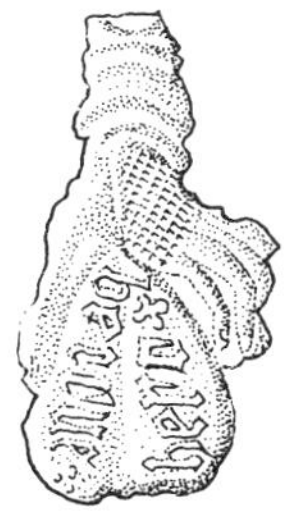

314

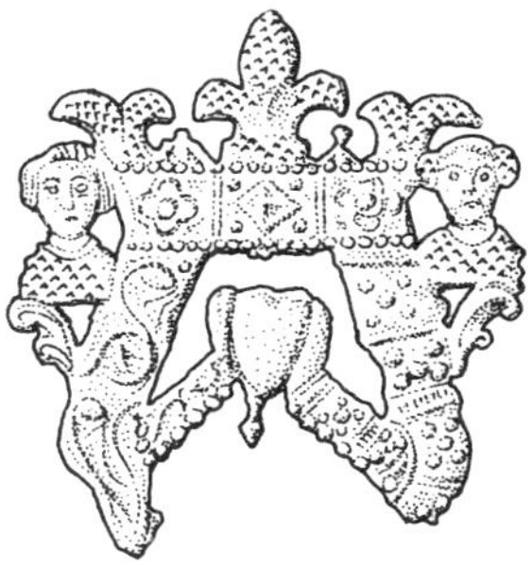

315

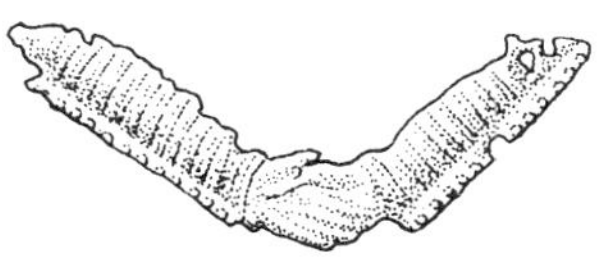

316

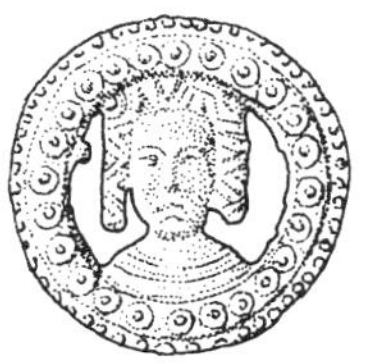

317

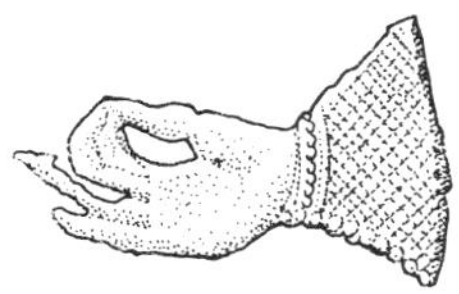

318

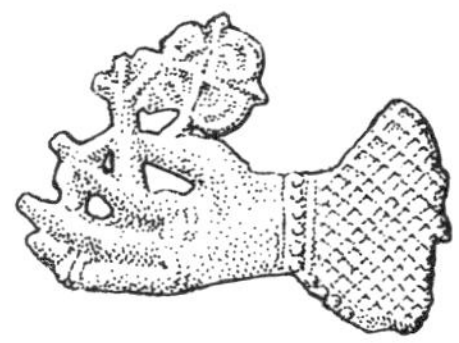

319

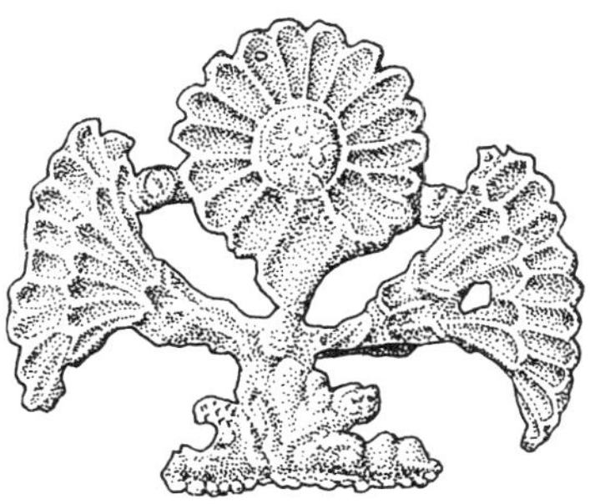

320

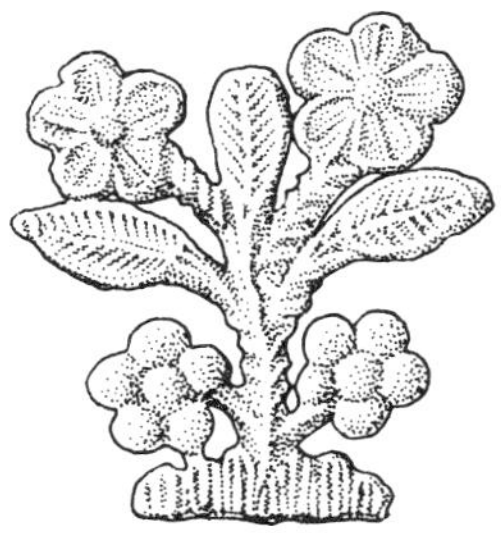

321

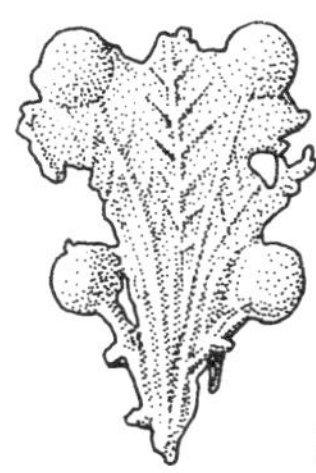

322

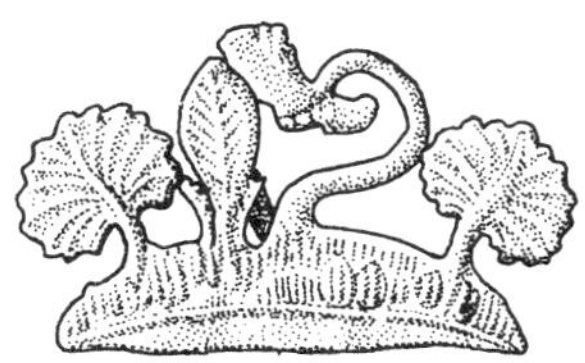

323

Secular badges. Figs 312-323. Scale 1 : 1

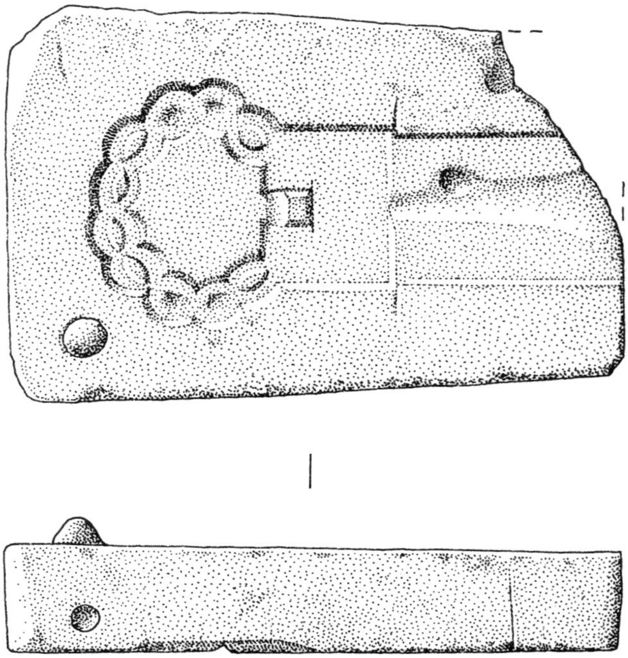

324

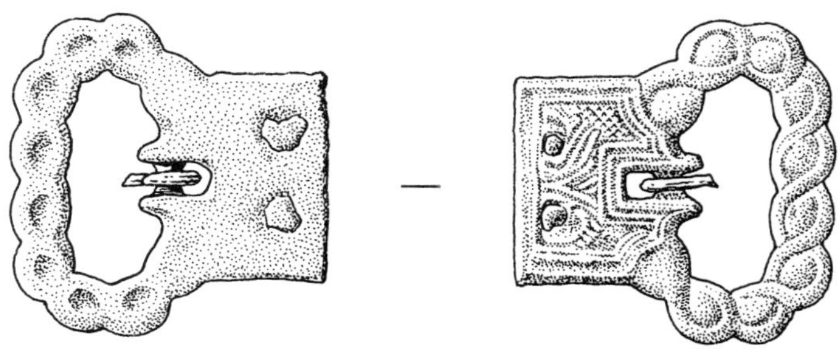

325

Stone mould and buckle. Figs 324-325. Scale 1 : 1

Bibliography

The place of publication is London unless otherwise indicated.

Alexander, J. and Binski, P. (eds) 1987: *Age of Chivalry: Art in Plantagenet England 1200-1400*

Akerman, J. V. 1855: 'Note on a variety of objects discovered during the progress of excavations for sewerage in Salisbury', *Archaeologia* **36**, 71-3

Akerman, J. V. 1857: 'On pilgrim signs found in Salisbury', *Wilts. Arch. Mag.* **3,** 94-7

Andersson, L. 1989: *Pilgrimsmärken och vallfart: Medeltida pilgrimskultur i Skandinavien* (Lund Studies in Medieval Archaeol. 7)

Baluzius, S. (ed) 1682: *Epistolarum Innocentii III*, I (Paris)

Barker, S. 1978: 'A Collection of Pilgrim Signs and Other Badges in Bristol City Museum', *Trans. Bristol & Gloucestershire Archaeol. Soc.* **95**, 47-50

Barnard, F. P. (ed) 1925: *Edward IV's French Expedition of 1475, the Leaders and their Badges, being MS.2M,16, College of Arms* (Oxford)

Beer, J. de 1932: 'Bedevaart- en pelgrimplaatjes', *Gedenkboek Frans Claes Museum 'De Gulden Spoor' te Antwerpen* (Antwerp), 53-69

Bentley, S. (ed) 1831: *Excerpta Historica*

Bergen op Zoom 1987: *Schatten uit de Schelde* (exhibition catalogue)

Biddle, M. forthcoming: *Winchester Studies* 7 (ii): *The Arts, Crafts, Industries and Daily Life of Medieval Winchester*

Blockley, K. *et al.* forthcoming: *Excavations in the Marlowe car park and associated areas: The Archaeology of Canterbury V*

Bond, M. F. (ed) 1947: *The Inventories of St George's Chapel Windsor Castle* (Windsor)

Borenius, T. 1943: 'The Cycle of Images in the Palaces and Castles of Henry III', *Journ. Warburg & Courtauld Inst.* **6**, 40-50

British Museum 1976: *Jewellery through 7000 years* (exhibition catalogue)

Burlington Fine Arts Club 1916: *Catalogue of Objects of British Heraldic Art to the end of the Tudor Period*

Byrne, M. St. C. (ed) 1981: *The Lisle Letters* (Chicago), 6 vols

Camille, M. 1987: 'Labouring for the Lord: the ploughman and the social order in the Luttrell Psalter', *Art History* **10**, iv, 423-54

Chambers, R. 1866: *The Book of Days*

Cherry, J. 1969: 'The Dunstable Swan Jewel', *Journ. Brit. Archaeol. Assoc.* **32**, 38-53

Cohen, E. 1976: '*In haec signa*: Pilgrim-badge trade in southern France', *Journal of Medieval History* **2,** 193-214

Cuming, H. S. 1867 & 1868: 'On Signacula found in London', *Journ. Brit. Archaeol. Assoc.* **23**, 327-34 and **24,** 219-30

Cumming, W. P. (ed) 1929: *The Revelations of St Birgitta* (Early Eng. Text Soc.)

Cunliffe, B. 1977: *Excavations at Portchester Castle* III (Soc. Antiq. Research Report XXXIV)

Davies, R. T. (ed) 1963: *Medieval English Lyrics*

De Witte, H. (ed) 1988: *Brugge Onder-Zocht: Tien jaar stadsarcheologisch onderzoek 1977-1987* (Bruges)

Druce, G. C. 1911: 'Notes on the History of the Heraldic Jall or Yale', *Archaeol. J.* **68**, 173-99

Dunham, W. H. 1955: 'Lord Hastings' Indentured Retainers 1461-1483', *Trans. Connecticut Acad. Arts & Sciences* **39**, 1-175

Eccles, M. (ed) 1969: *The Macro Plays* (Early Eng. Text Soc. 262)

Edgren, T. 1979: 'En pilgrimsampull från Letala i sydvästra Finland' *Finska Förnminnesföreningen*, 52-9

Edwards, K. 1967: *The English Secular Cathedrals in the Middle Ages* (Manchester)

Egan, G. 1986: 'Finds Recovery on Riverside Sites in the City of London', *Popular Archaeology* **6**, no 14, 42-9

Ellis, R. H. 1981: *Catalogue of Seals in the Public Record Office: Personal Seals* II

Evans, J. 1922: *Magical Jewels of the Middle Ages and the Renaissance* (Oxford)

Evans, J. 1949: *English Art 1307-1461* (Oxford)

Evans, J. 1969: *Life in Medieval France* (3rd ed)

Faber, F. 1896: *The Wanderings of Felix Fabri* trans. A. Stewart (Palestine Pilgrims' Text Soc. VII-X, 1892-7)

Finucane, R. C. 1977: *Miracles and Pilgrims*

Forgeais, A. 1863 & 1865: *Collection de Plombs Historiés trouvés dans la Seine* II & IV (Paris)

Fox-Davies, A. C. 1907: *Heraldic Badges*

Furnivall, F. J. (ed) 1868: *The Stacions of Rome* (Early Eng. Text Soc.)

Furnivall, F. J. & Stone, W. G. (eds) 1909: *The Tale of Beryn* (Early Eng. Text Soc.)

Gairdner, J. (ed) 1904: *The Paston Letters 1422-1509*, 4 vols

Gairdner, J. & Brodie, R. H. (eds) 1932: *Letters and Papers, Foreign and Domestic . . . Henry VIII: Addenda*, I, part 1

Gatty, C. J. 1882: *Catalogue of the Meyer Collection, Liverpool*, III

Gay, V. 1883 & 1928: *Glossaire Archéologique du Moyen Age et de la Renaissance* I & II (Paris)

Given-Wilson, C. 1986: *The Royal Household and the King's Affinity: Service, Politics and Finance in England 1360-1413* (New Haven & London)

Goubitz, O. 1988: 'Brugge op grote en kleine voet: Laatmiddeleeuws schoeisel en andere lederresten', in De Witte 1988, 151-9

Graham, R. 1930: 'The Order of St Antoine de Viennois and its English Commandery, St Anthony's, Threadneedle Street', *Archaeol. J.* **84**, 341-406

Gray, D. 1963: 'The Five Wounds of our Lord', *Notes & Queries* **208**, 50-9, 82-9, 127-34, 163-8

Greene, R. L. 1935: *Early English Carols*

Guildhall Museum 1908: *Catalogue of the Collection of London Antiquities in the Guildhall Museum*

Haedeke, H.-V. 1976: *Kunstgewerbemuseum der Stadt Köln: Zinn* (Cologne)

Halliwell, J. O. (ed) 1846: *Letters of the Kings of England*, 2 vols

Harvey, J. H. 1961: 'The Wilton Diptych – A re-examination', *Archaeologia* **98**, 1-28

Hector L. C. & Harvey B. F. (eds) 1982: *The Westminster Chronicle 1381-1394* (Oxford)

Heeringen R. M. van, Koldeweij, A. M. & Gaalman, A. A. G. 1987: *Heiligen uit de modder: in Zeeland gevonden pelgrimstekens* (Utrecht)

Hind, A. M. 1935: *An Introduction to the History of the Woodcut*

Hole, C. 1976: *British Folk Customs*

Hope, W. H. St. J. 1911: 'A Note on the Jall or Yale in Heraldry', *Archaeol. J.* **68**, 200-2

Hope, W. H. St. J. 1929: *Heraldry for Craftsmen and Designers*

Howard de Walden, Lord 1904: *Banners, Standards and Badges from a Tudor Manuscript in the College of Arms*

Hussey, A. (ed) 1907: *Testamenta Cantiana: East Kent*

Huth, H. A. (ed) 1908: 'Speculum Humanae Salvationis' in *The Mirroure of Man's Salvacionne* (Roxburghe Club)

James, T. B. & Robinson, A. M. 1988: *Clarendon Palace: The History and Archaeology of a Medieval Palace and Hunting Lodge near Salisbury, Wiltshire* (Soc. Antiq. Research Report, XLV)

Janson, H. W. 1952: *Apes and Ape Lore in the Middle Ages and the Renaissance* (Studies of Warburg Institute, 20)

Jessopp, A. & James, M. R. (eds) 1896: *The Life & Miracles of St William of Norwich by Thomas of Monmouth*

Johnston, F. R. 1969: 'House of Bridgettines' in J. S. Cockburn, H. P. F. King & K. G. T. McDonnel (eds) *Victoria History of the County of Middlesex* I, 182-91

Jones, M. 1989: 'The depiction of proverbs in late medieval art' in G. Gréciano (ed) *Europhras 88: Phraséologie Contrastive* (Strasbourg; Collection Recherches Germaniques no 2), 205-23

Jones, M. forthcoming: 'Folklore Motifs in Late Medieval Art II: Sexist Satires and Popular Punishments' in *Folklore*, supplementing his previous article on 'Proverbial Follies and Impossibilities', *Folklore* **100**, ii (1989), 201-17

Judge, R. 1979: *The Jack-in-the-Green* (Cambridge)

Kemp, E. W. 1948: *Canonization and Authority in the Western Church*

Koenigsmarková, H. 1980: 'Středověké poutní odznaky ze sbirek UPM' in *Acta UPM* XV *C. Comentationes 2 Sborník statí na počest 60. výroči narození PhDr. Dagmar Hejdové, CSs*, 54-71

Koenigsmarková, H. 1987: 'Práce z prostých kovû' in *Řemeslo umelěcké středoveké: ze sbírek Umělecko průmsylového Musea v Praze* (Museum of Decorative Arts, Prague), 18-27

Köster, K. 1957: 'Meister Tilman von Hachenburg', *Jahrbuch der Hessischen kirchengeschichtlichen Vereinigung* **8**, 1-206

Köster, K. 1965: 'Religiöse Medaillen und Wallfahrts-Devotionalen in der flämischen Buchmalerei des 15 und frühen 16 Jahrhunderts' in *Buch und Welt: Festschrift für Gustav Hofmann zum 65 Geburtstag dargebracht* (Wiesbaden) 459-504

Köster, K. 1972: 'Mittelalterliche Pilgerzeichen und Wallfahrtsdevotionalien' in *Rhein und Maas: Kunst und Kultur, 800-1400* (exhibition catalogue, Cologne), 146-60

Köster, K. 1973: *Gutenberg in Strassbourg: Das Aachenspiegel-Unternehmen und die unbekannte 'afentur und Kunst'* (Wiesbaden)

Köster, K. 1981: 'Pilgerzeichen und Pilgermuscheln' in *Sankt Elisabeth: Fürstin, Dienerin, Heilige* (exhibition catalogue, Sigmaringen)

Köster, K. 1983A: *Pilgerzeichen und Pilgermuscheln von Mittelalterlichen Santiagostrassen* (Ausgrabungen in Schleswig, Berichte und Studien 2; Neumünster)

Köster, K. 1983B: 'Gutenbergs Strassburger Aachenspiegel-Unternehmen von 1438/1440', *Gutenberg-Jahrbuch* **58**, 24-44

Köster, K. 1984A: 'Die Pilgerzeichen der Neusser Quirinus-Wallfahrt in Spätmittelalter' in *Neusser Jahrbuch für Kunst, Kulturgeschichte und Heimatkunde*, 11-29

Köster, K. 1984B: 'Mittelalterliche Pilgerzeichen' in Kriss-Rettenbeck & Möhler 1984, 203-23

Kriss-Rettenbeck, L. & Möhler, G. (eds) 1984: *Wallfahrt kennt keine Grenzen. Themen zu einer Ausstellung des Bayerischen Nationalmuseums und des Adalbert Stifter Vereins München* (Zurich)

Kurath, H., Kuhn, S. M. & Reidy, J. 1952+: *Middle English Dictionary* (Ann Arbor, etc.)

Laborde, Le Comte de 1852: *Les Ducs de Bourgogne* III (Paris)

Lamy-Lassalle, C. 1968: 'Recherches sur un Ensemble de Plombs trouvés dans la Seine', *Revue des Socs. Savantes de Haute-Normandie* **49**, 5-24

Lamy-Lassalle, C. 1969: 'Une collection d'enseignes de pèlerinage au Musée des Arts décoratifs de Lyon', *Bull. de la Soc. des Antiq. de France*, 264-70

Lamy-Lassalle, C. 1971: 'Les enseignes de pèlerinage du Mont St-Michel', in *Millénaire Monastique du Mont Saint-Michel* (Paris) III, 271-86

Lamy-Lassalle, C. 1973: 'Les représentations de Saint Jean-Baptiste sur les Enseignes de Pèlerinage' *Bull. trimestriel de la Soc. des Antiq. de Picardie* **4**, 156-64

Lawson, W. 1986: 'The boatswain's call: its role in the European maritime tradition' in *Second Conference of the ICTM Study Group on Music Archaeology* I *General Studies* (Royal Swedish Academy of Music), 131-40

Legg, J. W. & Hope, W. H. St. J. 1902: *Inventories of Christ Church, Canterbury* (Westminster)

Liebgott, N.- K. 1972: 'Frøslevklokkens Relieffer' in *Historisk Samfund for Praestø Amt: Årbog 1971-72*

Liebgott, N.- K. 1973: 'Døbefonten i Varde Jacobi kirke' in *Nationalmuseets Arbejdsmark*, 31-44

London Museum 1940: *Medieval Catalogue*

MacGregor, A. & Spencer, B. 1987: 'An ampulla mould from Pirton, Worcestershire', *Journ. Brit. Archaeol. Assoc.* **140**, 194-9

Malden, A. R. (ed) 1901: *The Canonization of St Osmund from the manuscript records in the Muniment Room of Salisbury Cathedral* (Wilts. Record Soc.)

Marks, R. & Payne, A. 1978: *British Heraldry from its origins to c. 1800* (exhibition catalogue, British Museum)

Mayes, P. & Butler, L. A. S. 1983: *Sandal Castle Excavations 1964-73*

Meckseper, C. (ed) 1985: *Stadt im Wandel: Kunst und Kultur des Bürgertums in Norddeutschland 1150-1650* (exhibition catalogue, Stuttgart), 4 vols

Meech, S. B. & Allen, H. E. (eds) 1940: *The Book of Margery Kempe* I (Early Eng. Text Soc. 212)

Meyer-Wurmbach, E. 1964: 'Kölner "Zeichen" und "Pfennige" zu Ehren der Heiligen Drei Könige', in *Kölner Domblatt*, 205-92

Mitchiner, M. 1986: *Medieval Pilgrim & Secular Badges*

Moses, E. 1930: *Der Schmuck der Sammlung W. Clemens* (Cologne)

Munich 1984: *Wallfahrt kennt keine Grenzen* (exhibition catalogue: see also Kriss-Rettenbeck & Möhler 1984)

Museum of London 1982: *The Museum of London: Second and Third Reports of the Board of Governors*

Nicholas, H. (ed) 1826: *Testamenta Vetusta*

Nichols, J. G. (ed) 1875: *Pilgrimages to St Mary of Walsingham and St Thomas of Canterbury ... by Desiderius Erasmus*

Nicolas, N. H. (ed) 1830: *Privy Purse Expenses of Elizabeth of York*

Palgrave, F. 1836: *Antient Kalendars and Inventories, of the Treasure of His Majesty's Exchequer*, 3 vols

Parks, G. B. 1954: *The English Traveler to Italy* (Rome), 2 vols

Page, W. (ed) 1925: *The Victoria History of the County of Buckingham*, III

Pollard, A. W. 1903: *Fifteenth Century Prose and Verse*

Randall, L. M. C. 1966: *Images in the Margins of Gothic Manuscripts* (Berkeley & Los Angeles)

Raine, J. (ed) 1835: *Reginaldi monachi Dunelmensis Libellus de Admirandis Beati Cutherberti Virtutibus* (Surtees Soc.)

Riley, H. T. (ed) 1868: *Memorials of London & London Life in the 13th, 14th and 15th centuries*

Robertson, J. C. (ed) 1875: *Materials for the History of Thomas Becket* II

Rodin, K. 1983: *Räven predikar för Gässen* (Studia Ethnologica Upsaliensia, 11)

Ross, C. 1974: *Edward IV*

Rydbeck, M. 1957: 'Ett Pilgrimsmärke från Alvastra och Gutenbergs Aachener Heiltumsspiegel', *Fornvännen* **52**, 294-304

Rydbeck, M. 1958: Review article in *Fornvännen* **53**, 210-18

Salisbury Museum 1973: *Salisbury Heritage: Illustrations from the Museum Collection* (Salisbury)

Saunders, P. 1986: *Channels to the Past: the Salisbury Drainage Collection* (Salisbury)

Schmitt, J.- C. 1979: *Le Saint Guinefort, guérisseur d'enfants depuis le XIIIe siècle* (Paris)

Seaby 1986 & 1987: Seaby's *Antiquities Forum* **2** & **5** (sale catalogues)

Secousse, D. F. (ed) 1745: *Ordonnances des Rois de France de la Troisième Race* VI (Paris)

Shortt, H. 1959: 'Three Early Episcopal Tombs in Salisbury Cathedral', *Wilts. Arch. Mag.* **57**, 212-19

Silverstein, T. (ed) 1971: *Medieval English Lyrics* (York Medieval Texts)

Smith, C. R. 1846: 'On Pilgrim Signs and Leaden Tokens', *Journ. Brit. Archaeol. Assoc.* **1**, 200-12

Smith, C. R. 1848, 1852, 1857 & 1880: *Collectanea Antiqua* I, II, IV & VII

Smith, C. R. 1854: *Catalogue of the Museum of London Antiquities*

Spencer, B. 1968: 'Medieval pilgrim badges' in J. G. N. Renaud (ed) *Rotterdam papers: a contribution to medieval archaeology* (Rotterdam), 137-53

Spencer, B. 1969: 'London-St Albans Return', *The London Archaeologist*, 34-5

Spencer, B. 1971A: 'A scallop-shell ampulla from Castor and comparable pilgrim souvenirs', *Lincs. Hist. & Archaeol.* **1**, no 6, 59-66

Spencer, B. 1971B: 'An ampulla of St Egwin and St Edwin', *Antiq. J.* **51**, 316-8

Spencer, B. 1974: 'The lead ampulla' (from Toppings Wharf, Southwark), *Trans. London & Middx. Archaeol. Soc.* **25**, 113-5

Spencer, B. 1975: 'The ampullae from Cuckoo Lane' in C. Platt & R. Coleman-Smith (eds) *Excavations in Medieval Southampton 1953-1969* (Leicester) II, 242-9

Spencer, B. 1978: 'King Henry of Windsor and the London pilgrim' in J. Bird *et al.* (eds) *Collectanea Londiniensia . . .* (London & Middx. Archaeol. Soc. Special Paper 2), 235-64

Spencer, B. 1979: 'Leaden pilgrim badge' in G. H. Smith 'The Excavation of the Hospital of St Mary of Ospringe', *Archaeol. Cantiana* **95**, 145-8

Spencer, B. 1980: *Medieval pilgrim badges from Norfolk* (Norwich)

Spencer, B. 1981: 'Two Leaden Ampullae from Leicestershire', *Trans. Leics. Archaeol. & Hist. Soc.* **55**, 88-9

Spencer, B. 1982: 'Pilgrim Souvenirs from the Medieval Waterfront Excavations at Trig Lane, London, 1974-6', *Trans. London & Middx. Archaeol. Soc.* **33**, 304-23

Spencer, B. 1983: 'The pewter brooch' in K. S. Jarvis *Excavations in Christchurch 1969 to 1980* (Dorset Nat. Hist. & Archaeol. Soc. Monograph 5) 81-2

Spencer, B. 1984: 'A Thirteenth-Century Pilgrim's Ampulla from Worcester', *Trans. Worcestershire Archaeol. Soc.* **9**, 7-11

Spencer, B. 1985: Catalogue entries in *Santiago de Compostela: 1000 ans de Pèlerinage Européen* (exhibition catalogue, Ghent), 293-319

Spencer, B. 1987: 'Pilgrim Souvenirs' in Alexander & Binski 1987, 218-24

Spencer, B. 1988: 'Pilgrim Souvenirs' in P. F. Wallace (ed) *Medieval Dublin Excavations 1962-81: Miscellanea* I (Fascicule 5) 33-48

Stevenson, J. (ed) 1847: *Libellus de vita et miraculis S. Godrici. . .* (Surtees Soc.)

Stow, J. 1908: *Survey of London* ed. C. L. Kingsford, 2 vols

Streeten, A. 1983: *Bayham Abbey: recent research including a report on excavations (1973-76) directed by the late Helen Soutermeister* (Sussex Archaeol. Soc. Monograph no 2)

Stroud, D. 1984A: 'The Cult and Tombs of St Osmund at Salisbury', *Wilts. Arch. Mag.* **78**, 50-4

Stroud, D. 1984B: 'Edith of Wilton (*c.*961-984): the millenary of a saint', *The Hatcher Review* **2**, no 18, 352-8

Stroud, D. 1987: 'Miracles of St. Osmund', *The Hatcher Review* **3**, no 23, 107-15

Thomas, A. H. & Thornley, I. D. (eds) 1938: *The Great Chronicle of London*

Tonnochy, A. B. 1952: *Catalogue of British Seal-dies in the British Museum*

Tricou, J. 1957: 'Enseignes de Pèlerinages et de Dévotions au Musée des Beaux-Arts de Lyon', *Bull. des Musées Lyonnais* **11,** no 2, 39-51

Tristram, E. W. 1929: *The Wall Paintings in Eton College Chapel and the Lady Chapel of Winchester Cathedral* (Walpole Soc.)

Tudor-Craig, P. 1973: *Richard III* (exhibition catalogue)

Vandenberghe, S. 1976: 'Pelgrimstekens uit Mechelse baggerwerken', *Handelingen van de Kon.Kring voor Oudheidkunde, Litteren en Kunst van Mechelen* **79**, 81-98

Vandenberghe, S. 1988: 'Metalen voorwerpen uit recent archaeologisch onderzock te Brugge', in De Witte 1988, 160-91

Vandenbroeck, P. 1985: 'Bubo significans. Die Eule als Sinnbild vor Schlechtigkeit und Torheit, vor allem in der niederländischen und deutschen Bilddarstellung und bei Jheronimus Bosch' in *Jaarboek van het Koninklijk Museum voor Schone Kunsten, Antwerpen,* 19-136

Varty, E. K. C. 1967: *Reynard the Fox. A Study of the Fox in Medieval English Art*

Venerabile 1962: *The Venerabile* XXI: *The English Hospice in Rome* (Exeter)

Vieillard, J. (ed) 1938: *Le Guide du Pèlerin de Saint-Jacques de Compostelle* (Mâcon)

Virgoe R. 1989: *Private Life in the Fifteenth Century: Illustrated Letters of the Paston family*

Wagner, M. L. 1937: 'Phallus, Horn und Fisch' in the *Jaberg Festschrift: Donum natalicum Carolo Jaberg messori indefessos exagenario* (Zurich & Leipzig) 77-130

Walters, H. B. 1920: *Church Bells of Wiltshire*

Wenzel, S. 1978: *Verses in Sermons: Fasciculus Morum and its Middle English Poems* (Cambridge, Mass.)

Whiting, B. J. & H. W. 1968: *Proverbs, Sentences and Proverbial Phrases from English Writings mainly before 1500* (Cambridge, Mass.)

Williams, G. (ed) 1857: *The Itineraries of William Wey, fellow of Eton College to Jerusalem, A D. 1458 and 1462; and to St James of Compostella* (Roxburghe Club)

Woodfield, C. 1981: 'Finds from the Free Grammar School at the Whitefriars, Coventry, *c.*1545-*c.*1557/58', *Post-Medieval Archaeol.* **15**, 81-159

Author's acknowledgements

I should like to join the curator and trustees of the Salisbury Museum in thanking all those, named in the introduction and catalogue above, whose gifts and loans of Salisbury finds have helped to make the catalogue as comprehensive as possible. I should also like to express sincere thanks to the many colleagues and friends who have helped in the preparation of the catalogue. I especially wish to thank the following for contributing information about Salisbury finds or about comparative material, thereby helping significantly to enrich the text and illustrations: Mr J. Auld, Mr H. J. E. van Beuningen, Mr R. Davis, Mr P. Elkins, Mrs A. Freeman, Mr R. A. Green, Mrs F. Hammer, Dr R. Homer, Mr R. Jones, Mr M. Kashden, Dr A. M. Koldeweij, Mr E. Law, Mr B. N. Lee, Mr C. Marshall, Mr N. Mills, Mr L. Milward, Mr J. Mullen, Mr A. G. Pilson, Mr I. Smith, Mr R. Smith, Mr E. Taylor, Mr C. Wainwright, Mr S. Wheeler, and Mr P. Woods. Thanks are also due to the trustees and governing bodies of the British Museum, the Museum of London, the Cuming Museum, Southwark, and the Royal Museum, Canterbury, for allowing items in their collections to be illustrated here and to be referred to in the text. My indebtedness to the late Dr Kurt Köster and other continental scholars will be evident from the bibliographical references. I am grateful to John Cherry for reading the text in draft and for making helpful suggestions. My biggest debt of gratitude, however, is owed to Malcolm Jones for his warm-hearted and unstinting help in the area of medieval secular imagery and for allowing me to read in draft the text of some of his forthcoming publications on the depiction of folklore motifs and speech idioms in late medieval art.

Index

This is an index of personal and place names. Non-specific references to Canterbury, London and Salisbury (which occur on nearly every page) are omitted, as are museums in these three places, and the names of donors and depositors. Most English places are identified by historic (pre-1974) county; most other places are identified by country. All references are to page numbers.